Report of the Hamilton-Wentv.

Review Commission

Report
of the
Hamilton-Wentworth
Review Commission

Henry E. Stewart, Chairman
Harold C. Dixon, Member
James A. Johnson, Member

May 1978

Copies of this report may be obtained from:

Ontario Government Bookstore
880 Bay Street
Toronto, Ontario
M7A 1N3

Price: $4.00 per copy

Printed and bound in Canada

352
.071352
H222.

MINISTRY OF EDUCATION, ONTARIO
COMMUNICATION SERVICES BRANCH
13TH FLOOR, MOWAT BLOCK
TORONTO, ONTARIO M7A 1L3

March 30, 1978

Her Honour
The Lieutenant Governor of the
Province of Ontario

May it Please Your Honour:

    We, the Commissioners of the Hamilton-Wentworth Review Commission, appointed under The Public Inquiries Act, S.O. 1971, c. 49, by Order-in-Council 2588-77 dated September 14, 1977, to inquire into and to report upon the organization, administration and functioning of local government within the Regional Municipality of Hamilton-Wentworth in accordance with the Terms of Reference set out in that Order-in-Council, have the honour to submit the accompanying Report.

Henry E. Stewart
Chairman

Harold Dixon
Member

James Johnson
Member

To The Honourable
Pauline M. McGibbon, O.C., LL.D., D.U.(Ott.)
Lieutenant Governor of the Province of Ontario

Report of a Committee of the Executive Council
on Matters of State

May it please Your Honour

Upon the recommendation of the Honourable the Treasurer of Ontario and Minister of Economics and Intergovernmental Affairs, the Committee of Council advise that pursuant to the provisions of The Public Inquiries Act, 1971 a commission be issued appointing:

    Henry E. Stewart as Chairman,
    Harold Dixon as Member and
    Dr. James Johnson as Member,

and designating them as the Hamilton-Wentworth Review Commission empowered and instructed to examine, evaluate and make appropriate recommendations on the structure, organization and operation of local government within the Regional Municipality of Hamilton-Wentworth area including all municipal governments, boards, and commissions, and without limiting the generality of the foregoing, to examine the issues set out in the Terms of Reference attached hereto.

Respectfully submitted,

14th September, 1977.

Deputy C.E.C.

Chairman.

O.C. 2588/77

Terms of Reference

The purpose of this review is to develop recommendations for the consideration of the Council of the Regional Municipality, the councils of the area municipalities and the Province of Ontario on the organization, administration and functioning of the system of local government within the Region. The Study will include the political systems, the administrative systems and the relationship between them. Without limiting the generality of the terms of reference, the Study will centre on improvements that can be made to the present system of local government based on criteria such as: accountability, responsiveness, cost effectiveness, efficiency, responsibility and accessibility. To this purpose, the commission is empowered and instructed to examine, evaluate and make appropriate recommendations on the structure, organization and operations of local government within the Regional Municipality of Hamilton-Wentworth area, including all municipal governments, boards and commissions with specific reference to the following:

(a) an examination of any duplication of costs within the local government system;

(b) the appropriate division of responsibilities and functions among:
   (i) the Province and the system of local government operating within the study area;
   (ii) the Region and the area municipalities;
   (iii) the Region and the area municipalities and all local boards and commissions;

(c) the retention of the two-tiered system of government and the practicality and applicability of dissolving the regional government system and substituting:
   (i) a single-tiered system in which all area municipal responsibilities are transferred to the Region; or
   (ii) a single-tiered system in which all local government responsibilities are transferred to the lower-tier municipalities;

(d) the method of selection of regional councillors and heads of councils;

(e) the costs and effectiveness of the systems of administration;

(f) the relationships between the members of municipal councils and residents of the regional area, with regard for the requirements of responsive local government and the accountability of members of councils and their boards and commissions;

(g) the relationship between revenue and expenditures in the Region; the area municipalities in the Region; the area municipalities and special purpose bodies, including the adequacy of Provincial grants policies and the priority-setting mechanism for expenditures;

(h) any other matter which the study commissioner considers relevant to local government in the regional area.

TABLE OF CONTENTS

Letter of Transmittal   v
Order in Council   vii
Terms of Reference   ix
Table of Contents   xi
List of Tables   xiii
List of Maps   xvii
List of Figures   xix
List of Recommendations   xx
Preface   xxxiii
Chapter   1:   Introduction   1
Chapter   2:   A History of Hamilton-Wentworth   9
Chapter   3:   A Demographic and Economic Description of the Region   20
Chapter   4:   The Basis for Reform   37
Chapter   5:   Ward Boundaries   58
Chapter   6:   Policy Development and Management   66
Chapter   7:   Municipal Finance   84
Chapter   8:   Planning and Development   132
Chapter   9:   Physical Services   145
Chapter 10:   Transportation   153
Chapter 11:   Public Safety Services   164
Chapter 12:   Social Services and Health   176
Chapter 13:   Parks, Recreation, Libraries and Cultural Facilities   195
Chapter 14:   The Implementation of Reform   209
Appendices
  1: Hamilton-Wentworth Review Commission — Research Reports   215
  2: Hamilton-Wentworth Review Commission — Public Participation   216
  3: Chronology of Hamilton-Wentworth Review Commission   224

LIST OF TABLES

3.1 Population, 1976 21
3.2 Region's "Most Likely" Population Projections 22
3.3 Projection of Population Distribution within Region, 1976-2001 23
3.4 Ethnic Origins and Religious Identification, 1971 24
3.5 Labour Force by Sector, 1971 25
3.6 Place of Work — Place of Residence Exchanges within Wentworth County, 1971 29
3.7 Growth in Population - Growth in Manufacturing Employment, 1976-2001 30
3.8 Average Household Income, 1970 31
3.9 Retail Trade by Business Group, 1971 32
5.1 Proposed Ward Structure for the City of Wentworth 60
6.1 Total Staff Complement by Municipality for the Years 1972 and 1975-1977 79
6.2 Total Staff Complement by Service for the Years 1972 and 1975-1977 83
7.1 Expenditures of Municipalities in Hamilton-Wentworth 1972, 1975-1977 86-87
7.2 Composition of Municipal Revenue Fund Spending by Types of Municipality 89
7.3 Municipal Revenue Fund Spending per Household by Types of Municipality in 1976 89
7.4 Comparison of Actual and Expected Expenditure Growth Rates from 1972 to 1977 90
7.5 Revenues of Municipalities in Hamilton-Wentworth 1972, 1975-1977 92-93
7.6 Composition of Municipal Revenue Fund Revenues by Types of Municipality 95
7.7 Changes in Residential Mill Rates by Types of Municipality 95
7.8 Average Gross Residential Property Taxes per Household by Types of Municipality 96

7. 9   Average Gross Residential Property Taxes and Incomes
        Per Household in 1976   97
7.10   Transitional Grants and Special Assistance, 1974-1977   97
7.11   Total Capital Expenditures and Financing in Hamilton-Wentworth   99
7.12   Municipal Capital Fund Spending per Household by
        Types of Municipality in 1975 and 1976   100
7.13   Municipalities Net Long Term Debt per Household by
        Types of Municipality   101
7.14   Debt Charges for General Municipal Purposes by
        Types of Municipality   102
7.15   Factors Contributing to Residential Property Tax Changes,
        1972 to 1977   104-05-06
7.16   Price Indices for Municipal Expenditures   107
7.17   Financial Effects of the 1974 Reorganization   108
7.18   Estimated Effects of Establishing Uniform Water and
        Sewage Charges   109
7.19   Financial Effects of 1977 Transfer of Hamilton Roads and
        Transit Functions   110
7.20   Residential Property Taxes, 1972 and 1977   113
7.21   City of Wentworth — Estimated Total Levy ..114-116
7.22   City of Wentworth — Tax Effects of Consolidation
        without Special Taxing Arrangements   117
7.23   City of Wentworth — Tax Effects on Residential Taxpayers of
        Consolidation without Special Taxing Arrangements   118
7.24   Schedule of Recommended Taxing Arrangements   125
7.25   City of Wentworth — Effects of Consolidation with
        Proposed Taxing Arrangements   127
7.26   City of Wentworth — Effects on Residential Taxpayers of
        Restructuring with Proposed Taxing Arrangements   128
7.27   Benefits for Typical Residential Taxpayers of Existing
        Transitional Adjustments   129
8. 1   Planning Expenditures   139
9. 1   Annual Water Costs for an Average Household   146
9. 2   Annual Sewage Costs for an Average Household   148
9. 3   Storm Sewer Maintenance and Operating Costs   150
10. 1   Road Expenditures, 1972-1978   155
10. 2   Public Transit Deficits   158
11. 1   Complement Data, Hamilton-Wentworth Regional Police, 1975-1977   166
11. 2   Municipal Policing Costs in Hamilton-Wentworth, 1975-1977   167
11. 3   Analysis of Costs of Hamilton-Wentworth Regional Police, 1974-77   168
11. 4   Municipal Net Operating Budgets for Fire Services in
        Hamilton-Wentworth Region, 1977   172
12. 1   Total Expenditures and Net Cost to Municipalities of Social Services

	Department Expenditures 179
12. 2	Payments Made, Municipal Cost, and People Served through Basic General Welfare Payments 180
12. 3	Payments Made, Municipal Cost, and Number of Cheques Issued for Supplementary Aid and Special Assistance 181
12. 4	Municipal Day Care Expenditures and Children Served 182
12. 5	Expenditures, Net Municipal Cost and Caseloads for Homemakers and Nurses Services 183
12. 6	Total Expenditures and Municipal Cost of Homes for Aged 185
12. 7	Expenditures by Area Municipalities for Services to Aged Persons and Services to Children, 1976 186
12. 8	Expenditures of the Hamilton-Wentworth Children's Aid Society and the Catholic Children's Aid Society of Hamilton-Wentworth 187
12. 9	Total Expenditures and Local Cost of Health Unit 191
12.10	Full-time Staff of the Hamilton-Wentworth Regional Health Unit 191
12.11	Contributions of Local Government to Capital Costs of Hospitals 193
12.12	Doctors in the Hamilton-Wentworth Region and in the Province of Ontario 193
13. 1	Parks and Recreation Departmental Budgets, 1977 197
13. 2	Comparative Statistics on Libraries 202

LIST OF MAPS

5.1   City of Wentworth Ward Boundaries   65
7.1   City of Wentworth Urban and Rural Areas   120-21

LIST OF FIGURES

6. 1 Municipalities in the Hamilton-Wentworth Region
Present Organizational Components   80-81
6. 2 City of Wentworth — Proposed Plan of Organization   82
7. 1 Hamilton-Wentworth Expenditures by Function 1972, 1975-1977   85
7. 2 Hamilton-Wentworth Revenues by Source 1972, 1975-1977   94

LIST OF RECOMMENDATIONS

Chapter 4: Basis for Reform

4.1   The lower-tier municipalities of Hamilton-Wentworth be abolished and a single-tier local government structure composed of one municipal council be established in the present Region of Hamilton-Wentworth.

4.2   No legislative or quasi-legislative political bodies be established in addition to the one municipal council.

4.3   The council of the municipality be composed of twenty-seven aldermen, each representing one ward.

4.4   Legislation provide that the wards of the new municipality initially be established within existing municipal boundaries.

4.5   Legislation provide that representation on the new council initially be fourteen members from the area of the present City of Hamilton and thirteen members from the rest of the Region.

4.6   Legislation provide that after two elections the council be empowered to alter ward boundaries under the provisions of The Municipal Act.

4.7   The new municipality be called the City of Wentworth.

4.8   The term of office of the council of the City of Wentworth be three years.

4.9   For the first election in the City of Wentworth the mayor be elected by the aldermen from among themselves, and the mayor should retain his ward seat.

4.10   For all elections thereafter, the mayor be elected at large.

4.11   There be no change in the statutory authority of the mayor and the mayor be ex officio a member of all committees.

4.12   Legislation require the establishment of a Policy and Finance Committee composed of the mayor, as chairman, the chairmen of the four standing committees and the council's representative on the Police Commission other than the mayor.

4.13   Legislation provide that the chairmen of the four standing committees be elected by council.

4.14   Legislation provide that the Policy and Finance Committee have authority to: develop and coordinate policy; review the activities of the standing committees of council; set priorities and guidelines for capital and current budgets; review capital and current budgets and budget recommendations; undertake such non-legislative tasks as are assigned by council, provided that such tasks are not also assigned to the Chief Administrative Officer of the municipality; and recommend to council the appointment of members of the standing committees other than the chairmen.

4.15   Legislation provide for four standing committees of council to deal with policy matters as follows: the Planning and Development Committee; the Social Services and Health Committee; the Parks, Recreation and Culture Committee, and the Physical Services Committee.

4.16   Legislation require the appointment of a Chief Administrative Officer whose role be defined by by-law.

4.17   The City of Wentworth be empowered to establish such other committees as it determines is advisable and to alter by by-law the committee structure presented in Recommendations 4.12 and 4.15.

4.18   The council of the City of Wentworth give careful consideration to the use of present municipal buildings as district offices to provide office space for aldermen and to provide as much decentralization of service delivery as is consistent with economical administration.

4.19   The tax burden of the City of Wentworth be distributed as far as possible in ways that ensure that those areas benefiting from services will pay for them through the use of: area rating, user charges, and an urban-rural tax differential in addition to a general levy.

Chapter 5:   Ward Boundaries

5.1   The City of Wentworth be divided into wards in accordance with Map 5.1.

Chapter 6:   Policy Development and Management

6.1   The council of the City of Wentworth develop procedural by-laws that allow the public to speak to the full council after appropriate procedures have been followed.

6.2   The council determine the use to be made of each district office, and initially, a representative of at least the Planning and Recreation Departments be located in each office.

6.3   A central data-processing facility be established for all the City of Wentworth's computing needs.

6.4   Personnel policies and procedures, including development of job descriptions and performance appraisal, be investigated, and recommendations made to introduce a comprehensive personnel administration system in the City of Wentworth that will assist elected representatives and appointed officials in monitoring and controlling staff performance and costs.

6.5 Administrative systems, data-processing, and management information systems be investigated and recommendations made for standardization of all systems within the City of Wentworth.

6.6 The operating cost and personnel implications of all proposed capital expenditures be identified and incorporated into all such proposals for council consideration.

6.7 Three-year forecasts of all local government revenues and expenditures be developed and kept up to date as part of the regular current budgeting process of the City of Wentworth.

Chapter 7: Finance

7.1 The Ministry of Community and Social Services bring its grant payment system into line with those of other ministries.

7.2 The City of Wentworth be enabled to pass any capital expenditure by-law by means of a vote of council, and no vote of ratepayers be required unless one is ordered by the Ontario Municipal Board.

7.3 The municipality's capital program quota application to the Ontario Municipal Board contain a list of the projects planned for development within the year for which the quota application is made.

7.4 The municipality be required to advertise each project in the normal manner and if no objection is received it be permitted to proceed without seeking approval of the Ontario Municipal Board.

7.5 If objection is received as a result of the advertisement of a proposed capital project, the municipality be then required to apply to the Ontario Municipal Board, which at its discretion may decide whether a hearing is necessary before making its decision.

7.6 Where no objection is received to a proposed capital project, and the project proceeds, an affidavit of the actions of the municipality be submitted to the Ontario Municipal Board.

7.7 A report from the municipality on each year's capital expenditure and borrowing activities accompany its application for the next year's capital expenditure quota.

7.8 Legislation provide that the City of Wentworth be divided, for taxation purposes, into an urban area and a rural area and, for purposes of financing the city's net expenditures on general government (salaries, materials, services and rents only), parks, recreation, local cultural services, and urban improvements the properties in the area designated as rural be taxed at 50 per cent of the tax rate for these services in the urban area.

7.9   The City of Wentworth be empowered to increase the differential between the rate of tax on properties in the rural and urban areas for the services specified in Recommendation 7.8.

7.10   For the purposes of urban-rural differential taxation the portion of the city that is initially designated urban be the following:
  i) the present City of Hamilton;
  ii) two portions of the Town of Stoney Creek: first, the portion of the Town of Stoney Creek that is adjacent to the City of Hamilton commencing at the northern boundary of the Town and Fruitland Road; thence southerly along Fruitland Road to Barton Street, thence in an easterly direction along Barton Street to Jones Road; thence in a southerly direction along Jones Road to the Toronto, Hamilton and Buffalo Railway right-of-way; thence in a westerly direction along the railway right-of-way to the City of Hamilton limits; and second, the portion of the Town of Stoney Creek adjacent to the City of Hamilton commencing at Green Mountain Road allowance and the city limits; thence easterly along Green Mountain Road to Second Road West; thence southerly along Second Road West to Mud Street; thence in an easterly direction to First Road West; thence southerly along First Road West to Highland Road; thence in a westerly direction to Mount Albion Road; thence northerly along Mount Albion Road to the city limits;
  iii) the portion of the municipality of the Town of Ancaster that is adjacent to the City of Hamilton and the Town of Dundas commencing at King's Highway No. 53 and the City of Hamilton limits; thence in a southwesterly direction along King's Highway No. 53 to Shaver Road; thence in a northwesterly direction along Shaver Road to Jerseyville Road; thence in a northeasterly direction to Marlin Road; thence in a northwesterly direction along Marlin Road to Sulphur Springs Road; thence in a northerly direction to the limits of the Town of Dundas; and
  iv) the portion of the Town of Dundas commencing where the Town of Dundas, Town of Ancaster and City of Hamilton limits meet; thence in a southwesterly direction along the limits of the Town of Dundas to the road allowance between the Township of Ancaster and West Flamborough (prior to 1974) on the western boundary of the town; thence in a northeasterly direction along the road allowance to King's Highway No. 99; thence in a northeasterly direction along King's Highway No. 99 to the eastern boundary of lot 11 in the 1st Concession; thence in a northerly direction to the present boundary of the Town of Dundas; thence in a northeasterly direction following the town limits to York Road; thence in a northeasterly and then southerly direction along the former boundary of the Town of Dundas (prior to 1974) to the present town boundary; thence in a southwesterly direction to the place of commencement.

7.11   The City of Wentworth review the urban area boundary at least once a year and be empowered to change that boundary at any time, subject to prior approval by the Ontario Municipal Board.

7.12   The municipality be empowered to apply to the Ontario Municipal Board to approve the designation of an area or areas within which any property for which a draft plan of subdivision is approved shall be automatically included within the urban area at the time of such approval.

7.13   The costs of the following services be area rated to preserve the existing basis of charge: transit, subsidization of bus fares for the elderly and students, garbage collection, street lighting, fire, libraries, storm drainage, special roadway work such as a higher level of snow clearance and sidewalks, special tax assistance to the elderly, parking, tree-planting and maintenance, weed control, dental treatment and neighbourhood improvements.

7.14   Changes in the boundaries of the parts of the city to be area rated for certain services require approval of the Ontario Municipal Board.

7.15   The net cost of all municipal services provided by the City of Wentworth, apart from those identified for special treatment in Recommendations 7.8, 7.13, 9.1 and 9.2 be financed by a general levy on all property in the city.

7.16   The transitional taxation and special financial assistance arrangements initiated by the Government of Ontario in relation to the 1974 restructure and 1977 transfer of functions to the Regional Municipality of Hamilton-Wentworth not be changed.

7.17   The City of Wentworth be deemed to be a lower-tier municipality for the purposes of The Ontario Unconditional Grants Act, 1975, in respect of resource equalization grants.

7.18   The City of Wentworth be deemed to be an area municipality for the purposes of The Ontario Unconditional Grants Act, 1975, in respect of density grants.

7.19   All grants receivable under The Ontario Unconditional Grants Act be credited generally to the benefit of all City of Wentworth taxpayers.

7.20   Any financial losses in grants arising directly as a result of the creation of the City of Wentworth be compensated for in special assistance arrangements made by the Government of Ontario.

Chapter 8:   Planning and Development

8.1   All relevant aspects of the Niagara Escarpment plan, when it is adopted, be incorporated into the official plan of the City of Wentworth, which shall be authorized to undertake complete responsibility for the implementation of the Escarpment plan within its boundaries.

8.2   The Social Services and Health Committee of the City of Wentworth take appropriate steps to ensure that the provision of social services and assisted housing is coordinated.

8.3   The council of the City of Wentworth be assigned all the powers of a planning board under The Planning Act.

8.4   The council of the City of Wentworth be authorized to appoint both a committee of adjustment and a land division committee, the two committees to be served by the same municipal staff.

8.5   The land division committee and the committee of adjustment of the City of Wentworth hold meetings in the district offices, whenever appropriate.

8.6   The council of the City of Wentworth be delegated the power of the Minister of Housing to approve plans of subdivision.

8.7   The City of Wentworth adopt a single, comprehensive official plan for the municipality, which, on its approval, will supersede all existing plans; and pending its approval, existing plans remain in full effect.

8.8   The council of the City of Wentworth give careful consideration to the placing of planning staff in district offices to provide basic planning assistance, to receive and process applications for planning permits and approvals, and to provide liaison with other municipal departments.

Chapter 9:   Physical Services

9.1   Water services in the City of Wentworth be provided on a common, user-pay basis.

9.2   Sewage services in the City of Wentworth be provided on a common, user-pay basis.

9.3   The costs attributable to operating storm drainage facilities in the city of Wentworth be area rated.

9.4   The council of the City of Wentworth continue the use of private contracting for solid waste collection, where appropriate.

9.5   The costs of solid waste disposal be generally rated, but costs of solid waste collection be area rated on the basis of existing area municipal boundaries.

Chapter 10:   Transportation

10.1   The costs of roads be generally rated throughout the municipality; but where higher than normal levels of service are provided with respect to snow clearing or sidewalks (where not financed as local improvements), council be authorized to provide for area rating of the consequent additional costs.

10.2   The costs of street lighting be area rated to preserve the existing basis of charge.

10.3   Road maintenance be provided on a decentralized basis by integrating existing regional and area municipal maintenance facilities.

10.4   The costs of transit service within the Urban Transit Area continue to be borne by the ratepayers living within it, and the costs of service outside the Urban Transit Area be area rated according to the area benefiting from the service. Council should be authorized to alter the boundaries of the Urban Transit Area without provincial approval, provided the change is connected with a change of service to the area affected.

10.5 The province subsidize on the same basis as GO Transit the analogous inter-urban and commuter services provided by the City of Wentworth.

10.6 All municipally owned transit operations servicing the Region be eligible for provincial subsidy.

10.7 The council of the City of Wentworth be assigned direct responsibility for the provision of transit services.

10.8 The council of the City of Wentworth take the appropriate steps to wind up the Hamilton Street Railway Company and Canada Coach Lines Limited, providing that there will be no adverse consequences of the dissolutions.

10.9 The power to establish a parking authority be abolished, and parking be the responsibility of council and of the Physical Services Committee.

10.10 Any net cost relating to parking facilities in any existing area municipality be rated to that area, or any surplus credited.

10.11 The City of Wentworth assume the operating responsibilities for Hamilton Civic Airport now undertaken by the City of Hamilton.

10.12 Existing taxicab licences continue to be effective only for the territory for which they were issued, and the City of Wentworth be authorized to attach territorial restrictions to licence renewals and to new licences.

Chapter 11: Public Safety Services

11.1 The mayor of the City of Wentworth be a member of the Board of Commissioners of Police, and the second municipal representative on the Board be made a member of the Policy and Finance Committee of Council.

11.2 Fire services in the Region be combined into a single department that will continue to use an appropriate combination of full-time and volunteer personnel, the cost of whose services will be area rated to take account of continuing and acceptable differentials in level of service.

Chapter 12: Social Services and Health

12.1 The Ministry of Community and Social Services give serious consideration to using the City of Wentworth for a pilot project to combine the administration of Family Benefits and General Welfare Assistance under the local Social Services Department, and full compensation be made to the municipality for the added costs that it will thereby incur.

12.2 Wentworth Lodge and Macassa Lodge report to the Social Services and Health Committee of Council through the Commissioner of Social Services and the two management committees be discontinued.

12.3　The cost of programs of tax relief for elderly people and municipal subsidization of bus fares for the elderly and students be area rated.

12.4　Municipal appointments to the District Health Council be chosen from members of the Social Services and Health Committee of Council.

12.5　The Board of Health be abolished, and its duties and functions assumed by the Social Services and Health Committee of Council.

12.6　Councillors appointed to the boards of public hospitals be chosen from the Social Services and Health Committee of Council.

Chapter 13:　Parks, Recreation, Libraries and Cultural Facilities

13.1　A Recreation Department be created for the City of Wentworth, reporting to the Parks, Recreation and Culture Committee of Council through the Commissioner of Parks and Recreation, and that it have staff located in the district offices assisted by local citizens' advisory councils for recreation.

13.2　A Parks Department be created for the City of Wentworth, reporting to the Parks, Recreation and Culture Committee of Council through the Commissioner of Parks and Recreation.

13.3　Expenditures of the Parks and Recreation departments be allocated throughout the municipality on a differential urban-rural basis.

13.4　Responsibility for municipal cemeteries be consolidated in the proposed Parks Department of the City of Wentworth, with a separate unit established within that department to look after matters of cemetery administration other than maintenance.

13.5　Immediate attention be given to improving the administrative efficiency of the present Hamilton library system.

13.6　The three present library systems continue, and the chief librarians report directly to the Parks, Recreation and Culture Committee of Council, which shall be authorized to appoint whatever advisory committees it thinks might be able to assist in fulfilling its responsibility.

13.7　Costs of library services be area rated to preserve the existing basis of charge so long as there is more than one library system in existence.

13.8　Immediate attention be given to reducing the current deficit incurred in the operation of Hamilton Place.

13.9　All municipal councillors from the City of Wentworth appointed to boards of special purpose cultural and recreational bodies be chosen from members of the Parks, Recreation, and Culture Committee of Council.

13.10　All contributions to special purpose cultural and recreational special purpose bodies now made by the Region be generally rated for tax purposes in the City of Wentworth, and all other such contributions be made as part of the urban-rural tax differential.

Chapter 14: The Implementation of Reform

14.1 The City of Wentworth be constituted effective the 1st day of January, 1979.

14.2 The election of the council of the City of Wentworth occur no later than early October 1978.

14.3 The council so elected have authority to hire and organize staff.

14.4 The major priority of the new council be the development of a system to assure the continuation from January 1, 1979 of all services already provided by the regional and area municipalities at present levels until the establishment of the City of Wentworth is in full operation.

14.5 Immediately after the coming into force of the legislation each area municipality and the Regional Municipality appoint one of its members to a Steering Committee, a function of which will be to study and make recommendations to the council of the City of Wentworth on staff, salaries, quality of personnel, early retirement and staff requirements.

14.6 The Steering Committee oversee the collection and organization of all policies now used by the Region and area municipalities to provide a basis for subsequent deliberations on, or changes in, policies in the City of Wentworth.

14.7 The Steering Committee in conjunction with the Province of Ontario appoint management consultants to aid in personnel selection, organization, and development of management systems, including staff salaries, number of personnel, quality of personnel, early retirement and staff requirements.

14.8 The Province of Ontario provide assistance to the Steering Committee and bear the cost of retaining management consultants.

14.9 The present Regional Coordinator and those of his staff appointed by him assist the Steering Committee.

14.10 As its first items of business the council of the City of Wentworth choose the mayor, heads of standing committees, and its representative on the police commission and thus form the Policy and Finance Committee.

14.11 The Policy and Finance Committee immediately upon its formation assume all responsibilities of the Steering Committee and the Steering Committee cease to exist.

14.12 The Policy and Finance Committee, with the help of the management consultants, consider and recommend to council the appointment of a Chief Administrative Officer for the City of Wentworth who will work with the Policy and Finance Committee and the management consultants on all further recommendations on staff requirements and appointments.

14.13 The existing municipalities freeze, except in emergency situations, the creation of new positions and the filling of vacancies from the date of the release of this report until January 1, 1979.

14.14   Existing staff employed by the Region continue to be employed in the same capacity by the City of Wentworth with the understanding that the staff review referred to in Recommendation 14.5 will include a review of all positions in the city, with particular attention to those areas where service is provided both by the Region and the area municipalities, so that where possible all positions are ultimately filled from the best-qualified employees in the total staff of all seven municipalities.

14.15   The Policy and Finance Committee endeavour to recommend all necessary staff appointments by January 1, 1979, and no later than March 31, 1979. All persons interested in pursuing positions not filled by January 1, 1979, be entitled to employment at their present salary in any capacity assigned to them until March 31, 1979. By March 31, 1979, all employees should be notified as to whether they are required by the City of Wentworth. If they are not required they should be given not less than six months' severance pay.

14.16   Negotiations be carried out between the City of Wentworth, the Government of Ontario and the Ontario Municipal Employees Retirement System regarding offering options of early retirement without detriment to interested members of existing municipal staffs who are nearing normal retirement age, and legislation be enacted to accommodate such arrangements.

14.17   The Government of Ontario bear all start-up costs of the establishment of the City of Wentworth, such as early retirements costs, road signs, vehicle identification, and stationery costs on a negotiated basis.

14.18   The tax increases for the urban parts of the towns of Ancaster, Dundas and Stoney Creek be phased in over the three years 1979, 1980 and 1981 so that the full burden of those increases not become payable until 1982.

14.19   Subject to any overriding province-wide transitional assistance policies that may be developed to deal with general tax or grant reform, the Government of Ontario pay in one lump sum the full costs of the transitional tax assistance required by Recommendation 14.18, estimated on the basis of the 1977 municipal budgets to total $806,000, and the City of Wentworth place this sum in a Reserve Fund, to be invested and used to reduce the appropriate taxes in each of the three years to 1981.

14.20   No existing municipality dispose of any assets worth more than $5,000 from the date of the release of this report.

14.21   All the assets and obligations of the Hamilton-Wentworth municipalities be assumed by the City of Wentworth on the date of its inception.

14.22   The audited surplus or operating deficit of each Hamilton-Wentworth area municipality at the time of the establishment of the City of Wentworth accrue to the credit of, or become a charge on, the assessment supporting such surplus or operating deficit.

14.23 The mayor and Chief Administrative Officer of the City of Wentworth publish a report annually on the state of the municipality of the City of Wentworth.

Preface

Upon our appointment we undertook an extensive inquiry into local government in the Hamilton-Wentworth Region. The terms of reference were broad. They required us to examine all aspects of the political and administrative systems of local government as now constituted and the relationships that exist within the Region and between the municipalities and the province.

In undertaking this task we were under substantial time constraints, having only six months to complete our report. We were able nevertheless to carry out a comprehensive program of public participation and research. We not only conducted an advertising campaign in the press and on radio and television, but we also mailed to every household and business within the Region a notice describing the role of the Commission and inviting comment on the functioning of local government in the Region. The response was most gratifying; we received more than one thousand written submissions from individuals. Sixty groups in the Region made submissions to us and we received almost five hundred telephone and personal calls from individuals giving their views. In addition, we spoke to the people of the Region over two radio programs and by way of speeches to numerous community organizations. It is abundantly clear that the people of the Region are interested in their local government.

We also went out to the community to hear the public's views. We held meetings in every one of the municipalities that make up the Region. The views of elected persons within the Region were also obtained. We met with municipal councils as a whole and twenty municipal representatives spoke with us on an individual basis, as did one former municipal representative and one member of the Legislative Assembly. The local municipalities of the Region formally presented their analysis and recommendations to us during three days of public hearings.

We instituted a broad but selective research program to aid in our deliberations. While some of this work was done by our own staff, by far the larger part was entrusted to outside specialists. Research studies examined not only six functional municipal service areas, but also municipal finance and management, political life, political organization, the economic base of the Region, and the communities which form the Region. Unlike other studies of local government that prepared collections of data before analysis was undertaken, these research studies were both descriptive and analytical in nature. Because of the shortness of time we have not prepared these studies for formal publication but have made summaries of them so that others may have access to the data in them. In addition, a copy of each of the full research reports has been placed in the reference library in Hamilton, in each of the municipal offices and with the Ministry of Treasury, Economics and Intergovernmental Affairs.

It has not been possible to present financial and other statistical data in an entirely consistent manner throughout the report. A variety of factors, such as differences in accounting practices and in administrative organization, resulted in some material not being readily available on a fully comparable basis for all services. In many instances we have accepted the limitations of the data available to us, recognizing that the time and cost of achieving complete comparability would be unjustified by the benefits of consistency, especially where such information would be merely illustrative. In other instances, where the information was essential to making full assessments and decisions, we have been able to obtain the necessary details.

We did not deal directly with boards of education and hydro commissions in our work. Our emphasis on municipal government as constituted was the reason for this. In addition, hydro commissions are now under separate study by others. Aside from these two matters, however, we attempted to deal with the entire field of local government, to evaluate the effectiveness of it in Hamilton-Wentworth and to make recommendations for change. This is reflected in our report which deals with the organization, structure and financing of local government in the Region and examines in detail management, planning and development, physical services, transportation, public safety, social services and health, and parks, recreation and libraries. It also makes suggestions for implementation.

This report is the result of six months of intense work. It was made possible by the involvement of the citizens of the Region and their elected representatives as well as the Commission's researchers. Any study of this nature must also draw on the ability and knowledge of those actively involved in municipal administration. The assistance of many of those working in the system of local government in the Region has been of great value to the Commission.

It would be impossible to list individually all those who contributed to our work in some way. We should like, however, to thank those people and organizations who made submissions to the Commission, the many municipal and provincial officials who provided information and advice, the consultants who prepared the studies, and those in the media who helped make the regional community aware of our work. Hugh Hanson, John Laskin, Barney McCoshen and Diane Mew provided assistance in the writing of this report. Three people have provided so much help to the Commission from the beginning of the review to the conclusion of the report that it is fitting to pay a special tribute to them: Alec Trafford, Executive Secretary; Stanley Makuch, Research Director; and John Jackson, Associate Research Director. Finally, we should like to acknowledge the hard work and dedication of all of our support staff: Patricia Benning, Les Brown, Jill Houston, Zeltite Suskovs and Charlene Waters.

Chapter 1

Introduction

This review of the Hamilton-Wentworth Region is not an isolated event. It is part of a series of studies and reforms that have brought about the evolution of local government in this area. To understand the work of this Commission and the problems with which it was faced, it is necessary to be aware of the history of the Region and its economic development. It is also necessary to understand the underlying values and perceptions we brought to our task. This chapter identifies the values the Commission viewed as important in analysing local government and in suggesting reforms. It describes the perspective we took during our deliberations, and the criteria we used in deciding on our recommendations.

In some ways the Commission's approach was similar to earlier local government studies. The previous studies on, and deliberations regarding, local government in Hamilton-Wentworth all examined the need for restructuring. The provincial government's *Proposals for Local Government Reform in the Area West of Metropolitan Toronto,* (1973), for example, considered boundary changes, the need for one or two tiers, and the consolidation of local authority. That report proposed strong, broadly based local governments that could provide a better strategy for growth, a more responsive government, better administration, better protection, and more effective dealings with the senior levels of government than prevailed under the existing government structure.

In all the earlier studies, however, the primary focus for reform was on boundary changes, and the need for regional governments with a broader geographic base. The report of the Hamilton-Burlington-Wentworth Local Government Review Commission (1969) had such an emphasis on boundaries:

> On the one hand there are municipal institutions originating mainly in an earlier century, designed only to carry out the public functions and to operate within the restricted area boundaries considered appropriate for that time. On the other hand, the continuous pace of change has brought about a complex transformation in functions of municipal government and

the complete obliteration of many previously significant territorial boundaries.

The earlier studies assumed that a redefinition of external boundaries would substantially solve the problems of outmoded municipalities.

The approach of the provincial government in its *Design for Development, Phase II* (1968) was similarly based. Its focus for the establishment of regional governments was on the setting of regional boundaries. The criteria of a sense of community, a balance of interests, an adequate financial base, a sufficient size, and inter-regional cooperation were used to draw the outer boundaries of regions. Indeed, to a large extent, the choice of a two-tiered structure for Hamilton-Wentworth was in keeping with this approach.

Today the concerns in the Region are not so much about the need for regional government and its boundaries as about the cost of the system, duplication within the system, and access to the system. Such concerns, though not dominant, existed previously, and were reflected in the prolonged debate on the specific nature of regional government in Hamilton-Wentworth prior to its establishment. Today, however, they are in the forefront. Consequently, the Commission's review of regional government is different from the earlier studies and is focused not on the appropriateness of outer boundaries but on the cost of regional government, its efficiency, and the problems of duplication and accountability inherent in a two-tier system.

In order to analyse such issues it was necessary for the Commission to ask two quite different questions. The first, and most complex, concerns the nature of local government and what it should be capable of doing. The second asks whether, given their current responsibilities, the local governments in Hamilton-Wentworth are administering their functions in an efficient and cost-effective manner. Pursuing this second question involved the Commission in an examination of whether there may be management techniques that could be used to improve efficiency. Zero based budgeting, reporting requirements and improvements in internal organization were all considered in this regard. This question is technically, rather than philosophically, based.

The first question has to do with what services should be provided, and leads to an examination of the nature and purpose of local government itself. The determination of whether regional government is too costly, results in too much duplication and is too complex or unaccountable required a re-examination of the reasons for establishing such a government. We were concerned that the cost of regional government might be higher than under some other system of local government and that there might be unnecessary duplication; but we were also aware that high costs and duplication might be justified if they allowed substantially improved access to government for the citizens. To evaluate the existing system of regional government in Hamilton-Wentworth, the Commission looked beyond the limited rationale for regional governments of providing a structure to govern a larger geographic area. We focused on the statement in *Design for Development, Phase II* (1968) that the basic aim of "establishing regional governments is to make local government as strong and meaningful as possible."

To adopt this approach meant that the role and needs of individuals within the Region, groups within the Region, and the province's interest within the Region had to be considered in conjunction with the purpose of local government. It was the purpose of local government, however, that had to be considered first in order to determine the suitability of the existing system.

The Purpose of Local Government

A number of reasons for local government have been suggested in the past, including the provision of more efficient administration and the education of citizens in the processes of government through participation in local government. These are important reasons for maintaining and strengthening local government. In the Commission's view, the most important reason for local elected government is that it ensures local political authority and control over services provided in the local area.

It is theoretically possible that a decentralized provincial administration could be established to service Hamilton-Wentworth efficiently. But such an administration would not be sensitive to the needs and desires of the people of the area because it would be responsible to the provincial government, not to the people. Thus, the purpose of local government must be to ensure local political control; in this way local services can satisfy the needs and priorities of this Region, which are different from those of any other part of the province. The local government structure for the Region must be the one that can best identify and respond to those needs and priorities.

It follows from using such an approach to local government that a regional structure is vitally important. Hamilton-Wentworth is much more than a grouping of individual municipalities; it is an interdependent, social, economic, cultural and political community. The needs and servicing requirements of the people of Hamilton-Wentworth are shaped by their regional community. Local government must extend beyond the small and fragmented governments of pre-regionalization. The historical evolution has been toward larger municipal boundaries to deal with increasing urbanization and municipal interdependence. It would be impossible now to reverse this trend and return to a situation where a multitude of independent municipalities exist in the Region. But more importantly, as the Ontario Economic

Council has stated, "because most of the basic services provided by government relate to people in a regional community, that community should be the basis of our political system."

Accordingly, the basic criterion applied by the Commission in evaluating the present structure of local government in Hamilton-Wentworth was: Is this the system that responds best to what local elected representatives perceive to be their regional needs? In applying this criterion, however, the Commission had to keep in mind other values.

The Protection of Minority Interests

Although it is important that regional government can respond to the needs of the area, there may be more than one view of what those regional needs are. The Commission recognized that there are several different communities of interest within Hamilton-Wentworth whose legitimate points of view must be taken into account in designing a system of regional government. The most obvious example of differing points of view is between urban and rural residents of the Region, though other differences based on such factors as class, ethnic origin, income and geographic location within the existing urban and rural communities must also be considered. Any regional government structure which is based on providing regional authority must be based on a consideration of how a regional view can be constructed from the various communities of interest within the Region.

Although responsiveness to regional concerns may be viewed as the most important criterion of any regional system, the Commission recognized that there are other legitimate concerns to be taken into account. One of the most important of these is the implementation of provincial standards to ensure minimum requirements with respect to certain services. The province requires, for example, that basic welfare payments be uniform across the province. The Commission has attempted to determine the extent of provincial interests and has taken these into account in assessing the system.

The protection of individual rights and indeed community rights, is also an important concern. Regional control should not be achieved at the expense of denying protection to people whose interests are damaged by its exercise. A person whose property is devalued by down zoning, for example, must have recourse to appeal. Similarly, while the Region should be able to determine the level and extent of servicing, consideration must also be given to those who do not benefit from the service. This led the Commission to examine carefully the allocation of the cost of services within the Region. In short, it is important that the system of local government provides for protection for minorities within the Region, be they individuals or groups.

The protection of minority rights can be affected by the structure of regional gpvernment. Boards of Control, mayors elected at large, and municipal boundaries all affect the articulation of minority interests and must be considered in this context. Moreover, we were aware that the more balanced the regional government is in its representation, both in terms of rural and urban communities and in terms of other communities of interest, the more comprehensive and legitimate is that government, and the more capable it is to assume new responsibilities.

The Commission realizes that the province has an important role to play in minority rights. The province, through the Ontario Municipal Board, provides protection for individuals and groups in the field of planning. In the matter of transit service, the Minister's determination of the boundary of the Urban Transit Area is an important mechanism to provide such protection. Determination of these matters at the provincial level, however, means that the goal of regional control over them is compromised since the province assumes responsibility for the policy decision itself.

Organizational devices sometimes used for protecting minority rights and ensuring provincial interests are special purpose bodies, such as library boards and Children's Aid Societies. The extent to which these bodies are necessary was also considered and measured against the goal of regional authority. Provincial grants were also viewed in such a light. Given a goal of regional authority to determine regional wants, the Commission considered the provincial granting system in relation to regional needs.

Efficiency in Regional Government

The second major concern of the Commission, in company with an examination of the system's ability to respond to regional needs, was the efficiency of administration. This concern flows directly from the general perception of high costs and inordinate increases in taxes in the Region. The Commission was aware that these costs and increases may be in part the result of inadequate management techniques. The influence of inflation and increases in the volumes of services also had to be considered, as well as the phasing out of provincial grants or services. A vital issue was whether duplication in the system contributes to higher costs. We had to determine whether the existence of two levels of government providing similar services, such as planning and roads, may result in excess servicing, or the loss of economies of scale because of divisions in jurisdiction. In addition, the Commission considered whether the two-tier system government had built into it a bias for increasing or expanding services at the local level because of the small number of services that are allocated to that level. A local municipality might spend more on a particular function because it, like a kind of special purpose body, has little else with which to occupy itself. In addition, it is clear that without one municipal council to control all municipal spending there is no overall focus for decision-making and evaluation of programs and budgets.

An additional aspect of efficiency the Commission considered was that of council control over special purpose bodies such as library boards and the Board of Health. Here the goal of enhancing regional authority could increase efficiency by ensuring better coordination, and control over budgets. Direct council control means a single body can more easily review the cost effectiveness of various services and be responsible to the electorate for them.

Efficiency is in some ways in conflict with the basic objective of having a regional council that can respond to a multitude of local needs. The Commission was anxious to ensure that, in the quest for administrative efficiency, the need for a political expression of local needs and wants within the Region not be lost, and that an appropriate balance between these competing objectives be struck.

Accordingly, there were two steps in our analysis of efficiency: first, the identification of those increases in costs that would have resulted irrespective of the governmental system — costs that result from inflation, increases in the volume of services, and changes in provincial grants, services and standards; and secondly, an analysis of those increases in cost that can be attributed to a two-tier system as such. In analysing the latter, we realized that care has to be taken to balance the possible increase in costs attributable to a two-tier system against the benefits of ensuring local participation in the formulation of regional needs and desires. In addition, the Commission was aware that costs might have risen as the system responded effectively to local needs and wants; in that case the higher costs incurred because of increases in the quality of services and extension in scope of services may well have resulted in improved political responsiveness and accountability.

The Perspective

In summary, the Commission examined local government in Hamilton-Wentworth from a perspective that sees the purpose of local government as being to ensure that the people are able to control regional services to meet their wants and needs. Such a suggestion is not a clarion call for a new era of municipal autonomy, but rather a recognition that regional government reform must be viewed from such a perspective in order to be meaningful. It is, moreover, a recognition that regional governments of some form are essential, and that their viability should be enhanced.

In addition, it was clearly recognized that this goal does not stand in isolation; there are other concerns in reforming local government. First, there is the provincial interest that must be identified in the delivery of the various services. Secondly, the protection of minority, individual and group interests must be dealt with, while recognizing the need to develop a regional perspective.

It is with these concerns in mind that the problems of duplication and excess costs were approached. They are crucial concerns to the citizens of the Region and to the Commission, but efficient administration cannot be examined in isolation from the goal and values mentioned above. The Commission makes its recommendations for local government reform in Hamilton-Wentworth in the hope that the structure recommended will encourage efficiency and fulfill the long-term goal of developing a regional government that can respond to and meet the needs of its citizens.

Alternatives

The Commission identified at the outset a number of alternative local government structures for the Region as follows:
- A return to the former system of local government with a City of Hamilton, a County of Wentworth and the local municipalities;
- A complete single-tier municipality of Hamilton-Wentworth so that the lower-tier municipalities are abolished;
- Six single-tier municipalities with equal authority so that the upper tier is abolished;
- An enlarged City of Hamilton to include that area that is now urbanized or will be in the not too distant future. The rest of the Region could be formed into a new county, annexed to adjacent counties and/or regions, or organized into a new rural municipality;
- A maintenance of the present two-tier regional municipality with certain modifications.

All of the Commission's researchers recommended against the options of returning to the pre-existing system of local government or to one based on six single-tier municipalities. The Commission's view that the purpose of local government is to ensure regional authority and control over services delivered in the regional area also makes these options inappropriate. These options would, in fact, preclude local control because of the geographical difficulties which were raised in the Steele Commission Report of 1969: local government services would cross municipal boundaries. Under these options, therefore, it would not be possible to deal adequately with planning, transit, water, sewage, and road services. Because of this, special purpose bodies and provincial control would be required and thus defeat the purpose of local government reform. The time and cost of dealing with inter-municipal problems would be increased, while municipal financial resources would be reduced.

The possibility of enlarging the City of Hamilton to include an area that might be urbanized in the near future was suggested to the Commission. It is not dissimilar to one of the options suggested in *Proposals for Local Government Reform in the Area West of Metropolitan Toronto*. That solution would provide a local government that can respond to local needs and that does not have built-in duplications and inefficiencies. Moreover, it would resolve the problem of conflicting communities of interest, at least as far as many rural citizens are concerned.

Planning, however, would be difficult to carry out under such an arrangement. The alternatives contained in the regional development patterns proposal suggest a development boundary. The enforcement of such a boundary requires that the same municipality have jurisdiction on both sides of it. Under an enlarged city option, this would not be possible. In addition, this option divides other communities of interest and does not recognize the integrated nature of the present Region. It ignores the criterion of having a government that can effectively respond to local needs, since the rural area, cut off from the financial base of the urbanized area, would lack the resources to act. If the present rural area were annexed to other governments, the problem of representing the interests of those in the annexed portion would arise anew. Accordingly, we discard this option.

The two remaining options available to the Commission are moving to a single-tier system, and maintaining or modifying the existing two-tier system. These options are most in keeping with the concept of a regional government to meet regional needs. In some ways, the differences between them are really ones of emphasis. The present regional structure in Hamilton-Wentworth is a relatively highly centralized one with a great deal of authority placed in the upper tier. The Region has important planning, water, sewage, solid waste, transportation, police, social service, and public health functions, while the only significant areas of local jurisdiction are local planning, parks and recreation, local roads, solid waste collection and fire. In the Commission's view, a movement to a single tier would, therefore, not be a substantial shift in the provision of services. Nevertheless, it must be justified. It is the option of a single-tier municipality that the Commission has chosen to recommend for Hamilton-Wentworth, as being the one that will best serve the goals of strong and efficient local government. The remainder of this report sets out the reasons for this view and describes and makes recommendations on how the new single-tier municipality should be organized, structured and financed in order to meet our criteria of efficiency, accessibility and accountability.

Chapter 2

A History of Hamilton-Wentworth

To provide a better understanding of the present structure of local government in the Region, and to present a background for the Commission's recommendations for reform, this chapter describes the origins and development of local government in Hamilton-Wentworth. The history of local government must be considered in conjunction with the social and economic development of the communities within the Region, for local governments are largely a product of the communities they govern.

The history of Hamilton-Wentworth reveals a pattern of a developing community of interest within the Region and a government structure that reflects it. It shows as well that there were different, narrower and sometimes conflicting perspectives within that community of interest.

Local government in Hamilton-Wentworth has developed, in part, in response to the desires of the people of the area to be governed by those who know and recognize their needs and priorities. One of the earliest reforms in local government in the Region — the establishment of the District of Gore in the early nineteenth century — was an attempt to respond to those desires to provide a separate administrative district for the area. The establishment of Wentworth County in 1849 as a separate political district was a further step in this direction. The rise of separate communities within the area in the early 1800s and the competition among them indicates the different and conflicting groups that make up the broader region. The early separation of Hamilton as a city from the rest of the area recognized the existence of a different and relatively more highly urbanized community. The development of cooperative arrangements in the late nineteenth and early twentieth century between city and county culminated in regional government, and demonstrated the economic, social and cultural interdependence and community of interest present within the Region.

The Pioneer Period

The first settlers in the Region were United Empire Loyalists who came from the

United States after the American Revolution. Although their roots were British and American, they were faced with a distant government centred in Quebec, French civil law, and seigniorial land tenure. There were no locally elected institutions, only a rudimentary government called the Court of Quarter Sessions administered from Quebec. All these characteristics were unsatisfactory to the new residents, and they quickly made their dissatisfaction known.

In recognition of the growing population of the western regions, and in the light of the petitions and grievances of the new settlers, a number of magistrates were commissioned in 1785 to serve the new settlements, and were given some limited jurisdiction to provide local civil services. Three years later the "Upper Country," formerly part of the District of Montreal, was divided into four districts: Lunenburg, Mecklenburg, Nassau (shortly thereafter renamed Home) and Hesse. For each district a judge, justices of the peace, or magistrates, a sheriff, court clerk and coroner were appointed. It was to the justices of the peace, or magistrates, that the most authority in local matters was given. Their powers included, for example, all local finances, road building, the construction and operation of jails and court houses, the regulation of ferries and the sale of liquor licences. They appointed all local officials. This development, therefore, was an attempt to respond to some of the concerns of the people of the new area through administrative decentralization.

In 1792 the four districts of Upper Canada were divided into nineteen counties for the purposes of the militia and of electing representatives to the new legislature. The counties had no other administrative significance. By legislation effective on the first day of the nineteenth century, the District of Niagara was created out of part of the Home District, and for land-granting purposes was in turn divided into townships that included Ancaster, Barton, Binbrook, Glanford, and Saltfleet. The townships of Beverly and the two Flamboroughs were left in the Home District.

Although the pressures of the settlers for a greater say in local affairs grew at the end of the eighteenth century, the government response was very cautious. The minor concession granted was contained in the terms of The Parish and Town Officers Act of 1793, which permitted the householders of any "parish, town or place" to elect annually by public meeting a small number of officials, such as overseers of highways, fence viewers, assessors, pound keepers, wardens and a clerk. These meetings, however, could only be called by agreement of two magistrates, and the officials elected were responsible to the magistrates, not the householders who voted. There was still no local government responsible to the people of the region.

By 1810 the population scattered around the head of the lake was becoming progressively more dissatisfied with the state of local government. The rapid increase of population, and the dispersal of settlement into the interior, combined with the deplorable condition of the roads, made access to local service and justice exceedingly difficult. Local government was centred in the district towns of either York (Toronto) or Newark (Niagara). Long and arduous journeys had to be made to them to visit the land registry office, to attend court, or to conduct official business. The magistrates in those towns had only a scanty knowledge of local conditions outside of them. Understandably, pressure built for the creation of a new district at the head of the lake.

Although there was a consensus about the need for a new district, there was no agreement about the site of the new district town. Each village at the head of Lake Ontario hoped that it would be chosen, in order to increase its wealth and importance by the location of the court house, the jail and the district's administrative offices. The rivalry seemed to be mainly between Brant's Block (Burlington), and the two flourishing mill villages of Ancaster and Cootes Paradise (Dundas). Other petitions came from Crooks' Hollow and Durand's Farm.

Because of the War of 1812, it was not until 1816 that the legislature again turned its attention to local government reform. In that year the District of Gore was created at the head of the lake, taking in parts of the existing districts of Niagara and Home. The new counties of Wentworth and Halton were established within the district. To most people's surprise, Durand's Farm was chosen as the site of the new district town, and named after its new owner, Mr. George Hamilton. Attempts by both Ancaster and Dundas to have the decision changed in their favour were of no avail, although Dundas did not give up easily; ten years later it tried to gain control of the Court of Quarter Sessions with the same end in view. Hamilton, however, was established, and has maintained its dominant position among lakehead communities ever since. A local administrative unit was thus established for the area that was to develop into Hamilton-Wentworth.

Apart from the administration of justice, the major concern of the ratepayers in Wentworth was roads. The magistrates were the ones who decided where roads should go. They divided each district into sections and assigned overseers, who had been elected at the township meetings, to each area. The overseers then summoned those required by law to work on the roads and superintended construction.

Dundas Street was constructed before this time because Governor Simcoe felt it was a military necessity. Local roads were slower to develop. The problem was money and labour. The local tax was restricted by law to no more than a penny to the pound of assessment and the wholesale evasion of taxation by absentee landlords reduced the proceeds substantially. In addition, the first proceeds had to go toward the jail and court house, to the expenses incurred in the administration of justice, and to all the incidental expenses of local government administration. Thus there was so little money left for local improvements that, beginning in the 1830s, the district had to rely on funding from the colonial government for sufficient monies for roads and bridges.

During this period, however, in spite of the difficulties and high costs, several communities in Gore decided to combine their resources to get needed roads completed. A mutual interest was developed in the area for commercial reasons. The Dundas and Guelph Turnpike Company, for example, was organized by commercial interests in the valley in 1827 and was loosely controlled by the local authorities. Two years later the Waterloo Road was financed by the freeholders in Waterloo, Beverly, West Flamborough and Dundas. A little later still the district councils of Gore and Wellington took out shares in the Guelph-Dundas Road. These roads were of particular importance to Dundas, Ancaster and Hamilton because they were the means of increasing the trading areas of those towns. The Hamilton-Port Dover plank road, for example, opened up Lake Erie and the Grand River region to Hamilton, while the Hamilton-Toronto plank road (1845) expanded Hamilton's influence to the east.

Better roads encouraged travel, and as the area became possible to travel, the settlers came more and more to the villages for commercial and social reasons. A stronger sense of community developed. This had an effect on the villages, when it was found that inns and staging posts were profitable enterprises because of the increasing numbers of travellers. As stops for the stage coaches, the inns often became the place where news could be gathered from the outside world, and local taverns became a sort of community centre. Often, indeed, religious services were held in these establishments before churches could be built.

Water transport, too, was important to the early trade in the colony. Traditionally, Dundas had been the major port at the head of the lake, with access to the bay through a natural creek. Hamilton, however, soon developed and challenged this position. In 1832 the Burlington Canal was opened, making the natural harbour of Hamilton accessible to the deep-water boats, and thus commerce soon flourished. Despite the building of the Desjardins Canal to Dundas, completed in 1837, Hamilton became the centre of the shipping trade for the region.

The Growth of Local Autonomy

In the two decades after the establishment of the District of Gore, Hamilton and the surrounding area grew and prospered. By 1833 Hamilton had a population of some 1,400, and was the established commercial and social centre of the area.

Although there was pressure for further government reform during this period, it centred on the desires for more democratic institutions. William Lyon Mackenzie's abortive Rebellion in 1837 was the clearest example of that desire. Nevertheless, in

1833 community leaders sought, and were granted, the authority to have Hamilton incorporated as a town, with the right to govern some of its own local affairs. An act of the legislature established a Board of Police for the town, composed of one member elected from each of four wards, and a fifth member chosen by those who were elected. Among the board's duties were the passing of by-laws, appointment of officials, issuing of licences, fire protection, measures to protect the health and welfare of the citizens, maintenance of streets and roads, provision of a public market, and assessment of taxes. Little other change in local institutions occurred during this period, although Dundas was authorized to hold its own separate town meetings in 1835.

The general lack of representative, responsible government institutions in the colony, and the resulting political unrest led to the appointment of Lord Durham to examine the affairs of the Canadas. Among his suggestions was the establishment of strong municipal institutions based on the principle of local self-government. As a result of his famous report the Act of Union was passed in 1841, creating Canada East and Canada West. In that same year the District Councils Act was enacted, providing for the transfer of much of the power of the Court of Quarter Sessions to elected councils in each of the province's districts. The freeholders in each township of Gore, therefore, were entitled to elect one councillor to the district council. Elected members held office for three years, with one third retiring annually. As a corporate body, the council was able to sue, hold property, enter into contracts, levy taxes, oversee schools and charitable institutions, and administer the functions of justice. The autonomy of these councils was restricted, however, by the power of the central government to appoint the warden, treasurer and district clerk, and to dissolve the council and disallow any by-law within thirty days of its enactment. Limited though it was, the practice of local democracy permitted under the District Councils Act gave invaluable experience that would be put to good use after the enactment of the more thorough reforms that followed eight years later.

During the 1840s the population growth within the District of Gore was rapid, especially in Hamilton, whose numbers reached nearly 7,000 by 1846. Following the lead of Toronto and Kingston, Hamilton was incorporated as a city in that year, with a mayor appointed by elected councillors. Thereafter Hamilton was a separate entity within the district. Elsewhere, Dundas was granted town status in 1847, while the unincorporated villages of Waterdown and Stoney Creek were empowered to build lock-ups and to elect councillors for local purposes. By the 1850s local government institutions reflected the identity of most of the communities at the lakehead. There had also developed a wider community based on the social and economic interrelationships in the area.

The Baldwin Act

Probably the single most important statute affecting local government in Ontario was The Municipal Corporations Act of 1849, commonly known as the Baldwin Act. The Act was the culmination of a long struggle for local autonomy and its provisions still form the basis of many of the municipal institutions of today.

Under the provisions of the Act, the township became the basic unit of local government. The townships, towns and villages became the lower tier of a new two-tiered system. The county, which formerly was an electoral district rather than a local government unit, replaced the district and became the upper of the two tiers. County council consisted of the reeves and deputy reeves from each of the constituent municipalities of the county. The City of Hamilton was not included in this two-tiered system; its incorporation in 1846 had given it the powers that in the rural areas were divided between the county and the constituent municipalities.

In the flurry of activity following the first elections under the new system in 1850, there was a reorganization and refining of the county units at the head of the lake to make them more closely respond to economic and social reality. In 1851 the County of Brant was formed and briefly joined to the United Counties of Wentworth, Halton and Brant. Brant was separated from the United Counties in 1852, and Halton the following year. One of the first actions of the new county government (January 1850) was the creation of the Village of Ancaster. From that decade until 1974, a century and a quarter later, the basic organization of Wentworth County remained the same, apart from some minor interior realignment and the emergence of Stoney Creek as an independent municipality after 1930. That organization reflected the overall community of interest within the area and the smaller elements that made it up.

Though separate local jurisdictions, Hamilton and Wentworth showed an early willingness to cooperate in the building of a common jail and court house. The joint venture was not entirely without conflict, since disputes over the relative contributions to the upkeep occurred on occasion, but an ability to cooperate was clearly evident.

The period after the passing of the Baldwin Act was one of further economic growth. Local government institutions were involved in fostering growth and responding to its consequences. The great engine of modernization and prosperity for Hamilton and the surrounding area was the railroad. It also tied the region together. The most important rail line in Wentworth was the Great Western, which linked Hamilton to London, Windsor, Toronto and Buffalo. In 1849 its promoters, who included the mayor, the Board of Trade, and Sir Allan MacNab, successfully persuaded the city government to purchase £50,000 of Great Western stock. For the next decade the city merchants backed almost every railroad venture that promised to help them tap the resources of the surrounding area. The city council took out stock in the Galt and Guelph Railroad (1853) and the Hamilton-Port Dover Railroad (1855). The latter was promoted by MacNab and the mayor of Hamilton, who promised that the line would secure the Lake Erie and Buffalo trade. In the 1870s increased traffic was facilitated by railways to Dundas and Georgetown, which not only aided the Hamilton merchants and the rural farmers, but allowed the townships to enjoy the commercial and cultural advantages of the larger city.

With the railways came the modern base of Hamilton as a major steel and manufacturing centre. The rolling of rails originally brought from England formed the basis of the iron and steel industry, and the manufacture of locomotive engines and cars soon followed. The Gurney Iron Foundry, Wanzer's sewing machine firm, and Sawyer's agricultural implements were among the early businesses to locate in the city. A sign of the dramatic growth of economic activity was the quadrupling of the city's population between 1846 and 1859.

This growth was not without problems, however. The heavy commitments of the council to railway stock, and the generous tax concessions given to attract business left the municipality with tax revenues unequal to civic needs. A brief experience of bankruptcy (whose most onerous consequences for the taxpayers was avoided by a temporary absence of both the city clerk and the tax roll) and a chronic inadequacy of funds kept many local services to a bare minimum.

The city fathers had not far to look for ways of spending the few dollars that were left. The requirements of hygiene dictated the building of sewer and water systems in the 1850s. In a situation not unfamiliar to municipal councillors today, the Hamilton council found itself responsible for the debentures of the independent board, in this instance for water, although it had no control over the decisions about the water supply system. In large part these sanitary measures were undertaken at the urging of the Board of Health, which was appointed in 1847. Under their persuasion, too, the first permanent hospital was purchased, though so small that it was overcrowded with four patients. It was soon replaced by a larger facility that combined hospital and workhouse.

Further Changes in Local Government

Problems of this kind were not to diminish in the decades ahead. The idea of establishing boards with a single field of responsibility to look after particular services did not disappear. Indeed, the special purpose body, as it is called, came to be used increasingly. Among the separate boards with power to draw funds from the local tax base that were formed in the following period were the Library Board (1882), the Parks Boards (1883), and the formal Boards of Health (1884). Other functions that were organized on a basis of political independence from council control but that drew on local property tax support over the decades were care of neglected children (the first Children's Aid Society of Hamilton was formed in 1894), juvenile courts (1910), sanitary inspectors (1911), suburban roads (1915), and relief (1935).

Although the broad foundations of local government as laid down in the Baldwin Act have remained intact for much of the province until today, the provincial government decided to take a more active interest in the overseeing of the operations of local government. In 1882 the Bureau of Industries was created to collect municipal statistics. Fifteen years later, after several instances of municipal auditing errors and defalcations, the office of Provincial Municipal Auditor was established to supervise municipal bookkeeping. The Ontario Railway and Municipal Board was created in 1906 to provide supervision of local public utilities. Four years later the Bureau of Municipal Affairs was established to centralize and coordinate provincial supervision of all municipal activity.

The large number of defaults during the Great Depression led to the creation of the Ontario Municipal Board, which was given authority over all capital expenditures and permanent improvements made by local councils. The Department of Municipal Affairs was formed shortly after, with final responsibility for administering all government legislation that affected municipalities and improving the conduct and administration of municipal affairs.

A recurring problem for the County of Wentworth over the years was the matter of representation on the county council. Since each municipality was represented by its reeve and deputy reeve, in the case of many of the smaller municipalities clearly their representation was not in proportion to their population or to their contribution to county taxation. A reform in 1896 tried to deal with this by having county councillors elected separately, independent of the township elections, and basing the new electoral districts on population, assessment and acreage. Whatever the theoretical merits of this system, in actual practice the separation of the county council from the municipal councils lessened the importance of the reeves, and many of the smaller townships were left without a resident representative on county council. Recognition of this weakness led to the restoration of the original county council system in 1907. The number of members was reduced by providing that each reeve should represent 1,000 voters. In a somewhat similar way, the method of selecting representatives on municipal councils was altered back and forth during the last half of the nineteenth century. By 1900, however, all mayors, reeves and deputy reeves in Wentworth were elected to their positions.

Throughout this period local government was responding to the demands of commercial and industrial development. It underwent reorganization to serve better those needs that the citizens of the time thought were important. Special purpose bodies were therefore instituted; local government became involved in public utilities; and the board of control, a separately elected body, was established in anticipation of streamlining and making more efficient the local government process.

The Past Century

Despite occasional difficulties in the form of economic recessions and epidemics, Hamilton and the surrounding county of Wentworth grew and prospered. Social and cultural facilities accompanied the increase in population. The city hospital was relocated to Barton Street in 1882, and the public library built in 1890. Another landmark was the establishment of the Hamilton Street Railway in 1874.

A lift was given to the iron and steel industry in the 1880s with the deepening of the Welland Canal, which allowed cheap water transportation of many of the city's products. It was not until 1895, however, that the first iron was actually smelted in Hamilton by the Hamilton Blast Furnace Company, which had benefited from a grant of seventy-five acres, $75,000 and tax concessions from the city. That company united with others from Montreal in 1910 to form the Steel Company of Canada — Stelco. Dominion Foundries was formed in 1912, and changed its name in 1915 to Dominion Foundries and Steel (Dofasco) when it began its own steel production.

The past century of economic growth, moreover, has been one of the increasing integration of the region. The growth of Hamilton and the surrounding area resulted in increasing intergovernmental relations among the region's municipalities. To a large extent the municipal involvement in the railway in the nineteenth century was replaced by similar involvement in the electric streetcar. Four electric lines carried farm produce, passengers and freight between Hamilton, Dundas, Ancaster, Stoney Creek, Burlington, Brantford, Oakville and Grimsby at the turn of the century. All four lines were owned by Dominion Power which also provided electric power to the region. The Hamilton-Grimsby-Beamsville line (1896) served the fruit and cannery businesses in the area and contributed to the development of a profitable milk industry. The city council thought the streetcar route would be important for the area and it gave the line $25,000 to get underway. By the 1920s this feeling had spread to Ancaster, Dundas and the other municipalities along the routes. Thus, when Ontario Hydro (which had taken over control of the radial lines in the 1920s) announced its plans to abandon the streetcar routes, the province was forced to extend its service several times because of the protest and complaints from the communities along the line. During the 1930s the intermunicipal electric streetcars were replaced by bus service.

Intermunicipal undertakings in streetcar transportation were an important recognition of the interdependence of the region, but there are other examples. In 1891, West Flamborough and other interested townships in the area purchased the old Dundas-Waterloo Turnpike and converted it into a free road. A decade later the county was given the authority to designate county roads, and by 1904, Wentworth had established a uniform system of free roads. These macadamized roads, however, could not bear the heavy and sustained traffic load of the expanding population, and asphalt or concrete-surfaced highways were too costly for the rural communities. The ultimate result was the creation of the Hamilton-Wentworth Suburban Roads Commission (1918) through which Hamilton had to make contributions for roads in its immediate area. The commissioners were appointed in equal numbers by the county and the city, and the costs were paid by Wentworth, Hamilton and the province. The first improvements were made along portions of King Street, Main Street, Barton Street and Beach Road.

In the area of pollution control and beautification, the city and county worked together in both official and unofficial ways. The Hamilton Board of Parks Management, which was established in 1900, designed Chedoke Winter Sports Park, King's Forest and Confederation Park. Environmental groups were responsible for the preservation of the Escarpment in its natural state from Chedoke Falls to Albion Ravine (1913), and the Royal Botanical Gardens (1930) was developed out of an unsightly stone quarry.

Other areas of intermunicipal cooperation include the operation of the county health unit and the Wentworth Library Co-operative. The library co-operative was formed in 1947 to purchase and distribute books and to stimulate library development throughout the rural townships. A short while later, a book van was added to facilitate book distribution in the outlying districts. Public health services for the entire region were consolidated in 1968. Further evidence of the citizens' willingness to cooperate for the general good is found in the establishment of the Hamilton-Wentworth Planning Area Board; the financial aid given to Wentworth County by the city to enable the county to rebuild and modernize its own court house (1955); and by such unofficial actions as the city and county clerks' decision to submit joint advertisements to the local newspapers.

After the Second World War it became increasingly evident that local government structures in Wentworth no longer corresponded to the realities of community life. Annexations were used in addition to the structures mentioned to solve problems of interdependence, but these proved unsatisfactory. The old concept that rural areas must be separate from urban places had to be re-evaluated. With little other than agricultural land as the basis for raising revenue, the rural townships were particularly hard hit by the decline in agriculture in the postwar years, while at the same time such monies as were available had to finance a much greater variety of responsibilities. What was needed was a consolidation of the financial resources of Hamilton-Wentworth to improve its effectiveness in dealing with urgent urban problems, and a restructuring of the local government system to promote greater efficiency in social and economic planning.

It was this recognition of the greater interdependence of the city and the surrounding municipalities that led both the city and the county to request the province to examine the need for local government reform in the area. Studies documented the increasing interdependence of the region and the need to break down the barriers within it. The establishment of regional government in 1974, which united the city and its surrounding neighbours, is a clear recognition of that interdependence. The continued development and the successes and failures of that union is the subject of the rest of this report.

Chapter 3

A Demographic and Economic Description of the Region

The analysis and design of government institutions must take into account not only the history of the area under study, but also the characteristics of the people, the growth and distribution of the population, and the economy of the area. By looking at the present and probable future composition and distribution of population and of the kinds and location of economic activity, one may gain a better idea of the sorts of problems that will probably be uppermost in the future deliberations of local government, and thereby gain some insight into what kind of municipal organization may be best able to deal with these issues.

This chapter, accordingly, is devoted to an analysis of the current economic and demographic characteristics of the region and of the changes in these characteristics that are about to occur in the future.

The statistical material presented in this chapter comes from many sources, including a boundary study we commissioned, census documents (of which some are no more recent than 1971), Ontario government studies, and the official plan documents of the Region. We have not ourselves undertaken the difficult and expensive job of preparing estimates of population and economic growth, but have relied wherever possible on the "most likely" projections contained in the regional draft official plan.

Demographics

POPULATION DISTRIBUTION

In 1976, the Regional Municipality of Hamilton-Wentworth had a population of 409,490, of whom just over three quarters (76.2 per cent) lived in the City of Hamilton. So overwhelming is the preponderance of Hamilton that the second largest municipality in the Region, Stoney Creek, had only 7.4 per cent of the total population.

Table 3.1: Population, 1976

Municipality	Population	Per cent of total
Ancaster	14,255	3.5
Dundas	19,179	4.7
Flamborough	23,580	5.7
Glanbrook	10,179	2.5
Hamilton	312,003	76.2
Stoney Creek	30,294	7.4
Region	409,490	100.0

SOURCE: Statistics Canada, Census of Canada, 1976.

The other significant feature of the population distribution is the concentration of all urban development at the centre of the Region, in the City of Hamilton and environs. The developed parts of Dundas, Ancaster and Stoney Creek are all immediately adjacent to Hamilton and development is almost continuous. For example, the only physical distinction between neighbouring parts of Hamilton and Stoney Creek is the road sign.

The numbers of rural residents of the Region are, of course, small. In the 1976 census, Statistics Canada classified only 39,081 people (or 9.5 per cent of the total population) as living in rural areas. All Glanbrook residents are classified as living in a rural setting as are 88 per cent of those in Flamborough, 30 per cent in Ancaster, and 15 per cent in Stoney Creek. All of Dundas and Hamilton are classified as urban. By no means all of the people classified by Statistics Canada as living in rural areas actually live on farms. In 1971, only 17.3 per cent of the population classified as rural residents lived on a farm (which is defined as a piece of land at least one acre in size and having sales of agricultural products within the previous twelve months valued at $50 or more). In reality, only 1.8 per cent of the population were farm residents in 1971. Although more recent figures are not available, we may assume that the proportion of farm residents now is even less, because the proportion of rural dwellers fell by one percentage point between 1971 and 1976.

POPULATION GROWTH

Although the population of Hamilton-Wentworth has grown from 312,924 in 1956 to 409,490 in 1976, the actual rate of growth has been declining since the late 1950s. In the five-year period between 1951 and 1956 the population grew by 18.9 per cent, while between 1971 and 1976 it grew by only 2.1 per cent. But all parts of the Region have not experienced the same growth rates. The two municipalities in which the growth rates between 1971 and 1976 were highest are Flamborough (12.7 per cent) and Stoney Creek (10.7 per cent). The Town of Ancaster actually had a decrease in population of 832. The population of Glanbrook and Dundas now seems to be rather stable. In the City of Hamilton, population is declining dramatically in the residential areas adjacent to the industrial and central business districts. But Hamilton also contains some high-growth areas near the edges of the city: south of Mohawk Road to the Glanbrook boundary, and below the Escarpment east of Red Hill Creek to the Stoney Creek boundary.

The growth rate of Hamilton-Wentworth has been lower than that of the province of Ontario as a whole since 1956; between 1966 and 1976 in particular, the population of Hamilton-Wentworth grew by only 7.1 per cent, while the population for the entire province grew by 18.7 per cent. This trend is expected to continue over the next two decades. Provincial government population projections indicate that among those counties and regions expected to have a population over 250,000 by 1981, Hamilton-Wentworth's growth rate will be the lowest. For the period 1981-1991, its growth is projected at 7.5 per cent; the next lowest growth is the Region of Niagara (12.7 per cent). By contrast, the population in the neighbouring Halton Region is expected to increase by 30 per cent during the same period.

The Regional Planning Department's "most likely" population projection for the Region is given in Table 3.2.

Table 3.2: Region's "Most Likely" Population Projections

Year	Projected population	% increase in 5-year period
1981	438,681	
1986	465,202	6.0
1991	492,520	5.9
1996	521,137	5.8
2001	551,107	5.8

SOURCE: "Population — Future Growth in the Hamilton-Wentworth Region," Regional Planning and Development Department, Regional Municipality of Hamilton-Wentworth.

This projects a somewhat higher growth rate than the Region experienced over the past decade but still not what could be called substantial growth. It means an annual addition of 5,000 to 6,000 people, or an average annual growth rate of approximately 1.4 per cent.

As tenuous and problematic as overall population projections may be, forecasts of the distribution of that population within the Region are even less certain. Nonetheless, Table 3.3 shows two sets of projected population distributions within

DEMOGRAPHIC AND ECONOMIC DESCRIPTION 23

Table 3.3: Projection of Population Distribution within Region, 1976-2001

Municipality	Actual pop. in 1976 (000's)	% of pop. in Region	If 1971-1976 trend continues				Planned for 2001 according to Region's draft official plan	
			pop. in 1981 (000's)	% of pop. in Region	pop. in 2001 (000's)	% of pop. in Region	pop. in 2001 (000's)	% of pop. in Region
Ancaster	14.3	3.5	14.3	3.3	14.3	2.6	18.0	3.3
Dundas	19.2	4.7	20.7	4.7	26.3	4.8	25.0	4.5
Flamborough	23.6	5.7	32.0	7.3	64.3	11.7	35.0	6.3
Glanbrook	10.2	2.5	11.1	2.5	14.4	2.6	14.6	2.7
Hamilton	312.0	76.2	321.0	73.2	355.5	64.6	382.0	69.5
Stoney Creek	30.3	7.4	39.6	9.0	75.2	13.7	75.4	13.7
Total	409.6	100.0	438.7*	100.0	550.0*	100.0	550.0*	100.0

* Total population for Region is based upon the Region's "Most Likely" projections.

the Region for the year 2001. The first set is based on a continuation of the present trends, the second on the proposed planning strategy of the regional government. The basic difference between the two is that fulfilment of regional planning intentions would result in Flamborough not growing as quickly as present trends indicate, and in Hamilton growing somewhat more quickly. Both indicate some decline in Hamilton's preponderant position in terms of population from its present three quarters of the Region's total to approximately two thirds by 2001. Nevertheless, Hamilton will remain the dominant area. In both projections, Stoney Creek is the major growth area, increasing from its present position of containing 7.4 per cent of the population of the Region to 13.7 per cent by 2001. The other possibly substantial change in distribution is the ranking of Flamborough. It now contains 5.8 per cent of the population; if the current trends continue, it will nearly triple its population by 2001 and will house 11.7 per cent of the Region's population. The carrying out of the Region's proposed plans would, however, radically change the growth situation in Flamborough Township; the Region's proposed population for Flamborough in 2001 is nearly 30,000 smaller than would result from a continuation of present trends.

POPULATION CHARACTERISTICS

By looking at certain characteristics of the people who live in each area municipality one may gain an impression of the relative homogeneity or heterogeneity of the Region. By examining the ethnic origins and religious affiliations of the residents, one obtains some understanding of their backgrounds and the different perspectives they may have.

Table 3.4: Ethnic Origins and Religious Identification, 1971

Municipality[1]	British Isles Origin	Protestant[2]
Ancaster	73.6%	68.7%
Dundas	71.8	67.6
Flamborough	67.8	66.4
Glanbrook	71.1	69.8
Hamilton	57.3	50.1
Stoney Creek	61.0	57.0
Total	59.6	53.1

[1] Consolidated from those of pre-regional government municipalities. No correction is made for annexations.
[2] We have placed Anglican, Baptist, Lutheran, Pentecostal, Presbyterian and United Church in the Protestant category.
SOURCE: Statistics Canada, Census of Canada, 1971.

Table 3.4 shows that in the 1971 census returns ethnic origin of the majority in all six municipalities was the British Isles. This group was less dominant in Hamilton (57.3 per cent) than elsewhere; with the exception of Stoney Creek, over two thirds of the population in the other municipalities identified themselves as of British origin. Almost three quarters of Ancaster's population made such an identification. The pattern is similar for religious affiliation. This Region is characterized by a predominantly Protestant population. Except in the cases of Hamilton and Stoney Creek, Protestants made up at least two thirds of the population in each of the municipalities in 1971.

Economic Structure

EMPLOYMENT

The dominant economic factor in the Region is steel. It is the largest industry, and as a result the manufacturing sector is the largest employer in Hamilton-Wentworth. Almost half the employment for men is in manufacturing, and 38.1 per cent for men and women combined (in 1971). The comparable figure for the whole of Ontario is 26.2 per cent. The relatively heavy dependence of this Region on the manufacturing sector is clearly demonstrated in Table 3.5.

Within the manufacturing sector, 34 per cent of the 1971 employment in manufacturing was in the iron and steel mills. This accounts for one eighth of the entire labour force of Hamilton-Wentworth. Moreover, a number of other industries are heavily dependent on the iron and steel mills, since they provide specialized services to that industry, or rely on its products for their inputs.

Table 3.5: Labour Force by Sector, 1971

	Hamilton-Wentworth % of total labour force	Ontario % of total labour force
Primary sector (agriculture, forestry, fishing trapping, mining)	1.7	5.6
Secondary sector (manufacturing and construction)	44.9	32.6
Tertiary sector (trade, finance, community services, public administration, etc.)	52.5	60.8
Unspecified	.9	1.0

SOURCE: Statistics Canada, Census of Canada, 1971.

This dependence on the steel industry is a cause of concern for many people in the Region. Although Hamilton's annual production of steel doubled between 1963 and 1974, the immediate prospects for the industry are uncertain, particularly in the face of proposed barriers to steel imports into the United States and a currently less buoyant domestic economy than existed during the 1960s. The steel requirements for gas pipelines in the Canadian north may raise the demand for structural steel, but it seems that even this is unlikely to boost the industry's employment locally because of competition from other areas and the restricted opportunities for expanding the existing plants due to the limited availability of land. Hamilton's competitive edge in the steel industry is lost if expansion cannot occur at the existing sites. In a study completed for the Region in 1977, Woods, Gordon & Co., Management Consultants, concluded:

> In the general area of economic viability it should be said from the outset that Hamilton-Wentworth will still continue to be a major centre for steel over the next 10-15 years and that employment growth in this major industry could provide an additional 2,000 new jobs. We do not foresee any rapid or disastrous decline in community economic prospects on the basis of the steel and related industries. Against this, however, we (a) cannot look to steel as the generator of substantial new jobs as heretofore, (b) must expect growing competition at least in the steel-related industries from Nanticoke after 1986-91, and (c) cannot look to the steel-related industries themselves to provide much new employment over the next 10-15 years. In short, Hamilton-Wentworth must look immediately to new manufacturing industries, major retail functions and especially the services sector for the expansion of employment opportunities in the future. (Hamilton-Wentworth Steel and Related Industries Substudy, March 1977).

Stated simply, although employment in the steel industry is not expected to decline over the next ten to fifteen years it will not increase in any major way. If employment opportunities are to grow substantially, they will have to be found in other industries.

Most of the Region's other manufacturing industries expect sluggish market conditions in the near future because of anticipated weak demand. The establishment of new manufacturing firms in the Region or the exodus of existing firms would have an impact upon the levels of employment opportunities. There are no current indications, however, of significant increases or declines in the manufacturing industries within this Region. The Region's Planning and Development Department reports an increase during 1977 over the previous year in the number of inquiries from firms considering locating in the area. The department did not report that any of these inquiries resulted in any new industry being established, though it did report the loss of two firms that moved from the Region to Halton in 1976. Projections for Ontario by the Ontario Economic Council and by the Ministry of Treasury, Economics and Intergovernmental Affairs point to a decline in the growth rate of manufacturing sector employment in Ontario during the next decade. On the basis of these projections for Ontario, it is difficult to be optimistic about the growth of manufacturing employment opportunities in the Hamilton-Wentworth Region.

It is in the tertiary sector — service industries, commercial enterprises and government — that employment is expected to increase most rapidly in Ontario during the next twenty years. Currently employment in the tertiary sector in Hamilton-Wentworth is a smaller proportion of total employment than in Ontario as a whole. During the 1960s, the growth in employment in this sector was slower in Hamilton-Wentworth than in the rest of Ontario. Unfortunately, only incomplete data are available for examining the growth of employment by sectors during the 1970s; these data cover the whole of the Hamilton Census Metropolitan Area, which comprises Hamilton-Wentworth, Burlington and Grimsby. This admittedly partial information indicates, however, that during the early 1970s the situation was showing signs of changing. Employment in the tertiary sector in the Hamilton census area grew at a more rapid rate than employment in other sectors, and also at a more rapid rate than in the rest of Ontario. During the period 1974 to 1977, however, the growth rate of the tertiary sector slowed down, although it was still faster than the rate of growth of other sectors. While the growth rate was slowing down in the Hamilton census area it was speeding up in Ontario as a whole, with the result that Hamilton's rate of tertiary employment growth is considerably slower than the average for all Ontario.

The prime concern about the condition of the local economic structure is its effect on job opportunities. It is commonly feared that if the economy is not constantly expanding, stagnation and indeed decline will set in and unemployment will become a serious problem. The unemployment rates for the Hamilton census area are available only since 1975. They show that during 1976 and 1977 the unemployment rate was lower in Hamilton-Wentworth than in the rest of the province. The average rate for January to November 1977 was 6 per cent in Hamilton and 7 per cent in Ontario. The Ontario Treasury reports that, on the basis of Unemployment Insurance Commission data for 1976, the Hamilton district had the lowest rate of unemployment of any Unemployment Insurance Commission district office in Ontario.

To get a longer-term perspective on probable employment opportunities, however, one must turn to the industrial composite employment index. That index gives an indication of the rate of job creation or loss in an area, although it is only an indication, since the survey on which it is based includes only industrial firms which employ at least twenty people. Between 1971 and 1974 the index rose steadily. From

1974 to 1977 it fell constantly, to the point that it is now lower than the 1973 level, indicating that there are fewer industrial jobs in the Hamilton census area now than there were at that time. This fall could be explained by an overall reduction in the level of economic activity; but a more disturbing conclusion that can be drawn from the employment indices is that the gap between the index for the Hamilton census area and the index for Ontario widens during periods of province-wide stagnation, showing that the rate of job loss in this area exceeds that for the rest of the province. During periods of growth in the rest of the province, Hamilton-Wentworth has experienced a rise in job creation but only at a rate similar to that for the rest of the province. If this index is truly indicative of the whole of the local economy, and if Hamilton continues to perform as it has in the recent past, it seems unlikely that the area will for long continue to enjoy its relatively low unemployment rate.

Another indicator of employment opportunities is the rate of participation in the labour force by people of working age. The participation rate is related primarily to two factors: the desire to work, and the ability to find work. When comparing participation rates among such culturally similar communities as those of Ontario one may assume that differences in desire to work do not have a substantial impact on the comparisons.

The 1971 census shows that 60.4 per cent of the working age population in Hamilton-Wentworth (people 15 years and over) were participating in the labour force. In Ontario, the participation rate was 62.1 per cent. The difference in these rates is caused by the relatively low participation rate of women in the Hamilton-Wentworth labour force compared to the whole of Ontario (41.3 per cent and 44.3 per cent respectively); the rate for men was almost identical (80.4 per cent and 80.3 per cent). The most likely explanation for this difference is a lack of opportunity for women to find employment, which discourages them from joining the labour force. Hamilton's specialization in heavy manufacturing means that there is a relatively low demand for female labour. Expansion of the service parts of the tertiary employment sector, and the establishment of new types of manufacturing, would undoubtedly result in an increased participation rate for women in this area.

Employment opportunities in the Hamilton-Wentworth Region are heavily concentrated in the City of Hamilton. Table 3.6 shows that of the 135,780 people resident in the city and in Wentworth County who also worked within this area in 1971, 88 per cent worked in the City of Hamilton while only 79 per cent of those employed in the area lived in the city. Sixty-two per cent of the employed people in Wentworth County worked in Hamilton. For every municipality in the county, more residents worked in the city than in their own municipality, indicating a close interrelationship between Hamilton and each of the other municipalities of the present Region. It is important to note, however, that even though more residents

Table 3.6: Place of Work — Place of Residence Exchanges within Wentworth County, 1971

Municipality lived in[1]	Municipality worked in (Percentages are % of those employed in Wentworth County and City of Hamilton combined)						Total number of Hamilton-Wentworth residents employed in Wentworth County and City combined	Outside Wentworth County and City	Partials[2]	Total employed residents
	Hamilton	Ancaster	Dundas	Flamborough	Glanbrook	Stoney Creek				
Hamilton	102,105 95.3%	385 0.4%	1,230 1.1%	395 0.4%	395 0.4%	2,540 2.4%	107,050	17,950	115	125,105
Ancaster	3,250 67.8%	1,185 24.7%	195 4.1%	45 0.9%	50 1.0%	50 1.0%	4,775	165	15	4,955
Dundas	3,570 60.5%	65 1.1%	2,070 35.1%	110 1.9%	20 0.3%	35 0.6%	5,870	910	25	6,810
Flamborough	2,850 47.1%	135 2.2%	630 10.4%	2,340 38.7%	10 0.2%	70 1.2%	6,035	3,270	35	9,315
Glanbrook	2,275 68.5%	40 1.2%	15 0.5%	5 0.2%	810 24.4%	155 4.7%	3,300	500	15	3,820
Stoney Creek	5,850 66.6%	5 0.1%	55 0.6%	10 0.1%	35 0.4%	2,795 31.8%	8,750	2,225	15	11,010
Wentworth County	119,900 88.2%	1,815 1.3%	4,195 3.1%	2,905 2.1%	1,320 1.0%	5,645 4.2%	135,780	26,015	215	162,010

[1] Consolidated from those of pre-regional government municipalities. No correction is made for annexations.
[2] Individuals who did not identify their municipalities of employment in the Census of Canada.

SOURCE: Statistics Canada, 1971 Census of Canada as compiled in "Economic Base, a Substudy of the Regional Official Plan" by the Planning and Development Department of the Regional Municipality of Hamilton-Wentworth, 1975. Columns do not always add up to totals. The figures do, however, correspond to those in the source.

worked in the city than in their own municipality, at least 30 per cent in each case did find employment in their home municipality. The municipality whose people are least dependent upon Hamilton for employment opportunities is Flamborough, which had almost as many people employed within its own boundaries (2,340, primarily in Waterdown) as in the city (2,850). It is interesting that more Flamborough people found employment outside the area, primarily in Halton (i.e. Burlington), than in Hamilton.

In terms of exchange of employment across regional boundaries in 1971, there were more Hamilton-Wentworth residents finding employment outside the Region than there were people from other regions employed in Hamilton-Wentworth. Sixteen per cent of employed Hamilton-Wentworth residents travelled out of the Region to work. The major destinations were Halton County, Metro Toronto and Waterloo County. The people who travelled into the area to work came mainly from Halton, Niagara Region and Haldimand County. Because of the incorporation of part of Beverly Township into the Region of Waterloo in 1974, the dependence on Waterloo for employment opportunities may now be less. The major exchange of residents for jobs was across the Hamilton-Wentworth / Halton Region boundary. In 1971, 11,180 Halton people worked in Hamilton-Wentworth and 6,905 Hamilton-Wentworth people worked in Halton.

The Region's proposed official plan includes recommendations that, if adopted, would affect the location of new employment, particularly new manufacturing employment, within the Region. Although it may be possible to dispute the figures as being based on overly optimistic employment expectations, they are of prime interest because they indicate where new manufacturing jobs will be located. Table 3.7 compares growth in population by municipality with growth in manufacturing

Table 3.7: Growth in Population — Growth in Manufacturing Employment, 1976-2001

	Growth in population, % of total growth in Region	*Growth in manufacturing employment, % of total growth in Region*
Ancaster	2.6	18.4
Dundas	4.1	—
Flamborough	8.1	7.9
Glanbrook	3.1	19.8
Hamilton	49.9	19.1
Stoney Creek	32.2	34.8

SOURCE: Regional Municipality of Hamilton-Wentworth, Planning and Development Department, "A Regional Development Pattern for Hamilton-Wentworth: Statistical Summary and Tables," September 1977.

employment opportunities. The table indicates that for manufacturing jobs the residents of the Region will likely become somewhat less dependent on industries located in the City of Hamilton.

INCOME

Undoubtedly, the main reason for people's concern about the economic structure of their community and the surety of employment opportunities is their concern about personal income. The average total family income for residents of the Hamilton area is slightly above the average family income for all urban Canada. The area has maintained this position over the past fifteen years, although in the past five years it has lost ground relative to other Ontario urban areas and some cities in Western Canada.

Although the most recent year for which a measure of income by individual municipality within the Region is available is 1970, there is no reason to suspect that the relative positions have changed significantly since that time. Table 3.8 shows that Ancaster had the highest average household income, being almost 30 per cent higher than the average for the county and city combined. Hamilton was the lowest, being about 3 per cent below the average.

Table 3.8: Average Household Income, 1970

	Average income	% different from average
Ancaster	$13,053	+ 29.9
Dundas	11,685	+ 16.3
Flamborough	10,819	+ 7.7
Glanbrook	10,978	+ 9.2
Hamilton	9,719	- 3.2
Stoney Creek	10,768	+ 7.2
County and city combined	10,049	

SOURCE: Statistics Canada, Census of Canada, 1971.

There are several ways of measuring income disparity within a region, of which only one is this comparison of average incomes between the constituent municipalities in the Region. Another way is to look at the proportion of families falling within each income category. Still another is to determine the degree of segregation of income groups, the clustering of poor or rich into exclusive areas. In each of these measures, the Hamilton-Wentworth Region shows a smaller degree of income disparity, differentiation and segregation than other Canadian urban areas of a similar size. One probable reason for this relatively even distribution of wealth is the heavy reliance of so many people in Hamilton-Wentworth on the manufacturing sector for their employment, and on the steel industry within that sector. Steel has a major impact on wage levels not only in its own industry but also, because of its proportionately large size, in other industries that must compete with it in getting employees.

RETAIL SALES

Another basic measure of the economic situation of an area is the sales of services and retail goods. Of particular interest to the Commission is the extent to which each community is self-sufficient in providing goods and services to its own population. One can get a rough estimate of this by looking at the distribution of sales of certain items and comparing it with the relative population of the municipalities in which those sales are made. Because of a lack of detailed information for the smaller communities, Table 3.9 compares only the sales in the City of Hamilton as a percentage of all sales in the Region with Hamilton's proportion of the total population.

The table shows that, for 1971, only in the areas of "Amusement and Recreation" and "Food Sales" was the percentage of expenditures in the city smaller than the city's relative population in the Region. All the other figures indicate that a substantial number of people outside Hamilton relied on sources in the city for consumer goods and services. This is an important indicator of the interdependence of the city and the other municipalities in Hamilton-Wentworth.

Table 3.9: Retail Trade by Business Group, 1971

Business group	Dollar value of sales in Hamilton as a % of dollar value of all sales in the Region
Services: total	89.4
Amusement and recreation	71.6
Service to business	97.3
Personal service	88.2
Accommodation and food	84.4
Miscellaneous	95.8
Retail sales: total	85.2
Food	76.9
General merchandise	94.3
Automotive	86.0
Apparel and accessories	91.2
Hardware and home furnishings	89.7
Other	82.5
Hamilton's proportion of total Region's population in 1971: 77.1%	

SOURCE: Statistics Canada, Census of Canada, 1971.

Impact upon Local Government

As mentioned at the outset, the reason for examining the population and economic characteristics is to give a wider perspective with which to understand existing local government structures in this Region and to consider changes. There are two broad types of observation that may be made about the material as it affects local government. The first is the nature of the relationship between the constituent parts of the Region. The second is the nature of some of the most important existing and emerging problems with which local government will have to deal.

INTER-RELATIONSHIPS IN HAMILTON-WENTWORTH

The strong bond between the people of the City of Hamilton and those of the surrounding municipalities is undeniable. Population is now heavily concentrated in the city and all urban growth outside the city lies in very close proximity to its borders. The 1976 Canadian census found that 90 per cent of the population of the Region of Hamilton-Wentworth lives in the urban core focused on the City of Hamilton, a situation that is unlikely to change in the next twenty-five years. While it is true that half the population growth is expected to occur outside the city, most of that will be extensions of, and filling in of, urban development now lying immediately adjacent to the city. The majority of the people share a common ethnic heritage and religious orientation.

The pattern of employment opportunities indicates that Hamilton-Wentworth is not an area of people in separate communities merely living near each other, but rather that the constituent municipalities are highly interdependent. The sales figures for consumer goods and services also indicate a substantial interaction between the people of Hamilton and the other municipalities in the Region.

This pattern of strong interactions within the area makes it clear that a municipal government structure that ignores the significance of that bond by trying to set up a government for the City of Hamilton totally separated from the government for the rest of the Region will not serve the best interests of either the people of the city or of the rest of the Region. A single social and economic community should have a local government structure that reflects and fosters that community of interest.

However, this relationship is not without tension. The strength of the interrelationship is undeniable, but there are differences between the people. As we observed, the outer municipalities contain farm residents (few in number, admittedly) and also a very sizeable group of rural non-farm residents (8.5 per cent of the Region's population in 1971). The people who make up this latter group often have chosen to live in a more rural setting in reaction to high densities, high taxes, and high cost of housing. Often similar motivations underlie the attitudes even of those who live in urban settings outside the city proper, for example, in Ancaster and Dundas.

There are additional differences in the characteristics of the people between municipalities. As we noted earlier in this chapter, the people of Hamilton and of Stoney Creek are relatively dissimilar from the residents of the other municipalities in the Region in terms of make-up by religious and ethnic identifications. There are also substantial differences in income levels; average incomes in Hamilton are the lowest in the Region while those in Ancaster and Dundas are the highest.

The Commission must try to balance the forces of integration and of division within the Region. In doing so, it must be aware of the differing concerns of people in different parts of the Region and also of the need to treat the Region as an integrated whole. This is the most difficult problem which the Commission and which the people of this Region must confront when considering what is desirable as a local government structure.

IMPACT ON LOCAL GOVERNMENT PROGRAMS

The dominant expectation from the foregoing sections is one of slow growth in population and in development of the local economy. An actual decline in the local economy or population, however, is not expected. The people of Hamilton-Wentworth are now reasonably prosperous and are likely to remain so.

The combination of slow population growth and strengthened planning controls now in use means that urban development will not be spread throughout the Region but will be quite concentrated. Accordingly, even though the provision of services has not caught up with areas already settled, the demand on municipal government to provide sewers, water and roads should not be heavy. The exceptions to this generalization are Stoney Creek and Glanbrook. Since it is in Stoney Creek that much of the new growth is expected in now undeveloped areas, certain new infrastructure services will be needed. Similarly Glanbrook may find itself with entirely new development areas to service. Overall, however, the dominant concern of local government does not have to be with securing the technical expertise and huge financial resources needed when undertaking major new infrastructure works.

The relatively stable population should have an important impact on politics in the community. At times when there is a major influx of new residents into a previously stable community, the accepted political structures, habits and personnel of the community come under strain. New people often do not understand and do not accept the old ways of doing things. Acting in accord with their own values and interests, they often come into conflict with those in power. Although it occurs to some extent in all municipalities, this conflict arises most sharply in rural municipalities that are undergoing urban development. Flamborough is currently experiencing some of these problems but, if the Region's proposed official plan is implemented, a slower growth rate should relieve these pressures substantially. Glanbrook, now an almost totally rural area, is likely to experience some transition problems if the regional plans for the development of Binbrook and along the present boundary with Hamilton are fulfilled and when the airport is expanded. In general, however, a slowing of population growth should lessen the strain, allowing new and old residents more time to come to understand each other, to establish effective working relationships, and to resolve their political differences.

In terms of the economic situation, Hamilton-Wentworth is relatively prosperous, although present trends indicate that compared to the rest of the province the Region will undergo a period of slower economic development. An outcome of this is likely to be an uneasiness among local people bred by the fear that lessened growth will ultimately lead to a downturn. As a result, municipal government in the Region will undoubtedly become more concerned about instituting positive promotional programs to strengthen and develop the regional economy than it has in the past. Every elected municipal representative who spoke at the Commission's public hearings indicated a desire to encourage the diversification and growth of industrial development within the Region. Hamilton-Wentworth requires a structure of local government that will facilitate such development.

Since an actual decline in the economic situation is not expected, municipally provided social services should not encounter serious new demands on them. The probable expansion of employment in service industries, however, with the accompanying rise in the participation rate for women, may well mean an increased demand for day care facilities. In addition, since such infrastructure problems as sewers, water service and roads are not likely to be major consumers of municipal energies once the necessary catching up has been completed, the future may be a period of concentration on restraint in spending or of the gradual introduction of expanded programs in such fields as social services, parks, recreation and public transit. Without steady economic growth in the Region, however, municipal government is not likely to feel that it has access to the extra funds required to embark on many new programs.

To summarize, economic and population factors will not confront municipal government with any particularly serious or unusual problems in the near future. It should be a relatively stable time, giving municipal government the opportunity to solve problems that have not been dealt with in the past, to restrain expenditures, and to use excess energies to institute specialized new programs, particularly in the area of encouraging further economic development and diversification. Above all, the period will provide local politicians and the local people with the opportunity to focus on the development of political processes to better the relationships between the residents and their government.

Chapter 4

The Basis for Reform

Introduction

The year 1974 is seen by many as a year of radical upheaval in local government in the Hamilton-Wentworth area. A new two-tier system of government was introduced, replacing a system that had been in existence for over 125 years. We are now recommending a shift from that two-tier regional government to a single-tier government covering the same geographical area. We recognize that many will look upon this recommendation as another radical transformation of local government structures and another dramatic break from the past.

The Commission does not view the changes of 1974 as being as major as they are sometimes portrayed. We think of them as changes that heavily emphasized boundary adjustments to take into account the changing nature of the relationships between the people and the municipalities in this region. Those changes simply continued, and in many cases recognized, changes that had already occurred during the 1960s. In addition, the reforms were attempts to adjust certain factors that were hindering the development of these new relationships. They were based to an extent on the objective of devising a government that can respond to regional needs and wants.

We have examined the municipal government in Hamilton-Wentworth and conclude that the reforms of 1974 have not resulted in a government that can fulfill this objective satisfactorily. Further structural changes must be made if local government in this area is to succeed in responding to the needs and desires of the people of this region.

Before describing in detail our recommended changes, it is necessary to analyse the present government in Hamilton-Wentworth.

The Reforms of 1974

The reforms of 1974 involved three major changes: the uniting of the City of Hamilton with the County of Wentworth for certain decision-making purposes; the joining of some lower-tier municipalities in the county with each other; and the shift of certain functions from the lower tier to the upper tier or new Regional Council. The first two of these changes were in effect boundary changes: the complete removal of some boundaries and the expansion of the boundary of the county government to a region-wide basis.

Underlying each of these structural changes was a major concern — land use planning. The pressures of the expansion of population during the 1950s and 1960s and the nature of the settlement patterns of those years led to the recognition that effective planning could not be carried out separately by each of the municipal jurisdictions then in existence. The municipal boundaries were much too narrow to deal with planning problems of a region-wide nature. At first, efforts were made to deal with this problem by setting up a joint planning body, the Hamilton-Wentworth Planning Area Board. This did not prove satisfactory, however, since there was no single council with the authority to approve or implement plans. New government jurisdictions were necessary.

The most dramatic break with the traditions of the past in the reforms of 1974 was the creation of a council composed of representatives from the City of Hamilton and the other municipalities in Wentworth County. Prior to 1974, the city interacted with these other municipalities by means of three mechanisms: special purpose bodies, intermunicipal agreements for sharing facilities, and annexations.

Several special purpose bodies were set up to act as the administrative and sometimes decision-making bodies to facilitate cooperation between the city and county. The major examples of these were the Suburban Roads Commission, the Children's Aid Societies, the District Health Unit, the Hamilton-Wentworth Planning Area Board, and the Hamilton-Wentworth Emergency Measures Organization. This approach to cooperation had serious disadvantages. Special purpose bodies with sufficient authority to adequately carry out their functions eroded the powers of the municipal councils. Special purpose bodies that did not have final decision-making powers were ineffectual because they were unable to reach binding decisions and carry out their functions.

The City of Hamilton had agreements with the individual municipalities immediately adjacent to its boundaries — Dundas, Ancaster, Glanford, Saltfleet and Stoney Creek. There was extensive provision of intermunicipal services, the most significant being water and sanitary sewage facilities. The city extended its water and sewage lines into Dundas, Ancaster, Saltfleet and Stoney Creek. But these arrangements often proved unsatisfactory to the municipalities involved. The future development of the municipalities adjacent to Hamilton relied upon the ability to persuade Hamilton to extend physical services. Simultaneously, the city disliked providing services to neighbouring municipalities without being able to control their development; in effect, the future demands on its own basic water and sewage treatment and trunk main facilities were beyond its control. Hamilton also often felt that the other municipalities were not covering their share of the costs of the services extended.

Annexations were never more than short-term solutions to the problem created by the lack of a common council to make decisions. Housing developments would soon extend once again beyond the boundaries of the municipality, with renewed demands for water and sanitary sewage facilities in the outlying municipality.

As a result of these inadequacies in the then existing relationships between the city and the county, and between the city and its adjacent municipalities, in 1974 elected people from Hamilton and from each of the other municipalities in the county were brought together to sit on a regional council. In effect, the city was made a member of the two-tiered county government system that had long been in operation in the rest of Wentworth County.

During the 1960s it became increasingly evident that the boundaries between lower-tier municipalities in the county did not correspond to actual service areas and that the municipalities were too small to provide services efficiently within their existing boundaries. As a result, there developed a growing interaction between townships and between rural and urban non-city municipalities, similar to the arrangements between Hamilton and the municipalities that surrounded it.

Two major limitations soon became evident in this type of intermunicipal cooperation. As with the intermunicipal agreements between the city and other municipalities, there were frequent frustrations and delays. But in the case of these smaller municipalities there was an additional problem with which intermunicipal cooperation could not deal. Local government was developing into an operation that required a broader and more detailed range of skills, especially as provincial regulations, grant structures and demands became ever more detailed and pervasive. It was no longer realistic to expect a clerk-treasurer to do all these tasks himself. But a more specialized administrative staff could not be justified to serve the small populations of the county towns and townships.

In recognition of both the growing interaction between municipalities for the provision of services and the limitations that existing municipal boundaries placed upon this cooperation, one important aspect of the formation of regional government in 1974 was the creation of larger governmental units at the lower tier. The number of lower-tier municipalities in the former County of Wentworth was reduced from ten to five.

The other major aspect of the reforms was the movement of responsibility for certain functions to the upper tier or Regional Council. During the 1960s there had been an expansion of the number of functions dealt with by the County Council.

Certain functions, such as welfare and assessment, could be provided in a better and more economical way if the County Council was given responsibility to make decisions about them, and to oversee their administration. The introduction of regional government continued the trend to shifting functions to a level of government with jurisdiction over a wider geographical area.

The upper tier or Regional Municipality of Hamilton-Wentworth is responsible for certain functions on a region-wide basis. Regional land use planning, industrial development, water works, sanitary sewage works, solid waste disposal, arterial roads, transit, social services, and debenture financing are the main functions that now lie with the Regional Municipality. Policing and public health services are provided on a region-wide basis, although they are not direct responsibilities of the Regional Council.

The six lower-tier or area municipalities — Ancaster, Dundas, Flamborough, Glanbrook, Hamilton, and Stoney Creek — retain all those powers not specifically delegated by The Regional Act to the upper tier and yet allowed by The Municipal Act to be carried out by municipalities in Ontario. Local land use planning, land drainage, area roads, solid waste collection, fire protection and parks and recreation are the most significant of these functions.

There is a Regional Council of twenty-eight members: the chairman, seventeen members of the City of Hamilton council, and two members from the councils of each of the other five area municipalities in the Region. Thus each of the members of the Regional Council, except the chairman, also has a seat on an area council. For the five municipalities outside the city, the mayor and the regional councillor sit on both councils. The mayor, the four members of the board of control, and twelve aldermen chosen by the members of city council represent the City of Hamilton on the Regional Council.

The head of the Regional Council — the regional chairman — is elected for a two-year term by the members of the Regional Council at their first meeting as a newly elected council. The person chosen as chairman may or may not already be a member of a municipal council. If the person chosen is already an elected council member, however, that person must resign the council seat.

The Present Problems

The Commission has examined the existing structure of local government in Hamilton-Wentworth and found that the present institutions do not fulfill our criterion of a government that can respond to the needs and desires of its citizens. In our view, there are three basic problems: there are serious conflicts between city and non-city politicians, which interfere with and retard the development of policies to serve the citizens of the Region; the structure blurs accountability and hinders accessibility, with the result that it cannot respond to the citizens easily; and finally, the structure of the system results in resources not being used as efficiently as possible.

POLITICAL CONFLICT

The most controversial aspect of the reforms of 1974 is the nature of the new relationship between the City of Hamilton and the other municipalities. As described in Chapter 3, the Region is very clearly focused on the Hamilton urban area. Almost all urban growth is either within the city or immediately adjacent to its borders. Understandably, the non-city municipalities fear that they would be submerged by the overwhelming weight of Hamilton's population and by the city's dominant influence if they were combined with the city for government purposes. Partly as a result of the very strong expression of this fear, the provincial government set up a two-tier system of regional government, although it had presented a single-tier alternative for consideration.

As a result, the smaller municipalities retain control over certain functions without having to worry about the city dominating their decisions in these areas. But, because some very important matters are decided by a council where Hamilton is dominant, the two-tier system has not soothed the fears of the outlying municipalities. The present structure of local government reflects those fears; special protective and balancing mechanisms have been put into the system. The city, though having 76 per cent of the population, has only 63 per cent of the seats on council. From the other perspective, 24 per cent of the population (those living outside the city) have 37 per cent of the representation on the Regional Council. In this way the province withdrew significantly from the principle of representation by population in order to counteract the fears of the non-city municipalities.

Even though the city is relatively under-represented in terms of its population, it does control seventeen of the twenty-seven seats on the Regional Council. Ottawa-Carleton is the only other regional municipality where one area municipality controls more than half the votes on a regional council. (Ottawa has 53 per cent of the voting strength on the Ottawa-Carleton Regional Council.)

In addition, special quorum features were put into The Regional Act to protect the smaller municipalities. A quorum for a regional council meeting requires fifteen members representing at least three area municipalities. Although this means that the City of Hamilton can end any meeting if all its representatives withdraw from the chamber (it is impossible to have fifteen members without having some city people present), this is not of concern, since the city has a majority of seats on the council and, if its members are unanimous, can control a vote. More importantly, it means that the five municipalities in the former county can end a meeting if all eight representatives of any four of those municipalities choose to withdraw or to be absent. For the outlying municipalities, therefore, the quorum provision is a significant protective mechanism. This quorum provision has been used by the noncity municipalities only once — in February 1975, over the issue of where regional council meetings should be held.

The Regional Council itself has introduced further balancing and protective mechanisms. Chief among these is the over-representation of the non-city municipalities on the committees of council, to correct the predominance of the city that would result if strict population criteria were applied. The procedural by-laws of the Region specify how many people on each committee will be from the city and how many will be from the other area municipalities combined. In each case, the city has a majority of the members. Except for the Social Services Committee, however, where the split is six and three, the city's majority is only one.

In this way, the present structure is designed to balance two of the concerns outlined in Chapter 1 of this report: making decisions from a regional perspective, and taking into account minority concerns. The unifying of the system for certain very important functions — especially some land use planning and physical services — so that the municipal government would be able to respond to the needs and desires of the people in the entire Region was the basis for establishing the Regional Council. Simultaneously, the protection of the interests and concerns of the smaller communities within the Region is achieved by retaining a second tier of smaller municipalities and by the special protective mechanisms introduced in the Regional Council. It was hoped that the compromises made in the setting up of a two-tier structure would encourage representatives to work together to operate a regional government that could lessen the strong suspicions that had necessitated these compromises. An understanding and acceptance of each others' differences, and the development of common concerns and perspectives were the expected outcomes.

The processes of learning to work together and of recognizing common interests have not gone very far. The main problem confronting municipal government in this area is the suspicion and the acrimony between city and non-city municipalities, which, in our view, are fostered by the present regional government structure. This was clearly illustrated by the public part of this review culminating in the municipal submissions in February 1978. The municipalities outside the City of Hamilton were able to come to agreement on a joint brief that supported the present two-tier system with only minor changes and praised the accomplishments of the Regional Council. The City of Hamilton's brief, however, was completely different, urging a single-tier government, with some question left open as to the position of the rural parts.

Over the past four years, the members of the Regional Council have been able to achieve substantial successes in terms of providing for the needs of this Region, even though the process has been long and arduous, and has often resulted in compromises that run counter to the best interests of the Region. There is evidence, however, that the task of developing policies to satisfy regional needs is often set aside as a result of the desire of each area municipality to protect its separate existence and to get what it considers the best deal possible for its own residents, even at the expense of the overall needs of the people of the Region. The Commission is convinced that it is the structure of the regional government that encourages this unfortunate attitude when municipal representatives are discussing regional problems.

A good case in point is the regional transit system. It was not until 1977, after years of negotiation between the city and non-city municipalities and the province, that the responsibility for the operation of the Hamilton Street Railway Company and Canada Coach Lines was transferred from the City of Hamilton to the Regional Municipality of Hamilton-Wentworth. The negotiations during that time focused not on developing mechanisms to foster the best transit system but on divisions between the city and non-city municipalities. As a result, the long process of working out a system for regional transit has actually resulted in a decision-making structure that makes it difficult for transit to be planned on a regional basis. Service into areas outside the City of Hamilton depends on the signing of an intermunicipal agreement by the Regional Council with each of the area councils in which the service is provided. This means that the Regional Council can determine neither the locations of service nor the frequency of service. As a result, there cannot be a regional transportation policy that the Regional Council has the power to implement.

Another example of the difficulty in reaching agreements is the transfer of some of the roads in Hamilton to the regional roads system. Again, it was not until 1977 that this occurred, although the Region had taken on the responsibility for many roads in the other area municipalities in January 1974. The agreement for this transfer occurred only after the provincial government agreed to make a substantial contribution to payment of the debt charges that would have been transferred to the non-city municipalities through the assumption of arterial roads by the Region. There are still complaints from non-city politicians that too many of Hamilton's roads were transferred to the regional level. Again, prolonged negotiations focused on the differences and conflicts between the city and non-city municipalities rather than on ways to serve best all the people of the Region.

Distrust also shows up in the transfer of special cultural facilities from the City of Hamilton to the Region, with the result that any deficits incurred fall on all taxpayers in the Region rather than on only those in the city. The Art Gallery, which is now likely to involve growing costs to the Region, is one example of this, and it seems likely that the city will request the transfer of other similar facilities to regional jurisdiction in the future. The non-city municipalities see such transfers as efforts by Hamilton to get rid of the responsibility for paying for some of the deficits incurred on money-losing projects that the city chose to initiate. The opinion of the non-city municipalities is that, not having been involved in the decision to construct these facilities, they should not have to help finance the losses incurred. But Hamilton feels that these facilities are for the benefit of all the people in the Region and therefore should be paid for by everyone. Here again, a municipal structure that does not promote joint decision-making and joint responsibility has encouraged the development of bitter feelings between city and non-city municipalities.

The single most important reason for establishing regional government is to permit region-wide planning. Nevertheless, the present structure has failed to allow the development of common perspectives, and there are indications that there may be some difficulty in securing general agreement to the proposed official plan. At our municipal hearings it became evident that the city and the other municipalities have quite different opinions of the "Recommended Pattern for Development in Hamilton-Wentworth" currently under discussion. The non-city municipalities lauded it as an example of the success of the regional government. By contrast, the representatives of the City of Hamilton thought the proposed plan was an example of the inability of the Regional Council to arrive at the most desirable region-wide solution.

We find these difficulties distressing examples of what happens in a structure that emphasizes protection of the separateness of municipalities. This emphasis on separateness in the structures is reflected in the behaviour of elected representatives on the Regional Council, who often stress their differences and exhibit attitudes that reflect suspicion of each other. We are convinced that there is no validity behind these suspicions. One example that leads us to this conclusion is the use of regional planning staff for local planning purposes by the Town of Dundas and the City of Hamilton. Despite the repeated declarations of the unworkability of such an arrangement by the other four municipalities, on the ground that the regional planners would not take into account the special local needs, both Dundas and Hamilton have expressed complete satisfaction with the service they receive.

The question we are left to consider is whether the present institutional structures, by being too concerned with protective mechanisms for the constituent municipalities, have resulted in hindering the development of a common perspective. For example, even though the mechanisms to protect various concerns have not actually been used in a divisive way, they were repeatedly pointed out to us as means used by the area representatives on the Regional Council to threaten each other. A system based upon threats, either stated or implied, and upon mistrust of the other partners is clearly not satisfactory, since it works against the defining of common goals and the providing of a united thrust for the Region.

Our analysis of the functioning of regional government indicates that a regional perspective has not developed, and we conclude that it cannot develop within the present structure. In our research study, *Political Life in Hamilton-Wentworth,* the municipal councillors were asked the following question: "Do you feel that the regional government of Hamilton-Wentworth has helped to foster a community of interest in your Region?" Forty-six, or 69.7 per cent of the respondents replied no. Only eighteen, or 27.3 per cent, said that it had. Of even greater interest is the study's finding that there is no significant difference in opinions on this question between those who sit on Regional Council and those who sit only on area councils. This shows that sitting together on Regional Council for the past four years has not resulted in a feeling of common purpose. Indeed, we conclude that the present municipal structures in Hamilton-Wentworth may actually be worsening the situation.

We are disturbed also by the unwillingness of many councillors to assume responsibility for the problems in the area. All too often we heard even Regional Council members accuse the Regional Municipality of not dealing with problems. These regional councillors did not recognize their responsibility to make the system work and to try to deal with the problems in the area. This lack of attention to the concerns of the Regional Council and of region-wide matters also showed up in the *Political Life* Study. When regional councillors were asked to estimate the relative proportions of their time spent on regional and area council matters, only three out of twenty-six respondents said that they spent more time on regional matters. Four said that they spent an equal time on regional and area matters. But nineteen, or almost 75 per cent, of the regional councillors said they spent more time on local than on regional matters. Indeed, some said they spent more than four times as much time on area matters. This focus on local rather than regional issues showed up again when they were asked if they had campaigned mainly on regional or local issues. Only one person said that he had campaigned mainly on regional issues.

This Commission has heard a great deal of negative comment about regional government. Rarely did these comments criticize specific policies; instead they focused on the loss of local autonomy that occurred when the new form of government was established, and emphasized the need to retain separate municipalities within the Region. The Commission is convinced that this attitude to regional government is the product of a structure that encourages politicians to look at regional concerns from a narrow perspective and to emphasize divisions. This situation leads the residents of the Region to believe that differences and the resultant conflicts are inevitable in regional government and makes them hostile to it. And because the prime loyalty of the politicians is to their local council, there is no one, with the exception of the chairman, to explain the Region to the people.

From all these foregoing observations we conclude that the prime objective of municipal government — ensuring that the people of the Region are able to control regional services to meet their wants and needs — will not be achieved within the present institutional structure. That structure facilitates and encourages acrimonious relationships that hinder the development of a regional perspective and divert Regional Council from its main purpose of meeting the needs of the Region.

ACCOUNTABILITY AND ACCESSIBILITY

The second series of problems that we have observed in Hamilton-Wentworth local government relates to the questions of accountability and accessibility — both of which we pointed out earlier as prime objectives in setting up and judging municipal government structures. Two basic ingredients for achieving these objectives are understandability by the public of government structures and responsibilities, and the assumption of responsibility by the elected people.

Our numerous contacts with the residents of this Region by telephone, letter and at public meetings showed us that there is a great deal of misunderstanding about the present system. The cause of most misunderstanding is the division of responsibility for functions. A detailed knowledge of the powers of each level of government is necessary if time and energy are not to be wasted in trying to have problems resolved. The lack of such knowledge results in frustration and a feeling of lack of access. Simultaneously, accountability is weakened since it is necessary to know who is responsible for specific functions if politicians are to be held accountable.

The other side of accountability is the assumption of responsibility by the elected people. Regional politicians direct most of their time to area council matters both during election campaigns and while in office. They often refuse to assume responsibility for what happens at the regional level. In the present structure, there is only one person whose full-time concern is with regional matters — the regional chairman. She makes it her regular task to explain the operation of the system and to give the reasons behind the activities of the Region. Most other regional councillors seem to see their prime constituency and major direct responsibility as being the area municipality on whose council they sit.

During the past six months we have heard a great deal of dissatisfaction from the public with the way in which the regional chairman is chosen. Repeatedly we were told that the regional chairman should be elected directly by all the residents of this Region. We believe that the unhappiness of the people with the way the chairman is now chosen is a product of the frustration they feel in their efforts to hold the regional government accountable. When their regional councillors stress their role in area municipal matters, the public identifies only one person as being truly responsible for regional problems — the regional chairman — and this person they do not elect. It is, of course, unfair to place all the blame for the Region's problems on the chairman, since the position does not carry significant legislative or executive powers.

EFFICIENCY

The third major problem we have been concerned with is the inefficiencies of the present system. Of the 1,500 written submissions and telephone calls received at our office, two-thirds said the system is too costly. In Chapter 7 of this report we examine the reasons behind tax increases over the past four yeas and suggest that they have not been inordinate. We believe, however, that there are two aspects of the present system that lead to inefficient expenditures of money: duplication, and the absence of a mechanism for overall priority setting.

The obvious duplication that exists in the present two-tier system is the existence of seven municipal councils and seven administrative staffs.

The other aspect — the absence of a mechanism for overall priority setting — has significant impact on the expenditure patterns in the Region. Ideally, each proposed expenditure should be examined to determine the total financial impact it will have on the residents of the Region. The decision-making body must then balance the various expenditure proposals and determine which should be approved within the overall limitations. Special purpose bodies in local government have long been the object of criticism because, being responsible for only one function, they do not need to take other programs into account when developing their expenditure plans. The two-tier regional government structure, by leaving fewer functions at the lower tier or area council level, has, in effect, made the area councils more like special purpose bodies. This has resulted in expenditures on some functional areas increasing more rapidly than previously. Parks and recreation is the best example of this. Since some of the other major functions were taken away from the area councils in 1974, it is understandable that these councillors now pay more attention to, and therefore put more money into, the parks and recreation functions.

Both of these factors contributing to the inefficient use of funds in the two-tier regional government system are discussed in more detail in chapters 6 and 7.

The Proposed Structure

The Commission is convinced that a single local government, assuming all municipal responsibilities for the entire region, is needed to provide a structure that is able to respond effectively and efficiently to the needs and wants of the citizens of the region. A single local government will best overcome the three most important deficiencies of the present system: acrimonious relations between the city and its neighbours; a lack of accountability resulting from uncertainty about the relative responsibilities of the various levels now existing; and inefficiencies resulting from duplication and the lack of any overall control of local government budgets.

A single local government should reduce the acrimonious political relations currently existing in the Region. The single tier of government would receive the undivided loyalties of all those elected to it, and it will be impossible to blame another level of local government for decisions. We are confident that the result of this will be a stronger local government, better able to respond to the needs of the citizens of the Region. Politicians will no longer be distracted by municipal divisions, as there will be no division within the Region along municipal lines. Acrimony, which has characterized much of the political debate within the Region, will be diffused by such a change, and debate focusing on municipal divisions will be replaced by debate focusing on other political considerations. The Commission is concerned that, unless changes are made to obviate the type of conflict that exists within the Region as now structured, conflict will continue and may well result in bringing local government into further disrepute and ultimately to a standstill.

Having one local government for the Region will obviously alleviate problems of divided responsibility resulting from seven municipal councils. No longer will citizens be forced to go from one level of local government to another to ascertain who has responsibility for dealing with their problem. A one-tier system of government will be easier for citizens to deal with and to understand. It will, therefore, make local government better able to respond to and meet their needs.

Although the Commission's research did not reveal any extreme inefficiencies, nor did it suggest that the two-tier system of government results in inordinate duplication, it did indicate that both planning and transit could be aided by a one-tier system. In addition, it is the Commission's conclusion that the establishment of a single-tier system may aid in industrial promotion, by reducing unproductive competition, and by providing a structure whereby a concerted and coordinated effort can be made. In our view, the duplication in the area of general government as a result of maintaining seven municipalities is unwarranted, given the political difficulties that the maintenance of these separate jurisdictions has created. We conclude that one body is needed to oversee all municipal spending in the Region and that, because of the large increases in spending that have resulted in some areas, it is inappropriate to maintain local municipalities with relatively few functions. Our most important concern, however, is that from the point of view of the ratepayer there is a need for one body that is responsible for, and that can control the ultimate tax burden. This need is made more important by the existence of the independent role of the Boards of Education. The relative increases in taxes and the impact of the Boards of Education on those taxes are examined in Chapter 7.

Recommendation 4.1: The lower-tier municipalities of Hamilton-Wentworth be abolished and a single-tier local government structure composed of one municipal council be established in the present Region of Hamilton-Wentworth.

To strengthen the local government structure, the Commission gave consideration to modifying the one-tier system in order to ensure both easy access for citizens and a wide representation of the diverse interests within the Region. We had research conducted into the operation of local government in the City of Winnipeg where under recent reforms community committees are retained. We gave consideration to a suggestion made to us for district committees. The Commission concludes, however, that there should be no political structures established by legislation other than the council of the new municipality. Our reasons for recommending a one-tier structure also led us to dismiss the notion of requiring committees at a community level and granting those committees even limited legislative authority. To solve the existing problems, the new council must be the only focus of authority and loyalty. If municipal boundaries are reintroduced under the guise of committees as legislative or quasi-legislative bodies, then the entire problem of municipal divisions and political acrimony will continue, and the difficulty of citizens understanding where authority lies will not be diminished.

Recommendation 4.2: No legislative or quasi-legislative political bodies be established in addition to the one municipal council.

There is a strong community of interest among all residents of the Region. Our economic study and the accomplishments of regional government to this time attest to that. We realize, however, that the conflict that has characterized much of the life of regional government in Hamilton-Wentworth is the result of differing interests and views within the Region. The Commission is also aware that such divisions are not merely ones of city versus non-city residents; other divisions and other communities of interest within the Region are even more important. Suburban and urban groups have different interests from those of rural people, interests that cross the present city-non-city division because of the planning, transit and development problems these two groups face. Their lifestyles as well have a great deal in common. The people of the urbanized part of Stoney Creek, for example, have more in common with residents in the City of Hamilton than with residents of the rural areas of Flamborough. Income groups have a community of interest that transcends city and non-city interests. We think that groups interested in planning, the environment, recreation and cultural activities, for example, are all based on common concerns far more basic and important than a city versus a non-city dichotomy.

It is the Commission's view that the best way to ensure that various interests are represented on council is by having a relatively large number of wards with one alderman per ward. This will mean that citizens or groups across the municipality can work to elect people to the council who represent their particular interest or point of view and not simply a city or area municipal point of view. Such a system will enable political groupings to form along policy lines. The ward system will maintain a geographic element in the electoral process, while the restriction of one alderman per ward will eliminate conflict and duplication between aldermen of the same ward. In addition, the Commission has concluded that, although a relatively large number of wards is required to reflect the multitude of interests within the Region, care must be taken to ensure that the size of the council is not so large as to inhibit effective decision-making.

Recommendation 4.3: The council of the municipality be composed of twenty-seven aldermen, each representing one ward.

The Commission cannot ignore the existence of the strong feelings expressed at its public hearings about the maintenance of existing municipalities. In addition we recognize that the existing municipal boundaries do in fact reflect legitimate and important communities of interest within the Region that should be given some recognition. Moreover, if a serious attempt is not made initially to reflect those communities of interest and those boundaries in the new municipality, the citizens may have difficulty in understanding and dealing with their new municipality. One way of giving recognition to existing municipalities without maintaining separate governmental bodies is to prevent the ward boundaries from crossing existing municipal boundaries, at least initially. The Commission is convinced, however, that the abolition of existing municipalities will mean that within a few years present municipal conflicts will disappear and the need to ensure that ward boundaries correspond to the former municipal boundaries will also disappear.

Recommendation 4.4: Legislation provide that the wards of the new municipality initially be established within existing municipal boundaries.

In addition to recognizing the importance of the existing boundaries within the Region, the Commission also accepts that there is a need to ensure that the present City of Hamilton does not, because of its population, initially dominate the new council. We are concerned about a need at the outset to protect the minority of non-city residents within the Region. We are confident that after the establishment and operation of the new municipality for a number of years, divisions on a city versus non-city basis will disappear because of the absence of those separate municipalities. When that happens there will no longer be a need to protect the non-city minority because political divisions will then occur, as we have suggested, on different bases. This process should be completed before the expiry of two terms of the council of the new municipality. Until that time, special representation provisions should be made in order to protect the minority living outside the city. We suggest that a principle of close to equal representation for the present city and non-city areas is appropriate for the new municipal council but that the principle of representation by population be recognized to the extent that representation from the present City of Hamilton form a majority of the council.

> Recommendation 4.5: Legislation provide that representation on the new council initially be fourteen members from the area of the present City of Hamilton and thirteen members from the rest of the Region.

> Recommendation 4.6: Legislation provide that after two elections the council be empowered to alter ward boundaries under the provisions of The Municipal Act.

The Commission had little difficulty in choosing a name for the new municipality. We felt that it should no longer be called a regional municipality because of the two-tier commotation of that phrase and because of the hostility that the term regional government provokes in the citizens of the Region. The municipality that we are recommending will have only one tier, it will be one of the largest municipalities in the province, and it will have all the powers of a city; we conclude that it should be described accordingly.

With respect to the geographic portion of the name, we suggest that an attempt be made to break with the acrimonious past. Our recommendations offer a new start for Hamilton-Wentworth under a new structure. We are not concerned to ensure the existence of the name of Hamilton or of any of the other area municipalities in the official designation of the new municipality. The names Dundas, Stoney Creek, Hamilton, Ancaster, Flamborough and Glanbrook are not dependent on their inclusion in the official title of the municipality for their acceptance and use. The name Hamilton Tiger-Cats can obviously continue as can the name Hamilton Place and the name Hamilton Philharmonic Orchestra. Similarly the name of the Stoney Creek Dairy, of the Dundas Merchants Hockey Team and of the Ancaster Agricultural Society can continue. The identity of communities depends not on municipal structures but on the traditions of community institutions.

The name Wentworth is suggested by the Commission as an appropriate one since it is not part of any area municipal name and yet is of substantial historical significance and connotes the entire area of the Region.

Recommendation 4.7: The new municipality be called the City of Wentworth.

The Commission is most anxious that the council of the new City of Wentworth organize itself and have the ability to work in a way that will provide strong leadership to the municipality and ensure that it achieves the Commission's goal of strong and efficient local government. The term of office in municipal government has an important impact on the ability of municipal councils to function well. There is a need to have a term that is short enough to encourage responsiveness to the electorate, particularly since there is no opportunity to vote no confidence in a municipal government. There is also a need to establish a term that is long enough to encourage political leadership and independence so that aldermen are not constantly concerned about the next election. The Commission concludes that the two-year term of office is clearly too short, and discourages a leadership role. Moreover, within a two-year term it is difficult for a council to establish goals and priorities and see them to completion. Many program decisions take longer than two years to complete.

Recommendation 4.8: The term of office of the council of the City of Wentworth be three years.

The Commission sees the role of the mayor as very important in ensuring that the City of Wentworth council functions well. The Municipal Act defines the powers of mayors and gives them a responsibility to enforce the laws of the municipality, to oversee the conduct of the municipality's affairs and to communicate and make recommendations to council. The mayor has a vote on council and traditionally has been ex officio a member of all committees. We do not think it is necessary to change the statutory authority of the mayor.

The strength of the mayor largely depends not on his legislative authority but on his leadership ability. A mayor who is able to bring together and lead individuals or groups on council is best able to serve the municipality. It is the Commission's view that such qualities will be of paramount importance during the first term of the new council of the City of Wentworth. During that period a great deal will have to be done to bring together individuals and groups who have spent much of their previous time in conflict. The mayor will have to encourage a new loyalty to the City of Wentworth on the part of all members of the council. The Commission suggests that, to ensure there is a mayor who can accomplish these tasks, the new council should choose the first mayor. The main consideration in choosing a mayor for the first term of the new council will be to find a person who has the support of council and can bring its members together in a common purpose. The council is best able to make such a choice. To ensure that the mayor has faced the electorate, the choice should be made from among council members.

The Commission is well aware, however, that the election of the mayor by the municipal council is foreign to our political traditions, even though wardens and regional chairmen are elected by their councils. In addition, we know that there is a strong tradition and belief on the part of the citizens of the Region that they should be able to choose their mayor directly. The Commission shares this belief. In addition, one of the major criticisms of regional government is that the chairman is not elected by the people. We want to ensure that there will be a symbol of the municipality whom all citizens can participate in selecting, because this will help overcome the divisiveness that has plagued regional government in Hamilton-Wentworth. Therefore, even though we think that in the first term of office it is imperative that the mayor be someone who can unify the council, after that term the election of the mayor should be at large. When a strong and unified council is established the mayor will have all of the aldermen to aid in creating a wider commitment to the new municipality.

> **Recommendation 4.9:** For the first election in the City of Wentworth the mayor be elected by the aldermen from among themselves, and the mayor should retain his ward seat.

> **Recommendation 4.10:** For all elections thereafter, the mayor be elected at large.

> **Recommendation 4.11:** There be no change in the statutory authority of the mayor and the mayor be ex officio a member of all committees.

In order to assist the mayor in his leadership role, the Commission suggests that the municipality should have a Policy and Finance Committee. The purpose of this committee is not comparable to the Board of Control, which has been both a policy and administrative body. The board, as discussed in greater detail in Chapter 6, has not been successful as either a policy or an administrative body in the City of Hamilton. All boards of control tend to create divisions within municipal councils and make aldermen second-class elected representatives. Accordingly, such a board should not be established in the City of Wentworth. The primary purpose of the Policy and Finance Committee will be to facilitate the coordination and development of policy for the municipality. This committee will also review the activities of standing committees and set priorities and review recommendations for capital and current budgets. It should also be able to perform non-legislative tasks assigned to it by council. Provision should be made, however, that council does not assign any authority to the committee that is also assigned to the Chief Administrative Officer: the committee's primary responsibility is for policy development and providing leadership. It should also have the authority to recommend to council the membership of the standing committees on the basis of the interests and abilities of the members of council. In order that the committee can fulfill these functions it should be composed of the mayor who will act as chairman of the committee, council's second representative on the Police Commission, and the aldermen who are elected by council to be chairmen of the four standing committees of council. (These committees are dealt with in greater detail in Chapter 6.)

> Recommendation 4.12: Legislation require the establishment of a Policy and Finance Committee composed of the mayor, as chairman, the chairmen of the four standing committees and the council's representative on the Police Commission other than the mayor.

> Recommendation 4.13: Legislation provide that the chairmen of the four standing committees be elected by council.

> Recommendation 4.14: Legislation provide that the Policy and Finance Committee have authority to: develop and coordinate policy; review the activities of the standing committees of council; set priorities and guidelines for capital and current budgets; review capital and current budgets and budget recommendations; undertake such non-legislative tasks as are assigned by council, provided that such tasks are not also assigned to the Chief Administrative Officer of the municipality; and recommend to council the appointment of members of the standing committees other than the chairmen.

The details of the standing committees of council and the relationship of the administration of the municipality to the council and its committees, and particularly the need for the role of the Chief Administrative Officer, are discussed in detail in Chapter 6. It is important to stress here, however, that there is a clear need to have an appointed Chief Administrator with a degree of independence from council to oversee the administrative arm of the new municipality. The standing committees of council must focus their attention on policy matters. There is also a need to ensure that the number of committees established by council is kept to a minimum so that overall coordination is possible and decision-making does not bog down in a labyrinth of committees, as appears to have happened in the City of Hamilton. The implementation of our recommendations with respect to the mayor, the Policy and Finance Committee and the standing committees will ensure a strong and well-organized policy role for the new council in responding politically to the needs and wants of the citizens of Wentworth. We see the establishment of a Chief Administrative Officer as a means of ensuring a strong administrative operation that is able to carry out council's wishes and thus respond to those needs and wants as well.

Recommendation 4.15: Legislation provide for four standing committees of council to deal with policy matters as follows: the Planning and Development Committee; the Social Services and Health Committee; the Parks, Recreation and Culture Committee, and the Physical Services Committee.

Recommendation 4.16: Legislation require the appointment of a Chief Administrative Officer whose role be defined by by-law.

The Commission is aware that the committee structures of councils are not usually set out in legislation in Ontario. We recognize that municipal councils should be able to establish a committee structure that reflects their particular needs and that those needs may change over time, making some flexibility necessary. The total and immutable provision of a committee structure in legislation is neither desirable nor practical because of changing circumstances. The Commission nevertheless views its suggestions as realistic and necessary and thinks that the council of the City of Wentworth should follow them until the need for change becomes apparent.

Recommendation 4.17: The City of Wentworth be empowered to establish such other committees as it determines is advisable and to alter by by-law the committee structure presented in Recommendations 4.12 and 4.15.

The Commission considered recommending in detail a decentralized administrative structure for the City of Wentworth. We have chosen not to do this. There is a great deal of decentralization within the Region through the delivery of regional and local services and through various groups conducting and managing local programs such as recreation. There is nothing in the recommendations of the Commission that inhibits the continuation of such decentralization. Decentralized activities depend not on existing municipal boundaries but on various communities of interest that are sometimes smaller than a municipality — such as running an arena, or managing a softball league — and sometimes larger than existing municipal boundaries — as in the case of the Hamilton Philharmonic Orchestra or the Royal Botanical Gardens.

The need for decentralized administration will therefore vary substantially from one function to another and from one community to another, and it would be inappropriate to try to suggest a single, uniform approach throughout the City of Wentworth. Because of the small size of wards, local aldermen will be able to assist in the development of the most effective links between the administrative arm of the municipality and the communities they represent.

We think that existing municipal buildings can be used to assist in the development of such links. Such buildings can provide meeting places for citizen groups and activities. They will also provide office space where an alderman can meet with his constituents and help them with their problems. Those facilities, however, should also be used, where appropriate, to decentralize the administration of the City of Wentworth. It may be that taxes can be paid in them, or that applications may be made for particular matters in them. It is not the Commission's function to specify the particular services that must be provided in every district office, but rather to indicate that these offices may be used for such purposes.

The new council should approach these facilities with the view that as many services should be provided in them as is consistent with economical administration. It seems likely, for example, that at a minimum, at least one person from the recreation staff and one person from planning staff could be located in these offices. The planning staff could provide general information on services and assist citizens in dealing with all administrative departments of the municipality. The Commission, however, leaves overall staffing in such offices to be determined by the new council on the basis of the needs of particular communities. There is further discussion of this matter in Chapter 6.

Recommendation 4.18: The council of the City of Wentworth give careful consideration to the use of present municipal buildings as district offices to provide office space for aldermen and to provide as much decentralization of service delivery as is consistent with economical administration.

In recommending a single-tier structure for the City of Wentworth, the Commission was faced with the difficulty of the increased financial burden that this could place on residents outside of the present City of Hamilton. An analysis of these difficulties and the solutions to them are dealt with in detail in Chapter 7. The problem is especially acute, however, because many rural inhabitants do not want or require the same level of service found in urban and suburban areas. One of the benefits of a regional government system is that the difference in levels of service and costs of services can be partially dealt with by two tiers of government. The Commission concludes, however, that this problem can be dealt with very effectively within the City of Wentworth by using area rating for a number of services such as transit and fire, by continuing user charges for water and sewer services, and by providing for a differential between the urban and rural tax burdens. To provide a basis for the tax differential the city can be divided into an urbanized and rural portion. In the rural portion expenditures for certain services of general government, parks, recreation, local culture and for urban improvements which are lower or non-existent in the rural areas, can be charged at a reduced rate. Using these techniques will minimize any increase in the overall municipal taxes of residents that might otherwise result from the establishment of a one-tier system.

The Commission is convinced, moreover, that the use of area rating, user charges and the urban-rural tax differential along with a general levy will result in an equitable tax burden; taxpayers in different parts of the municipality will generally shoulder the burden for only those services they actually receive. In addition, such an allocation of the tax burden will result in a better realization and understanding of the relationship between municipal costs, taxes and services.

> **Recommendation 4.19: The tax burden of the City of Wentworth be distributed as far as possible in ways that ensure that those areas benefiting from services will pay for them through the use of: area rating, user charges, and an urban-rural tax differential in addition to a general levy.**

Conclusion

The Commission is recommending a number of substantial changes in the local government structure in Hamilton-Wentworth to overcome present divisions, disharmony, lack of accountability and inefficiencies. In doing so, we are presenting an integrated system where a one-tier government, with a strong leadership and administration, can meet the needs of the people of Wentworth. We are cognizant of the differences within the Region. We have taken those differences into account and provide for them in our recommendations on representation, district offices and financing. In our view, the system we propose incorporates the correct balance of the abilities to respond to needs of its citizens, to be efficient, and to take into account the various interests that make up the City of Wentworth.

Chapter 5

Ward Boundaries

In Chapter 4 we make general recommendations for the establishment of electoral wards for the City of Wentworth. Recommendations 4.3, 4.4 and 4.5 suggest that the wards are to be drawn within existing municipal boundaries and should provide fourteen wards from the existing City of Hamilton and a total of thirteen wards from the other municipalities. The drawing of electoral boundaries is always a difficult and sensitive task, requiring skill combined with considerable local knowledge. Apart from the general guidelines mentioned above, there are three important criteria that we think should be taken into account in drawing ward boundaries.

First, it is important that ward boundaries be drawn to reflect both geographic and social communities of interest. Residents of a ward should, as much as possible, share similar social outlooks and be concerned with common local problems. To accomplish this, ward boundaries should, wherever possible, follow recognizable physical divisions within the City of Wentworth such as major roads, railway lines, and the Escarpment. In addition, the drawing of boundaries should try to take into account such matters as income groupings, ethnic backgrounds, historic associations, and urban or rural orientation. We suggest names in addition to numbers for the wards we propose in this chapter as a way of emphasizing the relationship between the new ward boundaries and communities within the Region.

Drawing ward boundaries with this criterion in mind will result in the election of representatives who can both reflect and respond to the views of their constituents. Under the present system of government, regional councillors are, to a large extent, delegates of their respective municipalities. Those municipalities, however, do not represent one community of interest. Most of the non-city municipalities, for example, have both urban and rural portions, each with different needs and views. The needs of the citizens of Hamilton, moreover, are not uniform. Wards based on a community of interest will thus provide more effective representation than is possible now at Regional Council.

A second important criterion is that wards within the existing City of Hamilton be of approximately equal population. The reason for not moving immediately to full representation by population, as explained in Chapter 4, is to provide initial protection for non-city residents. It is important, however, that representation by population be adhered to as much as possible after that basic protection is assured.

The third criterion that should be taken into account in drawing ward boundaries is the relative difficulty, especially in terms of demands on a councillor's time, of representing rural areas rather than urban ones. The large size of rural wards and the low density of population means that travelling time, for example, will be a heavier burden for rural representatives than for their urban counterparts.

The Commission has applied these guidelines and criteria to the Region, and has developed a detailed proposal for a ward system for the City of Wentworth. We conclude that five rural or farm-oriented wards should be established, one in each of Stoney Creek, Flamborough and Ancaster and two in Glanbrook. These wards will allow for the reflection of an important community of interest as well as for the particular demands of representing rural areas. We also suggest that the wards in the City of Hamilton should have populations ranging between 18,000 and 28,000.

The wards proposed for the existing municipalities, with their populations, are shown in Table 5.1.

The total number of twenty-seven wards suggested for the City of Wentworth are accordingly drawn from the existing municipalities in the following proportion:

Hamilton	14
Ancaster	3 (1 rural)
Dundas	2
Flamborough	3 (1 rural)
Glanbrook	2 (2 rural)
Stoney Creek	3 (1 rural)

The actual ward boundaries on Map 5.1 are the result of the application of these overall allocations and of the criteria previously outlined.

The details of the ward boundaries and the reasons for them are as follows:

1. *Beverly Ward* includes the former Township of Beverly, which is essentially an area of farms and small villages. Although its population is below the average it is the largest of all the wards in area.

The boundary on the south is the present Flamborough/Ancaster municipal boundary. On the east the boundary follows the former Beverly/West Flamborough line except that from Kirkwall Road (the 8th Concession) to the Christie Reservoir the east side of Townline Road (up to a depth of 100 metres) is included in Beverly, whereas south of the Reservoir the west side of the road is included with Flamborough Ward.

Table 5.1: Proposed Ward Structure for the City of Wentworth

Wards	Approximate population
FLAMBOROUGH	
1. Beverly — RURAL	5,500
2. Flamborough	9,000
3. Waterdown	9,500
ANCASTER	
4. Jerseyville — RURAL	3,000
5. Mineral Springs	6,000
6. Ancaster	5,000
DUNDAS	
7. South Dundas	10,000
8. North Dundas	9,000
HAMILTON	
9. Westdale	20,300
10. Aberdeen	21,300
11. North End	22,400
12. Stinson	22,000
13. Barton	28,000
14. Ottawa	23,000
15. Rosedale	20,300
16. Glendale	19,200
17. Eastgate	25,500
18. West Mountain	21,400
19. Mid Mountain	24,200
20. East Mountain	22,900
21. Ryckmans	22,100
22. Hannon	18,000
GLANBROOK	
23. Glanford — RURAL	7,000
24. Binbrook — RURAL	5,000
STONEY CREEK	
25. Stoney Creek	13,600
26. Winona (or Fruitland)	13,000
27. Saltfleet — RURAL	5,200

2. *Flamborough Ward* includes the former West Flamborough, with the above-mentioned adjustments with Beverly, and with the addition of Concessions x, xi, xii, and xiii of former East Flamborough. This ward is composed principally of non-farmers living in the country; it includes two large villages — Greensville and Freelton.

The boundary with Beverly is given previously. The boundary with Waterdown follows the 10th Concession of former East Flamborough, with both sides included in Flamborough Ward; and Highway 6 to just north of Clappisons Corners. In order to keep the Clappisons cluster together, lots 24, 25 and 26 of the 3rd Concession of former West Flamborough are included within Waterdown.

3. *Waterdown Ward* includes Waterdown, Carlisle, Flamborough Centre, and Clappisons Corners, and is thus the most heavily urbanized portion of present Flamborough.

The western and southern boundaries are given previously. The boundary to the east and to the north follows the present municipal boundary.

4. *Jerseyville Ward* consists of the rural, farm-oriented portions of present Ancaster. The boundary has been drawn so as to exclude not only the suburban clusters but also the strips of non-farm people living in the country.

The boundary begins just west of the Copetown Corners and follows the line between lots 29 and 30. It then runs eastward so as to place Power Line Road within Jerseyville and Mineral Springs Road within Mineral Springs Ward. It makes a slight zigzag southward along the line of Martins Road, Jerseyville Road, and Shaver Side Road as far as Highway 53, which it then follows eastward to the Hamilton city limits. Both sides of Martins Road, Jerseyville Road, Shaver Side Road and Highway 53 to a depth of 100 metres (or 100 yards) are to be excluded from Jerseyville Ward, since their strip developments make them more urban than rural.

5. *Mineral Springs Ward* includes the postwar suburbanized portions of urban Ancaster west of the Hamilton Golf and Country Club.

As described above, the western and southern limits include Mineral Springs, Martins, Jerseyville and Shaver Side Roads, and Highway 53. The eastern boundary follows the line between lots 44 and 45 through the golf course, along Halson Street (both sides to be in neighbouring Ancaster Ward), into the regional conservation lands.

6. *Ancaster Ward* includes the old village centre, Ancaster Heights, and the developments along Old Dundas Road, Mohawk Road, Golf Links Road, and Highway 53.

The western and southern boundaries are given above. The boundary to the north and east follows the present boundary for the Town of Ancaster.

7. *South Dundas Ward* consists of those portions of the existing Town of Dundas south of Spencer Creek. Most of the housing has been built since 1950.

The boundary follows Spencer Creek with two slight exceptions. At the western end the line is forced to leave the creek and runs between Mill Street (industrial) and Mercer Street (residential). In the eastern end the small area south of the Thorpe Street bridge is included with North Dundas because this area has no road contact with South Dundas.

8. *North Dundas Ward* includes the historic parts of the existing Town of Dundas. The boundary is given previously.

9. *Westdale Ward* is probably the most clearly demarcated and recognized sub-part of Hamilton. The boundary follows the line of Highway 403 in the Chedoke Ravine.

10. *Aberdeen Ward* includes the old, fashionable southwestern part of Hamilton, with its concentration of modern highrise apartments. Main and James Streets, both of which are broad and busy, form the limits, as well as the Escarpment to the south.

11. *North End Ward* consists of the old northern and northwestern portions of Hamilton. It is well known for its ethnic concentrations and urban-renewal projects.

The boundaries are Wellington Street on the east, Main Street on the south, Westdale Ward on the west and Hamilton Harbour to the north.

12. *Stinson Ward* consists of a cluster of small neighbourhoods, generally middle class, between King Street and the Escarpment. It is bounded by Gage Park and James Street.

King Street East has been selected as the northern boundary, rather than Main Street East, because King Street is the social and economic divider; the residential areas between King and Main resemble those south of Main. Also, the use of King Street allows for a fairer division of population between the Stinson and Barton wards. The eastern limit follows Gage Avenue (the edge of the park) south of Main Street. In the short extent between Main and King the boundary follows the railway track instead of Gage Avenue, to allow both sides of this residential street to be in the same ward.

13. *Barton Ward* is a working-class district close to major industries, and is the cultural centre of many European groups, notably the Italians, Poles and Ukrainians.

The boundaries are Wellington Street on the west, King Street on the south, and the Toronto, Hamilton and Buffalo Railway track on the east (with the line extended to the Bay).

14. *Ottawa Ward* includes the major commercial concentrations of the old east end of Hamilton — Ottawa Street and the Greater Hamilton Shopping Centre. It is a working-class district.

The boundaries are the Toronto, Hamilton and Buffalo Railway on the west, Highway 8 (Main Street and Queenston Road) on the south, and Parkdale Avenue on the east.

15. *Rosedale Ward* is a middle-class area between Highway 8 and the Escarpment and King's Forest Park. It is surrounded by parks on three sides.

The limits are Gage Park on the west, Highway 8 on the north, Red Hill Creek on the east, and the Escarpment on the south.

16. *Glendale Ward* is an area of new housing between Red Hill Creek and the old village of Stoney Creek. Located between King's Forest Park and the Escarpment, it is a popular location for new housing.

The limits are King's Forest Park on the west, Highway 8 on the north, Stoney Creek on the east and the Escarpment, including the Glendale Golf Club, on the south.

17. *Eastgate Ward* is the new east end of Hamilton, notable for its large commercial mall, and for new industries.

The western limit is Parkdale Avenue, the south side of Highway 8. The Beach Strip is included in this ward since it has a considerable similarity to Confederation Park.

18. *West Mountain Ward* is a fashionable area that includes the Scenic Drive, Mohawk College, and the Hillfield-Strathallen private school.

The boundary begins in the northeast and travels along Upper James Street south to Mohawk Road. It follows Mohawk Road westward to Garth Street, which it follows southward to a line serving as a continuation of Limeridge Road (thus including the Fessenden and Gilbert neighbourhoods). The other boundaries are the Escarpment and the city limits.

19. *Mid Mountain Ward* includes the oldest and most densely populated parts of the mountain, as well as the Concession Street and Mountain Plaza shopping areas.

The limits are Upper James Street on the west, the Escarpment on the north, Upper Sherman Avenue on the east and Mohawk Road on the south.

20. *East Mountain Ward* is centred on the fashionable strip along Mountain Brow Boulevard.

The Escarpment forms the limit on the north and east. The other boundary begins in the northwest on Upper Sherman Avenue, which it follows to Fennell Avenue. It then runs east along Fennell to Upper Gage Street, then south to Mohawk Road, and eastward along Mohawk Road to the Escarpment.

21. *Ryckmans Ward* consists of the partially built-up southwestern portions of the mountain. The name is taken from Ryckmans Corners, the well-known junction of Highways 6 and 53.

The limits are Upper Wentworth Street on the east, West Mountain and Mid Mountain wards on the north, and the city limits on the south and west.

22. *Hannon Ward* includes the southeastern portions of the mountain, south of East Mountain and Mid Mountain, and east of Ryckmans Ward. Although generally south of Mohawk Road, the Macassa neighbourhood north of Mohawk (the Sherman-Fennell-Gage-Mohawk block) has had to be included as well, to equalize the

population totals between East Mountain and Hannon.

23. *Glanford Ward* consists of the former Township of Glanford. This is the half of present Glanbrook that has known and can expect most of the southward thrust of urbanization. It includes the Mount Hope Airport and Highway 6, as well as the paths of projected highways towards Nanticoke.

24. *Binbrook Ward* .comprises the former Township of Binbrook. This is still an essentially rural area with a central village.

25. *Stoney Creek Ward* includes the former Town of Stoney Creek, extended eastward to Green Road.

The northern boundary is Queenston Road (Highway 8), the eastern is Green Road, the southern the Escarpment, and the western the present municipal boundary. Between Queenston Road and King Street the houses on the east side of Green Road should be included so as to have both sides of a residential street in the same ward.

26. *Winona Ward* includes the subdivisions just east of Eastgate and Stoney Creek wards, the villages of Winona and Fruitland, and virtually all the Niagara fruit belt remaining within the Region.

The limits are the Escarpment on the south, the lake on the north, the regional boundary on the east, and the Eastgate and Stoney Creek wards on the west.

27. *Saltfleet Ward* includes all of the present Town of Stoney Creek above the Escarpment. Despite the unavoidable inclusion of the "new City" (Albion Estates, etc.) in the western end, this is essentially a rural area.

The Commission recognizes that it is impossible to be completely objective about the drawing of electoral boundaries; subjective considerations are bound to intrude. Nevertheless, we are confident that the ward boundaries we propose for the City of Wentworth reflect the considerations that we think are most important at this time. The boundaries suggested should, therefore, serve satisfactorily for the first two terms of the council of the new city.

Recommendation 5.1: The City of Wentworth be divided into wards in accordance with Map 5.1.

WARD BOUNDARIES 65

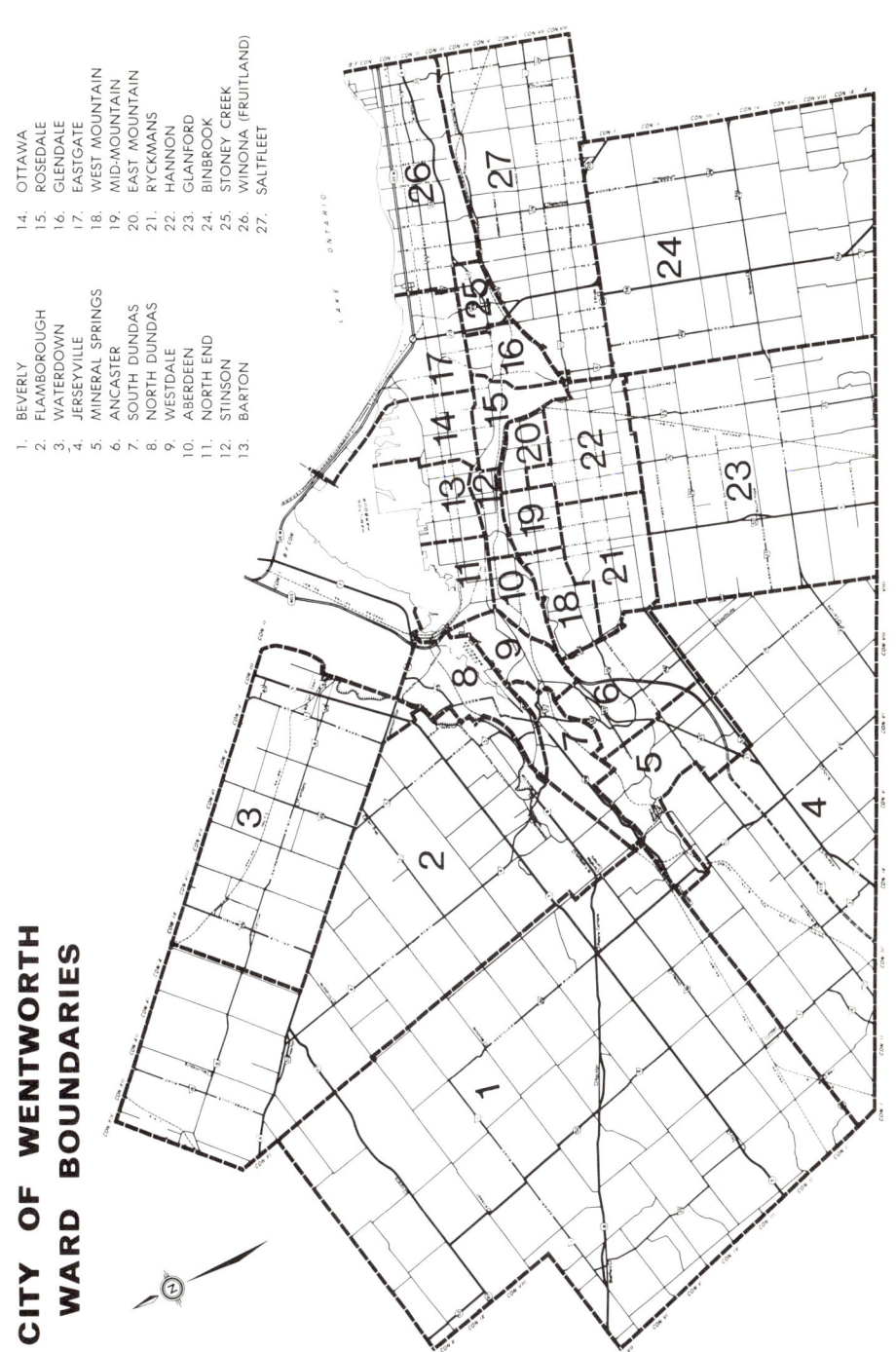

Map 5.1: City of Wentworth Ward Boundaries

Chapter 6

Policy Development and Management

In this chapter we discuss the way the City of Wentworth should organize itself to discharge its responsibilities to the people of the Region. There are two broad aspects of the process of government that must be considered in this connection: the determination of policies, and the administration of programs and services in keeping with these policies. Our objective is to suggest an organization that will assist the City of Wentworth in devising policies that best identify the needs of the Region and in establishing priorities among the possible programs that can be used to meet those needs. The system must also ensure that the programs are administered in an effective and economical manner, and that the means exist to achieve the necessary coordination between the various programs.

Effective management of the affairs of a government requires that there be a clear understanding of the respective roles of elected representatives and appointed officials. In the field of local government, the definition of these roles is not so clearly or universally understood as it is in senior governments; the division between policy and administration is often very indistinct. Differences in the perception of these roles are well illustrated by the organization of the existing municipalities in Hamilton-Wentworth.

It is important to recognize that institutions attempt to structure relationships but that the actual operation of the institution relies upon people. As a result, municipalities with similar formal structures may operate in very different ways because of the attitudes and abilities of the people on council and of the administrative staff. The structure is, nevertheless, important, for it encourages certain kinds of behaviour.

Present Organizational Structures in the Region

The seven municipalities in Hamilton-Wentworth have three distinct types of organizational structure: the chief administrative officer system (Ancaster, Dundas, Flamborough, Stoney Creek, and the Regional Municipality of Hamilton-Wentworth), the committee of council system (Glanbrook), and the board of control system

(Hamilton). Figure 6.1 (pages 80-81) shows the present organizational structure of these seven municipalities.

In the chief administrative officer system, the council delegates most of the responsibility for administration to the chief administrative officer, whom it appoints. It is a system that aims at freeing the municipal councillors to focus on policy matters. The system often has committees of council whose role is to discuss policy matters in particular functional areas, not to oversee the administration of those functions. The chief administrative officer is the head of the administration and is responsible for coordinating and overseeing the administration of the municipality. In each municipality that has a chief administrative officer, the council has passed a by-law outlining his powers and functions. Our management study indicates that the system is not operating equally effectively in each of the five municipalities in Hamilton-Wentworth that use it. In some instances, there has not been a sufficient delegation of administrative authority by the council to the appointed officers. Also, in some cases, channels of communication between administrators and council are not clearly defined.

The Township of Glanbrook operates under the committee of council system — a system frequently found in small municipalities. In such a system, the council members become involved in the details of administration. Unlike committees of council in the chief administrative officer system, these committees act in effect as the administrative heads of the various functional areas. There is always a clerk or a clerk-treasurer who, in some respects, plays the role of the chief administrative officer. This person does not have any special delegated powers, however, nor does he have explicit responsibility for coordination of the administration. Often he is expected to act as the coordinator but lacks the authority to do so.

The third type of management structure found in the municipalities of Hamilton-Wentworth is the board of control system. Hamilton is one of a decreasing number of larger municipalities in Ontario using it. In the board of control system, the municipal council is divided into two groups: the members of the board of control including the mayor, and the aldermen. The board of control is responsible for directing and coordinating the affairs of the municipality from the point of view of both policy and administration. The members of the board of control have special statutory powers defined in The Municipal Act, and any additional powers entrusted to them through municipal by-laws. These powers result in substantial authority in the areas of finance, personnel and other aspects of administration.

The board is not simply a body that makes suggestions and recommendations to council. It has the power to make binding decisions or recommendations in some areas subject to change only by a two-thirds vote of council. The members also have an independent power base, being directly elected at large by the people.

The board of control system also has committees of council, each of which assumes responsibility for an administrative area. In the City of Hamilton there are more than forty such standing committees of council, although most of them do not meet on a regular basis. Most staff departments, including the clerk's office, treasury, purchasing, legal and real estate departments report directly to the board of control, while line departments, including parks, recreation, cemetery, fire, engineering, streets and sanitation, traffic, and building and the personnel department report directly to standing committees of council.

There are several weaknesses in the board of control system. From the viewpoint of residents in the community, it is extremely complicated, and therefore a difficult system to understand. From the perspective of a member of council, it also creates difficulties by encouraging the involvement of council members in administrative detail. This can be very time-consuming and thus detracts from council members' ability to work on policy matters. Some council members in Hamilton complained to us of the awkwardness and inefficiency of the system. Further, it creates a potential conflict situation by setting up two classes of council members: controllers elected at large and with special statutory powers, and aldermen elected by ward who often feel they play a secondary role to the board of control.

The board of control is, in effect, the body responsible for direction and co-ordination in the municipality, performing in some respects the role of the appointed chief administrative officer. There are, however, two serious shortcomings in having this body perform such a role. The first results from some departments reporting directly to the board, while others report to one of the numerous committees of council. This situation gives rise to inconsistencies in decision-making practices among departments, including such areas as the resolution of personnel problems, establishment of work standards, performance appraisal, and supervisory methods. In addition, there exists no direct means to resolve problems or disputes between appointed officers. The second shortcoming of the system is that there is no guarantee that the people elected by the residents of the community to the board of control will have the special administrative skills needed to operate a large municipality.

Our review of management within Hamilton-Wentworth shows that those municipalities with a chief administrative officer who has appropriate delegated authority are better managed than the others. This was the case in Ancaster, Stoney Creek and the Region. The system allows council and its committees to be more effective, since council members are able to involve themselves more in the task of policy-making and are relieved from many tasks of the day-to-day administration. The administration of these municipalities is greatly enhanced through good communication among appointed officers and between appointed officers and council. The design of the system itself ensures that the lines of communication are clearly understood by all. Appropriate delegation of authority can allow appointed officers to make decisions effectively within the scope of duties, responsibilities and limits of authority vested in them.

Necessary Elements of a Management System

This analysis of the management organizations now used in the Region provides support for the Commission's basic approach in this field. We think it is important to make a distinction in the respective roles of elected representatives and appointed officials similar to the distinction made at senior levels of government.

The members of council must have a structure that allows them to focus their energies upon policy matters. Elected politicians must have sufficient time to spend on policy development and review; too much involvement in administrative matters makes this impossible.

The involvement of elected representatives in administration interferes with the proper management of the municipality. People who have been hired on the basis of their technical knowledge and administrative skills should be given the appropriate authority for administering the municipality, and be held accountable to council for their performance. The council members are not elected on the basis of their administrative expertise. Accordingly, they should neither pretend nor be expected to be involved in, or responsible for, the day-to-day administration of the municipality. It is important, however, that the council members have sufficient contact with the administration to be aware of substantive issues and problems that do arise, and to be sufficiently knowledgeable to approve the guidelines by which the administration is operated.

In most instances, and certainly for the City of Wentworth, the entire council is too large a forum for the sort of discussions necessary to develop policy proposals. Detailed analysis of proposals should be undertaken by a smaller group, whose members can each come to grips with the issues and contribute usefully to the development of solutions. Some form of committee structure is required for council, based on functional policy areas.

The structure should give aldermen the opportunity to specialize in a certain range of policy matters. If, on the one hand, each alderman feels equal responsibility for all functional areas, he is unlikely to develop sufficient expertise in any field to contribute meaningfully to debate. This situation often results in aldermen becoming overly dependent on appointed staff because of a heavy reliance on their advice. If, on the other hand, the structure requires an alderman to specialize in a narrow area, he becomes too limited in his perspective and fails to understand how his policy area fits in with and affects others.

No matter how the committees are structured, the complicated nature of today's problems and solutions makes it essential that aldermen have access to people with professional and technical expertise. It is not realistic to expect each of the council members to have all the technical knowledge necessary for addressing these problems. Staff must be available to advise and support the policy committees.

Once a clear understanding of the role that council and staff play in the management of the municipality's affairs is reached, the line of authority within the administration may be established to ensure the appropriate coordination of all the administrative matters of the municipality.

Organizational Structure of the City of Wentworth

COMMITTEES OF COUNCIL

It is on the basis of the considerations outlined above that the Commission recommends the setting up of council committees and the appointment of a Chief Administrative Officer (see Recommendations 4.12, 4.15 and 4.16). The committees of council are to be responsible for policy matters; the Chief Administrative Officer is to be responsible for directing and coordinating the administration of the municipality. Figure 6.2 shows the proposed organization of the City of Wentworth.

The City of Wentworth should have five committees of council: a Policy and Finance Committee a Planning and Development Committee, a Social Services and Health Committee, a Parks, Recreation and Culture Committee, and a Physical Services Committee. As stated in Chapter 4, the chairmen of the last four committees will be chosen by the city council. These four chairmen, the mayor, and the other council representative on the Police Commission will form the Policy and Finance Committee. The Policy and Finance Committee will recommend to council the remaining appointments to the other committees after taking into consideration the needs of the individual committees and the interests of the members of council. The whole council will make the final determination of committee memberships. We suggest that the number of members on the four functional committees be similar, since we expect the workloads of the committees will be reasonably equal.

The purpose of the Policy and Finance Committee is to coordinate the policy of the municipal council from two special perspectives: the impact that policy recommendations from a council committee in one functional area may have on other areas; and the financial situation of the municipality. This committee will provide leadership in bringing together the various concerns within the City of Wentworth. The leadership role will be fostered by the fact that all of the Policy and Finance Committee's members, at least during the first term, will have been chosen by the council. After the first term, the election at large of the mayor by the residents of the whole city will obviously give that committee member a leadership role for the entire municipality.

The fact that four of the six members are the chairmen of the other committees will facilitate coordination by a two-way flow of information: having the chairman of each committee on the Policy and Finance Committee assures that this coordinating and leadership body will always be aware of the special concerns in each functional area; and having a member of the Policy and Finance Committee chairing each functional committee assures that more specialized committees will not deal with their own functions in a vacuum caused by ignorance of the overall priorities and concerns of the municipality. The presence of the council's appointee to the Police Commission on the Policy and Finance Committee will ensure that the Police Commission and council will be mutually aware of each other's concerns while still maintaining the traditional separation of the police function from control by municipal council.

The Policy and Finance Committee will comment to council on the recommendations of the other committees if it thinks that important considerations have not been brought forward. This committee will also play the central role in the preparation of budgets, both current and capital. It should play the initiating role, laying out the guidelines to departments and other committees for the coming year in terms of acceptable overall expenditure levels and priorities. It will then review the budget recommendations arriving from each committee of council and make its own recommendations to council for the overall budget. The Policy and Finance Committee may also undertake additional tasks assigned to it at the discretion of the council. The council must be sure, however, that tasks assigned to this committee and to the Chief Administrative Officer do not overlap.

The Planning and Development Committee will be responsible for planning, by-law enforcement, zoning, licensing, industrial promotion, tourism and conventions, and fire protection and prevention. The Social Services and Health Committee will be responsible for the social services function, including Macassa Lodge and Wentworth Lodge, and for public health. The Parks, Recreation and Culture Committee will be responsible for parks, cemeteries, recreation, libraries and for considering requests from those special purpose bodies that operate cultural facilities and programs. The Physical Services Committee will be responsible for sewage, waste collection and disposal, water, land drainage, roads and traffic, transit, parking and the airport. Each of these committees will be responsible for developing policy in its subject area. Each will be assisted in this function by senior administrative staff. The committees, having considered the advice of staff, and having listened to delegations from the public, where appropriate, will make recommendations to the council for its decision.

We recognize that, as it works with this committee structure, the council may find that adjustments are necessary. Nonetheless, we urge the new council to give this system a fair trial before making substantial changes. We are particularly concerned about an expansion in the number of committees; for, if they become more numerous, we fear that the understandability of the system and the possibilities for coordination in the municipality will both be seriously handicapped. Each committee member should have to be concerned with a reasonably broad spectrum of matters, and therefore, it is important that committees not specialize in fields that are too narrow.

The Commission observed that in some of the existing municipalities in this Region, residents are allowed to speak to committees of council but not at meetings of the whole council. We think this situation lessens the access of the citizen to council; for when speaking to a committee one is speaking only to a minority of council. It is possible that a committee's reaction to a delegation's expressions of concern may not be representative of the reaction the whole council would have. Accordingly, we urge the council of the City of Wentworth to consider means by which the public can be given the opportunity to speak at meetings of the entire council.

Recommendation 6.1: The council of the City of Wentworth develop procedural by-laws that allow the public to speak to the full council after appropriate procedures have been followed.

CHIEF ADMINISTRATIVE OFFICER

As recommended in Chapter 4, the most senior appointed official in the new City of Wentworth will be the Chief Administrative Officer. The Chief Administrative Officer will be accountable to council under a by-law which provides for his appointment and dismissal, his duties, responsibilities and limits of authority. We pointed out earlier that appropriate delegation of authority can greatly enhance the effectiveness of the total municipal operation. The delegation of too much authority can erode to some extent the duties and responsibilities of elected representatives in the management of the municipality; too little delegation can restrict the Chief Administrative Officer position to that of the ineffectual figurehead of an uncoordinated and ineffective organization. The Commission suggests that the powers delegated and responsibilities assigned to the Chief Administrative Officer be no less than now exist in the regional coordinator's by-law in the Regional Municipality of Hamilton-Wentworth.

The reporting relationships of appointed staff within the proposed structure are discussed in parts of chapters 8 through 13. The five commissioners (Commissioner of Planning and Development, Commissioner of Social Services, Commissioner of

POLICY DEVELOPMENT AND MANAGEMENT   73

Parks and Recreation, Commissioner of Physical Services and Commissioner of Finance), the Medical Officer of Health, the three chief librarians and the fire chief will each have a dual reporting situation. They will report to their respective committees of council on policy matters; on administrative matters, they will report to the Chief Administrative Officer.

DISTRICT OFFICES

A complaint we have heard frequently from residents of the Region is that regional government has lessened their access to local government. Along with this complaint usually came the comment that a single-tier government for the Region would worsen the situation. We are convinced, however, that the structure of government in the City of Wentworth will actually make the citizens' access to their local government easier. The main reason for this is that a basic part of accessibility is understandability. In a single-tier government it is clear to the residents who is responsible for dealing with their problems.

Setting up the recommended district offices will also add to accessibility for the public. We suggest that district offices be located in existing municipal buildings — quite likely in the town or township halls of Ancaster, Dundas, Flamborough, Glanbrook and Stoney Creek. These offices will be places where the citizens can communicate both with their local aldermen and with the city's administration.

The district office will contain office space for the aldermen who live in that area. It will be the responsibility of individual aldermen to determine how that office space is utilized to service residents. In addition, consideration should be given to providing aldermen with access to secretarial assistance in these district offices.

Those aldermen who live in the central part of the city should be provided with office space in the existing city hall. If for some reason the needs of some aldermen cannot be adequately taken care of in city hall, an allowance could be provided to them to cover their costs of obtaining office space elsewhere.

The district office will be the usual point of contact between the administration of the new city and residents of the outlying areas. The administrative staff in the office will receive inquiries and complaints from citizens, provide information and, for matters that cannot be dealt with on the spot, be responsible for relaying the matter to the central office or telling the resident how to pursue it himself. We envision these district offices, however, as being much more than just information offices. Applications for the various types of licences could be made available and submitted at these offices. In routine matters, the staff in the district office could be given authority to approve applications at that point. This is likely to occur only in situations where staff are dealing with subjects for which policies have been clearly defined by council. Nevertheless, even where approval cannot be given immediately, the function will be an extremely important one, since the role of the staff member will be to facilitate the resident's application by making sure that the forms have been properly filled out while the applicant is still present, thus avoiding undue delays and frustration. It also may be useful in some types of applications to have the staff members in the district office comment to the central office on the merit of the application since that member will have had direct contact and thus perhaps gained a better understanding of the situation.

One of the important staff members at the district office will be a representative of the Recreation Department. This person will be responsible for giving residents information on assistance that is available for recreational programs. The member will be a facilitator, not necessarily the actual operator of the programs.

We think that it will be useful if there is also a member of the Planning Department in each district office. This person will be able to explain to the public the planning policies of the municipality and the planning process. Assistance can be given to residents in filling out application forms for such planning items as building permits, minor variances and severances.

In addition, the district office will be a place where meetings can be held. A committee of council, for example, may be discussing a matter that is of particular concern to people in one part of the city. It would, then, make good sense to hold a committee meeting in the district office in that area to make it easier for the concerned residents to attend and express their views. The Land Division Committee and the Committee of Adjustment also might decide to hold meetings in district offices. These offices could also provide meeting places for residents groups.

The district offices, then, offer a substantial opportunity for the City of Wentworth to improve the accessibility of local government services in the Region. These opportunities should be given early and careful attention by council.

Recommendation 6.2: The council determine the use to be made of each district office, and initially, a representative of at least the Planning and Recreation Departments be located in each office.

We wish to express, however, a word of caution. These district offices must not be seen by residents as new points of decision-making. There is only one municipal council in this city, and only one point at which decisions requiring council consideration can actually be made.

Also, we caution the municipal council to be sure that these offices do not interfere with the objective of cutting back on the duplication of administration that we observed in two-tier government. Administrative decentralization can result in a more efficient administration only if wisely used. Therefore, we urge the new council to take careful account of the financial implications of their actions in setting up district offices. The council of the City of Wentworth must remember the latter part of Recommendation 4.18: "to provide as much decentralization of service delivery as is consistent with economical administration."

The Chief Administrative Officer should be responsible for the coordination of the district offices as well as being accountable for their cost-effectiveness. Each of the employees stationed in a district office will be a member of one of the departments in the central office of the municipality. Therefore, each person in the district office will report directly or indirectly to his or her respective department head. For example, the planning officer will report to his superior in the head office of the Planning Department. Similarly, the recreation officer will report to his own department. Each department head will be accountable to the Chief Administrative Officer for the performance, quality and level of service provided by his representative in the district office. While local elected representatives may choose to discuss certain issues with the district office staff, under no circumstances should they direct the activities of the staff or interfere with the operations of these offices without going through the appropriate channel, that is, the Chief Administrative Officer.

The Management Advantages of Unified Government

The Commission recommends that the seven municipalities in HamiltonWentworth be reduced in number to only one — the City of Wentworth. One of the reasons for this recommendation is our recognition that the existing municipal structures do not result in the optimal use of the available resources for the fulfilment of the needs of the people in this Region. Reorganizing the administration in the Hamilton-Wentworth area on a single-tier basis provides a number of opportunities for developing a more highly effective management system.

Unification will remove the need for paralleling certain positions, both elected and appointed. For example, at present each of the seven municipalities must have a clerk and support staff to perform certain general government functions. The setting up of only one Clerk's Department will eliminate some duplication and provide an opportunity for cost reduction. This situation will also apply in the other basic staff support areas such as financial and legal services. These are services that each municipality must now have available and that could be provided at less total cost in a unified system.

In the roads function, where both the area municipalities and the Regional Municipality have jurisdiction, equipment and manpower are not always used as efficiently as they could be used in a unified system. Similarly, there is some inevitable duplication of overhead costs in this service (for example, garages, maintenance, managerial and supervisory staff).

While establishing a central administration will eliminate some duplication, and in this way will result in potential reductions in cost, more significant savings opportunities will be available because of the access to special equipment and skilled personnel for the benefit of all municipal government operations. A very important example of this is data processing. Our research studies indicate that little effort has been made by other municipalities within the Region to take full advantage of the City of Hamilton's capability to process data and generate management information. The Regional Municipality uses the city's computer facilities, but each of these two municipalities has developed independent systems to satisfy what it considers to be its own unique requirements. Dundas, Stoney Creek and Flamborough each operates its own mini-computers, while Ancaster and Glanbrook restrict their operations to manual methods because of their smaller size. With the exception of the City of Hamilton, each area municipality has its tax bills prepared by an outside computer service bureau. In light of Hamilton's decision to upgrade its data-processing capability by obtaining a larger computer, centralizing the system under a one-tier system will provide opportunities for reducing overall data-processing costs by eliminating the need for both mini-computers and the use of an outside service bureau, and for standardizing information systems to a uniformly high level.

> **Recommendation 6.3:** A central data-processing facility be established for all the City of Wentworth's computing needs.

In a unified system the different specialized skills in the staff of municipalities will no longer be available to only one of the municipalities; instead all people in the Region will have the advantages of these highly competent personnel.

Our research indicates that collectively the Hamilton-Wentworth community has a very competent management resource base. However, the effectiveness of that base is being hindered by the two-tier system. A single-tier government will allow for the maximum use of this base at minimal cost for all residents of the Region.

Additional Opportunities for Development

Based on our examination of management in the existing municipalities of Hamilton-Wentworth, we have come to the conclusion that management practices in two areas should be given special attention in the City of Wentworth. These are personnel administration and budgeting.

As can be seen in Table 6.1 and 6.2, in 1972 municipal councils in the Hamilton-Wentworth area employed 3,797 people full-time and 837 part-time, a total of 4,634. In 1977 the corresponding figures were 4,300 full-time (an increase of 13.2 per cent) and 848 part-time, (an increase of 1.3 per cent) for a total of 5,148 (an increase of 11.1 per cent). Total salaries and wages increased from $44,800,000 in 1972 to $95,500,000 in 1977, or 113 per cent. The 1977 budgeted salaries and wages account for 45 per cent of the total local government expenditures within the Hamilton-Wentworth area.

The number of municipal employees in the Hamilton-Wentworth Region, and the current level of expenditure in wages and salaries, clearly demonstrate the need for administrative attention being placed on personnel policies. Our studies show that personnel practices and policies vary considerably among the different municipalities. The consolidation of local government in the Region will provide both the opportunity and the need to implement consistent and effective procedures to handle personnel matters. Of particular importance are procedures for handling job descriptions, classifications, and evaluation of job performance.

Recommendation 6.4: Personnel policies and procedures, including development of job descriptions and performance appraisal, be investigated, and recommendations made to introduce a comprehensive personnel administration system in the City of Wentworth that will assist elected representatives and appointed officials in monitoring and controlling staff performance and costs.

Well-developed budgeting, monitoring and data-processing systems now exist in some municipalities in Hamilton-Wentworth. In the City of Wentworth, such systems can be extended to all municipal operations, with resulting benefits and savings.

Recommendation 6.5: Administrative systems, data-processing, and management information systems be investigated and recommendations made for standardization of all systems within the City of Wentworth.

We want to make two specific points in connection with budgeting. At present, though capital budgets are drawn up for periods of five to ten years, the operating cost implications of capital expenditure proposals are not always identified. Since the long-term operating costs of many capital expenditures may be much greater than the initial cost of the facility, this is a grave weakness in the budgeting system. In all instances, the operating cost and personnel implications of proposed capital expenditures should be identified and taken into account at the same time that the actual capital expenditure is considered.

Recommendation 6.6: The operating cost and personnel implications of all proposed capital expenditures be identified and incorporated into all such proposals for council consideration.

Most governments with sizeable budgets now recognize the value of long-term forecasting of expenditures and revenues. This practice is not generally adopted in Hamilton-Wentworth for operating costs, though the total amount of these expenditures is large indeed. Though long-range budget forecasts can never be fully accurate, they provide a valuable basis for helping with financial planning and establishing priorities for current and proposed programs. In our view, the total amount of local government expenditures in the Region fully warrants the introduction of three-year financial forecasting to provide a framework within which financial planning and current priority-setting can be done. The consolidation of all local government expenditures within one municipal budget will greatly facilitate this process, as well as making it even more necessary.

Recommendation 6.7: Three-year forecasts of all local government revenues and expenditures be developed and kept up to date as part of the regular current budgeting process of the City of Wentworth.

POLICY DEVELOPMENT AND MANAGEMENT 79

Table 6.1: Total Staff Complement by Municipality for the Years 1972 and 1975-1977

Municipality	1972[2] Full-time	1972[2] Part-time[5]	1972[2] Total	1975 Full-time	1975 Part-time[5]	1975 Total	1976 Full-time	1976 Part-time[5]	1976 Total	1977 Full-time	1977 Part-time[5]	1977 Total
Regional Municipality of Hamilton-Wentworth[4]	—	—	—	1,875	153	2,028	1,947	155	2,102	2,025	145	2,170
County of Wentworth[1]	177	94	271	—	—	—	—	—	—	—	—	—
Town of Ancaster	64	9	73	39	15	54	41	15	56	42	12	54
Town of Dundas	126	143	269	76	11	87	79	13	92	78	13	91
Township of Flamborough	—	—	—	40	15	55	40	15	55	42	15	57
Township of Beverly	9	2	11	—	—	—	—	—	—	—	—	—
Township of East Flamborough	6	1	7	—	—	—	—	—	—	—	—	—
Township of West Flamborough	9	—	9	—	—	—	—	—	—	—	—	—
Village of Waterdown	3	1	4	—	—	—	—	—	—	—	—	—
Township of Glanbrook	—	—	—	24	11	35	25	11	36	25	11	36
Township of Binbrook	9	1	10	—	—	—	—	—	—	—	—	—
Township of Glanford	8	2	10	—	—	—	—	—	—	—	—	—
City of Hamilton[3,6]	3,235	584	3,819	1,882	373	2,255	1,871	441	2,312	1,989	632	2,621
Town of Stoney Creek	25	n.a.	25	76	11	87	91	18	109	99	20	119
Township of Saltfleet	126	n.a.	126	—	—	—	—	—	—	—	—	—
Total[7]	3,797	837	4,634	4,012	589	4,601	4,094	688	4,762	4,300	848	5,148
Increase Over 1972				5.7%	(29.6)%	(0.7)%	7.8%	(20.2)%	2.8%	13.2%	1.3%	11.1%

[1] County of Wentworth data were not available for 1972. Figures shown represent the number of county employees as at December 31, 1973.
[2] Data for the Townships of East Flamborough, West Flamborough and Beverly and the Village of Waterdown were not available for 1972. Figures shown represent 1971 data for these former municipalities.
[3] City of Hamilton data were not available for 1972. Figures shown represent the number of employees as at December 31, 1973.
[4] Figures exclude transit staff from the Hamilton Street Railway Company (1972, 1975 and 1976), and the Region (1977).
[5] Part-time staffing data should be considered as estimates only, since in many cases, municipalities were unable to calculate actual equivalent man-years for part-time employees. Part-time figures for the City of Hamilton are as at December 31st for each year.
[6] Some 154 out of the total 632 part-time staff in 1977 at the City of Hamilton can be attributed to the operation of Hamilton Place.
[7] Volunteer firemen are excluded.
SOURCES: Woods, Gordon & Co., Finance Research Study, February 1978 and Data Schedules as completed by municipalities.

Figure 6.1: Municipalities in the Hamilton-Wentworth Region —

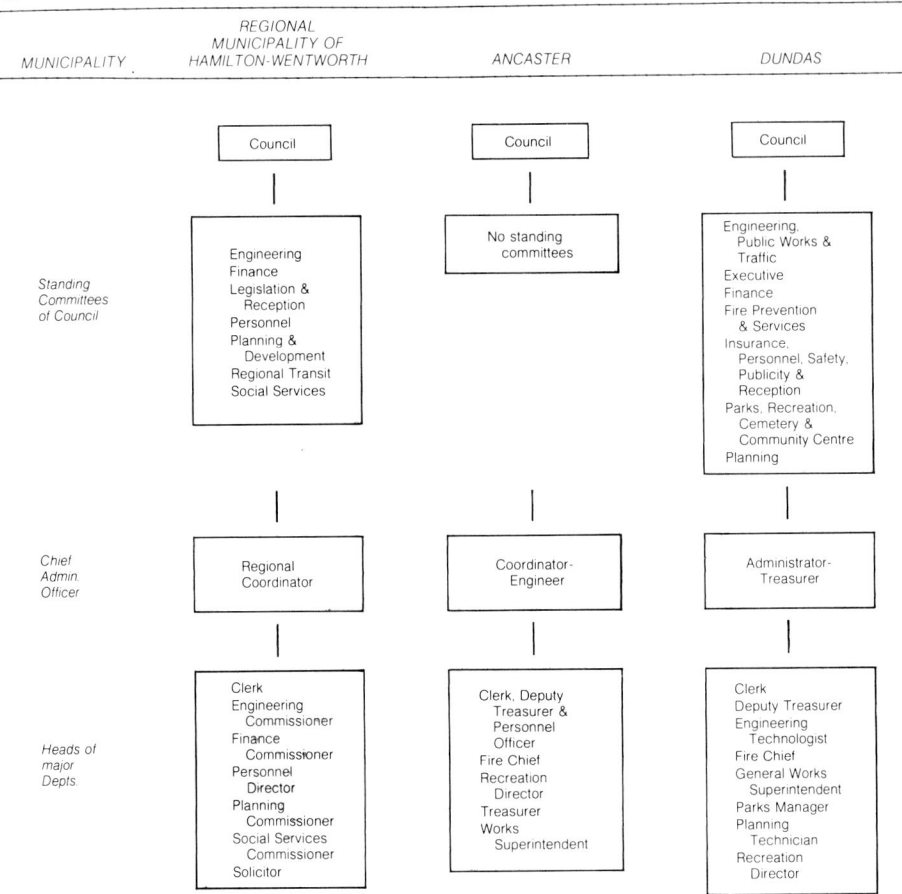

	REGIONAL MUNICIPALITY OF HAMILTON-WENTWORTH	ANCASTER	DUNDAS
MUNICIPALITY			
Standing Committees of Council	Engineering Finance Legislation & Reception Personnel Planning & Development Regional Transit Social Services	No standing committees	Engineering, Public Works & Traffic Executive Finance Fire Prevention & Services Insurance, Personnel, Safety, Publicity & Reception Parks, Recreation, Cemetery & Community Centre Planning
Chief Admin. Officer	Regional Coordinator	Coordinator-Engineer	Administrator-Treasurer
Heads of major Depts.	Clerk Engineering Commissioner Finance Commissioner Personnel Director Planning Commissioner Social Services Commissioner Solicitor	Clerk, Deputy Treasurer & Personnel Officer Fire Chief Recreation Director Treasurer Works Superintendent	Clerk Deputy Treasurer Engineering Technologist Fire Chief General Works Superintendent Parks Manager Planning Technician Recreation Director
NUMBER OF EMPLOYEES			
Full-time	2,025	42	78
Part-time	145	12	13
Total	2,170	54	91

POLICY DEVELOPMENT AND MANAGEMENT 81

Present Organizational Components

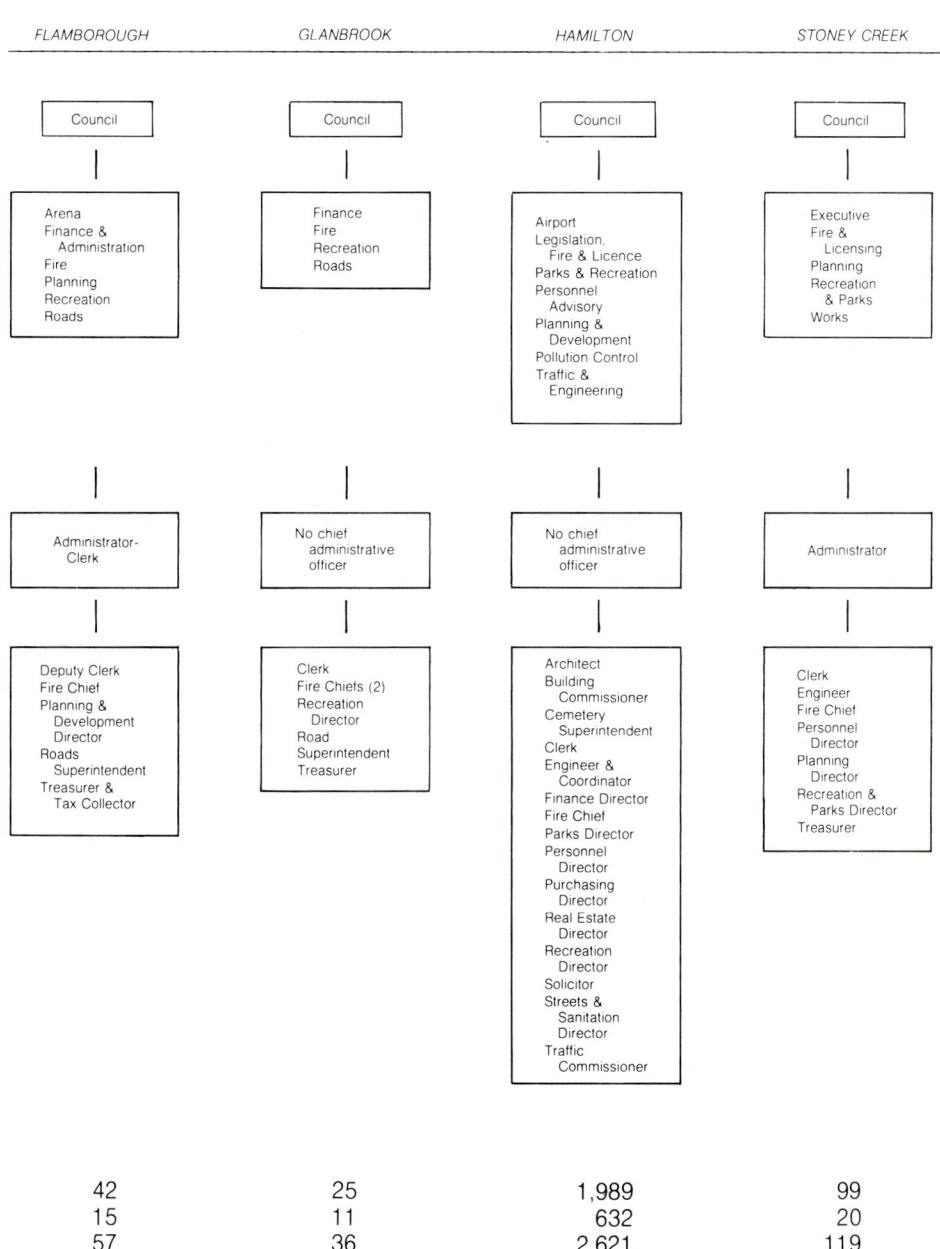

Figure 6.2: City of Wentworth — Proposed Plan of Organization

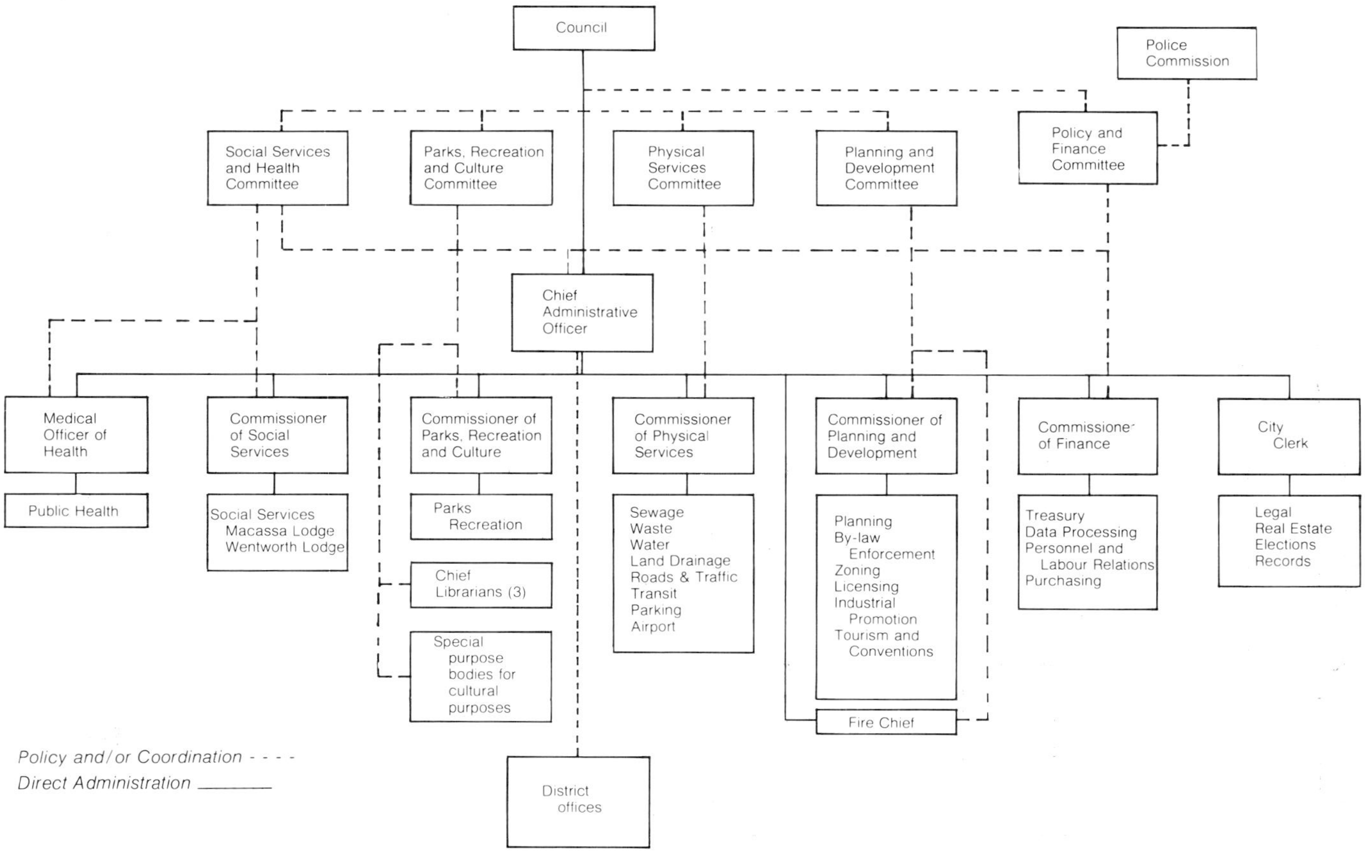

Policy and/or Coordination - - - -
Direct Administration ⎯⎯⎯⎯

POLICY DEVELOPMENT AND MANAGEMENT 83

Table 6.2: Total Staff Complement by Service for the Years 1972 and 1975-1977

Function	1972[2] Full-time	1972[2] Part-time	1972[2] Total	1975 Full-time	1975 Part-time	1975 Total	1976 Full-time	1976 Part-time	1976 Total	1977 Full-time	1977 Part-time	1977 Total
General Gov't												
– No. of Staff	398	138	536	452	42	494	467	41	508	479	41	520
– % Increase Over 1972				13.6	(69.6)	(7.8)	17.3	(70.3)	(5.2)	20.4	(70.3)	(3.0)
Transportation Services[3]												
– No. of Staff	1,093	41	1,134	679	20	699	696	25	721	748	30	778
– % Increase Over 1972				1.0	(9.8)	0.6	3.2	(12.2)	2.6	8.5	(2.4)	8.1
Protection to Persons and Property												
– No. of Staff	1,238	12	1,250	1,184	33	1,217	1,253	37	1,290	1,301	36	1,337
– % Increase Over 1972				(4.4)	175.0	(2.6)	1.2	208.3	3.2	5.1	200.0	7.0
Social and Family Services												
– No. of Staff	295	83	378	353	60	413	360	62	422	386	55	441
– % Increase Over 1972				19.7	(27.7)	9.3	22.0	(25.3)	11.6	30.8	(33.7)	16.7
Environmental Services[1]												
– No. of Staff	Inc. in Transp. Serv.			425	17	442	432	11	443	438	10	448
– % Increase Over 1972												
Health Services												
– No. of Staff	220	2	222	210	3	213	210	1	211	221	1	222
– % Increase Over 1972				(4.5)	50.0	(4.1)	(4.5)	(50.0)	(5.0)	0.5	(50.0)	0
Recreation and Cultural Services												
– No. of Staff	433	555	988	565	406	971	530	479	1,009	576	657	1,233
– % Increase Over 1972				30.5	(26.8)	(1.7)	22.4	(13.7)	2.1	33.0	18.4	24.8
Planning and Development												
– No. of Staff	120	6	126	144	8	152	146	12	158	151	18	169
– % Increase Over 1972				20.0	33.3	20.6	21.7	100.0	25.4	25.8	200.0	34.1
Total – No. of Staff	3,797	837	4,634	4,012	589	4,601	4,094	668	4,762	4,300	848	5,148
– % Increase Over 1972				5.7%	29.6(1)%	(0.7)%	7.8%	(20.2)%	2.8%	13.2%	1.3%	11.1%

All notes on Table 6.1 are applicable.
[1] Environmental Services staff could not be segregated from Transportation Services because these services were combined in one department in the City of Hamilton prior to January 1, 1974.
[2] Staffing data by service classification in 1972 were not available for Stoney Creek and Saltfleet. Figures used for these two municipalities were estimated by pro-rating the total staff figure by service according to the amounts spent in 1972 for salaries, wages and employee benefits.
[3] Percentage increases over 1972 are for the combined total of Transportation Services and Environmental Services Staffing.

SOURCES: Woods, Gordon & Co., *Finance Research Study, February 1978* and Data Schedules as completed by municipalities.

Chapter 7

Municipal Finance

A widespread concern about municipal finance, and particularly about the increases in local tax rates experienced since the introduction of regional government, created a major impetus for the establishment of this Commission. High property taxes and increases in municipal costs were identified as the prime causes of dissatisfaction by two out of every three people who expressed their views to us during our inquiry. Accordingly, we devoted a substantial portion of our research work to the general field of municipal finance in an effort to determine exactly what has happened and why, and to discover ways of ensuring that municipal services are provided in as economical a manner as possible and that costs are distributed equitably throughout the area. This chapter deals with the financial aspect of our findings and recommendations in this regard.

The chapter is divided into two parts. In the first part the changes in expenditures, revenues and tax levels between 1972 and 1977 are examined to determine the impacts regional government has had on local finances. In the second part of the chapter, we present the details of our financial recommendations for the new City of Wentworth and show some of the financial impacts that these reforms will have.

Two very important areas of reform in municipal finances are currently under consideration by the provincial government: property tax reform, and provincial-municipal grants reform. Since no firm policies have yet been adopted for these two fundamental elements of municipal finance, our analyses have to be based totally on the assessment information and provincial transfer payment arrangements as they stand at the moment.

The Years 1972 to 1977

The years under review have brought difficulty for most municipal governments in Canada. The country's inflation rate has accelerated, putting severe upward pressures on expenditures. In addition, since 1975 the provincial government has been constraining the grants it gives to municipalities in an effort to limit its own

Figure 7.1: Hamilton-Wentworth Expenditures by Function 1972, 1975–1977

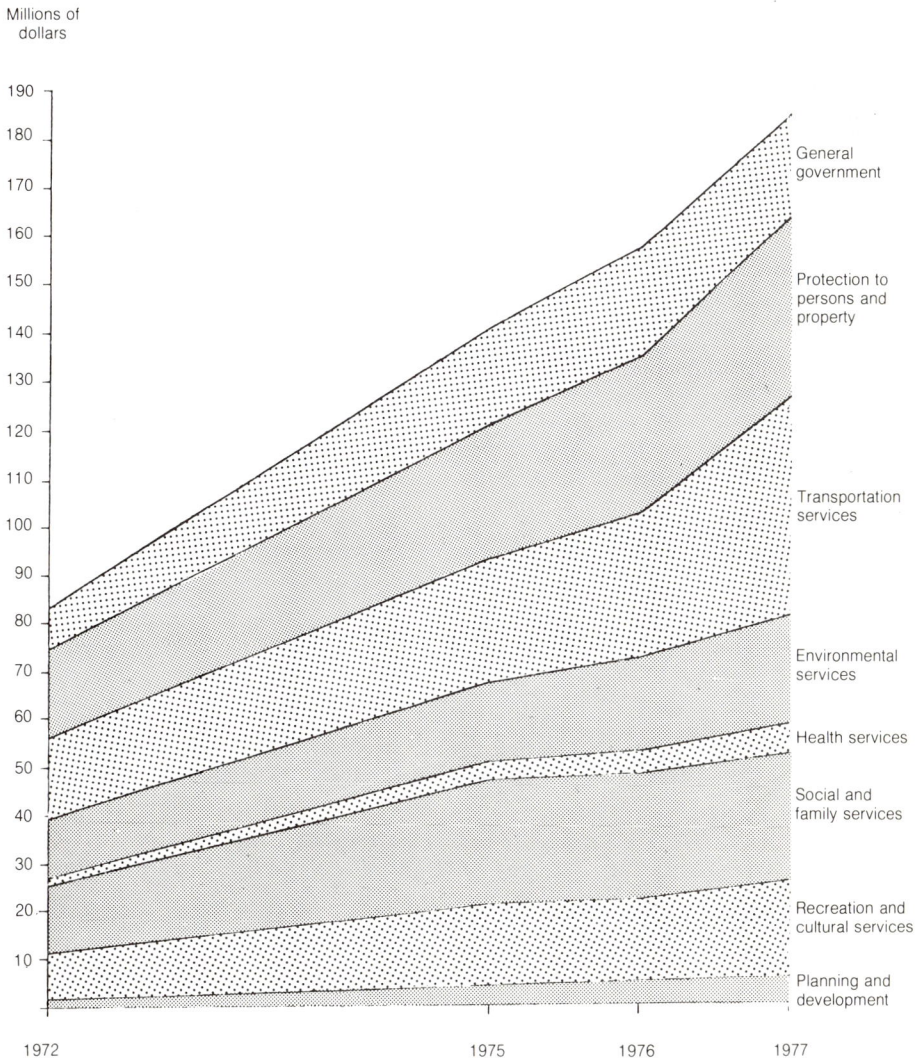

Table 7.1: Expenditures of Municipalities in Hamilton-Wentworth, 1972, 1975–1977

(thousands of dollars)

Municipality	Year	General gov't.[1]	Protection to persons and property	Transportation services	Environmental services	Health services	Social and family services	Recreation and cult. svcs.	Planning and dev'pment	Total expenditures
Ancaster	1977	333	165	742	181	118	13	356	88	1,996
	1976[3]	414	189	603	139	74	9	345	111	1,884
	1975[3]	348	131	519	52	78	8	267	78	1,481
	1972[2]	351	100	361	35	43	–	153	–	1,043
Dundas	1977	465	517	721	125	48	29	1,041	24	2,970
	1976[3]	480	469	691	141	64	26	1,104	27	3,002
	1975[3]	451	482	644	149	44	14	865	24	2,673
	1972[2]	335	352	397	96	–	–	337	–	1,517
Flamborough	1977	396	267	866	122	3	–	578	121	2,353
	1976[3]	468	227	795	119	1	–	467	89	2,166
	1975[3]	504	194	622	111	1	–	381	102	1,915
	1972[2]	274	100	540	58	–	–	54	8	1,034
Glanbrook	1977	156	79	736	71	4	–	299	68	1,413
	1976[3]	277	152	607	64	3	–	291	75	1,469
	1975[3]	182	64	537	45	3	–	187	72	1,090
	1972[2]	109	28	291	–	–	–	18	4	450
Hamilton	1977	13,309	12,404	16,131	2,937	964	611	16,106	2,948	65,410
	1976[3]	14,892	10,703	11,448	2,642	782	562	14,065	2,783	57,877
	1975[3]	10,072	9,734	10,596	2,288	703	549	13,757	2,924	50,623
	1972[2]	6,199	7,289	7,222	1,910	95	1,368	7,223	1,596	32,902
Stoney Creek	1977	1,102	569	1,641	552	67	65	842	130	4,968
	1976[3]	1,072	428	1,334	236	57	45	626	135	3,933
	1975[3]	732	373	1,038	242	62	11	606	125	3,189
	1972[2]	381	262	655	83	2	1	305	33	1,722

MUNICIPAL FINANCE 87

	Year									
Total area municipalities	1977	15,761	14,001	20,837	3,988	1,204	718	19,222	3,379	79,110
	1976[3]	17,603	12,168	15,478	3,341	981	642	16,898	3,220	70,331
	1975[3]	12,289	10,978	13,956	2,887	891	582	16,063	3,325	60,971
	1972[2]	7,649	8,131	9,466	2,182	140	1,369	8,090	1,641	38,668
Regional Municipality of Hamilton-Wentworth	1977	5,627	23,389	24,180	18,796	4,390	25,999	1,296	1,678	105,355
	1976[3]	5,239	20,583	14,485	15,278	4,245	25,028	1,246	1,211	87,315
	1975[3]	7,765	16,401	12,661	12,798	3,749	25,033	1,394	942	80,743
	1972[2]	779	10,573	7,445	9,693	1,569	13,325	747	537	44,668
Total (all municipalities)	1977	21,388	37,390	45,017	22,784	5,594	26,717	20,518	5,057	184,465
	1976	22,842	32,751	29,963	18,619	5,226	25,670	18,144	4,431	157,646
	1975	20,054	27,379	26,617	15,685	4,640	25,615	17,457	4,267	141,714
	1972	8,428	18,704	16,911	11,875	1,709	14,694	8,837	2,178	83,336

[1] General government includes irregular financial expenses such as transfers to capital and reserve funds.
[2] 1972 figures have been adjusted to reflect changes in responsibilities up to and including 1977 to afford valid comparisons.
[3] Transportation services: figures for 1975 and 1976 have been adjusted to reflect the 1977 changes in road and transit responsibilities to afford valid comparisons.

SOURCES: 1972, 1975, 1976 figures: Municipal financial statements.
1977 figures: Municipal budgets.

expenditure levels. These two factors have combined to make it difficult for municipal governments to keep mill rate increases down.

For the purpose of examining what has actually happened in the field of municipal finance we have gathered comparative data for 1972, 1975, 1976 and 1977. We chose 1972 as the base year as it preceded any effects on municipal decisions of the impending 1974 restructure. Figures for 1974 are generally omitted in this chapter, since it could by no means be considered a normal year. In addition, 1975 provincial reporting requirements changed extensively and valid comparisons could not easily be developed. All the 1972 figures have been adjusted, however, to take account of those changes.

In the tables where tax levels and mill rates are shown, the present area municipalities are sub-divided on the basis of the pre-1974 municipalities. This has been done because local assessment levels varied among the former municipalities. These differences were recognized when the new area municipalities were established, with the result that mill rates now vary among the merged areas within each new area municipality. In addition, we think that showing tax changes in this way will help individual taxpayers to see more precisely the tax impacts that regional government has had on them.

Current Expenditures

The total operating expenditures of the municipalities in Hamilton-Wentworth for the period 1972 to 1977 are shown in Figure 7.1, broken down by broad program area. The same information, with details for each of the municipal governments in the Region is given in Table 7.1, for the years 1972, 1975, 1976 and 1977.

A comparison with expenditures in other Ontario municipalities in recent years, shown in Tables 7.2 and 7.3, shows that the overall levels of the expenditure in this Region are not out of line with what might be expected in such a large and diverse area. Nonetheless, it is important to examine the expenditure performance in the Region to determine if there are areas where costs have been allowed to increase inordinately.

By taking into account inflation and expected changes in volume of services resulting from population growth, we were able to calculate expected annual expenditure growth rates between 1972 and 1977. These were then compared with the actual rates of growth. Table 7.4 gives the results of this analysis. Except in environmental services and health services, the actual increases in expenditures are higher than the expected increase in each functional area. The two categories that are furthest above the expected increase are recreational and cultural services (58.3 per cent higher than expected) and general government (57.7 per cent higher than expected). The analysis by object of expenditures shows that increases in

Table 7.2: Composition of Municipal Revenue Fund Spending by Types of Municipality

Function	Hamilton-Wentworth 1975 %	Hamilton-Wentworth 1976 %	Metro Toronto 1975 %	Metro Toronto 1976 %	Regional Gov'ts 1975 %	Regional Gov'ts 1976 %	Cities 1975 %	Cities 1976 %	Province 1975 %	Province 1976 %
General government	13	14	9	9	11	12	9	9	11	11
Protection	20	21	24	25	20	20	24	24	20	20
Transportation	18	18	21	19	24	23	20	19	24	23
Environment	11	11	10	10	11	11	12	13	10	11
Health and social services	23	21	21	21	19	18	20	19	20	20
Culture and recreation	12	12	13	14	12	13	13	13	12	12
Planning and development	3	3	2	2	3	3	2	3	3	3
Total	100	100	100	100	100	100	100	100	100	100

SOURCES: Ministry of Treasury, Economics and Intergovernmental Affairs, *Local Government Finance in Ontario, 1975 and 1976*; Supplementary data from Ministry of Treasury, Economics and Intergovernmental Affairs, Municipal Finance Branch.

Table 7.3: Municipal Revenue Fund Spending per Household by Types of Municipality in 1976

Function	Hamilton-Wentworth 1976 $	Hamilton-Wentworth 1976 over 1975 %	Metro Toronto 1976 $	Metro Toronto 1976 over 1975 %	Regional Gov'ts 1976 $	Regional Gov'ts 1976 over 1975 %	Cities 1976 $	Cities 1976 over 1975 %	Province 1976 $	Province 1976 over 1975 %
General government	159	20	108	15	123	13	92	7	107	13
Protection	232	14	292	11	207	8	239	11	203	7
Transportation	204	9	222	–	242	4	192	6	228	2
Environment	127	15	123	10	119	11	126	11	107	11
Health and social services	237	–	245	10	186	2	194	6	195	4
Culture and recreation	124	2	161	13	130	10	129	11	125	14
Planning and development	33	(6)	24	(4)	33	10	26	30	29	12
Total	1,116	8	1,175	8	1,040	7	998	9	994	7

SOURCES: See Table 7.2.

Table 7.4: Comparison of Actual and Expected Annual Expenditure Growth Rates from 1972 to 1977

Function	Actual	Expected[1]
General government	22.4%	14.2%
Transportation services	14.7	12.0
Protection to persons and property	16.7	14.1
Environmental services	11.1	13.2
Social and family services	11.5	9.9
Health services	8.5	11.3
Recreational and cultural services	17.1	10.8
Planning and development	18.7	15.1
Total Expenditures	14.7%	12.4%
Object	*Actual*	*Expected*
Salaries/wages	16.3	13.0
Materials/supplies	22.4	10.7
Contracted services	12.9	10.0
Financial expenses	9.4	13.8
Total transfers	12.6	13.4
Other	5.5	9.9
Total Expenditures	14.6	12.3
Direct Revenue	8.8	11.6
Net Expenditure	14.7%	12.4%

[1] Expected was calculated using (i) Price indices for Municipal expenditures (Table 7.16) to calculate price increases and (ii) volume parameters to calculate service level increases.
SOURCE: Woods, Gordon & Co., *Finance Research Study, February 1978.*

expenditures on materials and supplies are the furthest above the expected increase. The next two highest items are contracted services, and salaries and wages.

Our research studies indicate that between 1972 and 1977 there were major extensions of recreational services, particularly in the areas outside the City of Hamilton. We suspect that the higher than expected growth in recreational expenditures is partly attributable to the new two-tier system of government. When other major functions were elevated to the upper tier, recreational services became a relatively important item to area councils and probably received more attention and funds than they had previously.

General government expenditure is the other area that is substantially above the expected level. An increase of 20 per cent in the number of full-time staff performing general government functions, coupled with increases in levels of remuneration, undoubtedly contributed to the unexpected increases in these costs. The magnitude of the increase in general government expenditures is a cause for legitimate concern. It is the only function for which expenditures in Hamilton-Wentworth are substantially above those in other Ontario municipalities. Additionally, they are growing at a faster rate than elsewhere. We think that general government should not consume so large a proportion of municipal expenditures. By cutting out the duplications made necessary by a two-tier system of government, we are confident that significant savings can be made in these expenditures.

Revenues

As may be seen in Figure 7.2, taxation and provincial grants are the two largest sources of revenue for the municipalities in Hamilton-Wentworth. In 1977, the municipalities raised $88.5 million by their general levies, accounting for 47.9 per cent of their total revenues. A breakdown of revenues for the individual municipalities is given in Table 7.5. An analysis of the impact of tax changes on the individual parts of Hamilton-Wentworth, and on typical households in the area, is given in a following section of this chapter.

Tables 7.6 to 7.9 give comparisons of levels of taxes for Hamilton-Wentworth and other Ontario municipalities in recent years. As with expenditures, the tables show that the Region is not far out of line in its revenue and tax situation. Certainly the differences are not so great as to cause particular concern.

It is worth noting, however, that taxation makes up a greater proportion of total revenues in Hamilton-Wentworth than in the average of all municipalities in Ontario. As can be seen from Table 7.8, average residential property taxes and charges (excluding school taxes) in Hamilton-Wentworth are higher than in other municipalities when grouped by type, although average taxes in Metro Toronto were $3 higher than in Hamilton-Wentworth in 1976. The comparison of average property tax with average household income indicates that property taxes consume a slightly higher proportion of income in Hamilton-Wentworth than in the whole of Ontario. The figures are identical with those for all regional governments and very slightly lower than in Metro Toronto.

Provincial grants now make up a higher percentage of revenues in Hamilton-Wentworth than they did in 1972. In 1972, Ontario grants were 19.8 per cent of all revenues; in 1977, they accounted for 31.6 per cent. This increase in the relative importance of grants is partly caused by special assistance grants and transitional grants given to all regional municipalities in their early years of operation. In the first four years of this region's operation, provincial financial commitments of this nature

Table 7.5: Revenues of Municipalities in Hamilton-Wentworth 1972, 1975–1977

(thousands of dollars)

Municipality	Year	Taxation General levy	Taxation Other taxation	Payment in lieu of taxes	Ontario grants Unconditional	Ontario grants Conditional	Other revenues	Applied reserves surpluses, (deficits), etc.	Total revenues
Ancaster	1977	893	220	19	160	375	329	–	1,996
	1976[2]	754	190	21	150	378	290	101	1,884
	1975[2]	747	93	20	177	291	230	(77)	1,481
	1972[1]	458	93	16	–	254	222	–	1,043
Dundas	1977	2,032	81	54	304	201	468	(170)	2,970
	1976[2]	1,616	92	50	282	275	529	158	3,002
	1975[2]	1,593	100	15	499	160	440	(134)	2,673
	1972[1]	1,187	30	42	–	129	129	–	1,517
Flamborough	1977	1,139	159	10	301	340	366	38	2,353
	1976[2]	698	196	10	224	333	534	171	2,166
	1975[2]	867	165	4	196	189	628	(134)	1,915
	1972[1]	516	63	8	–	241	206	–	1,034
Glanbrook	1977	578	92	8	207	363	216	(51)	1,413
	1976[2]	460	83	8	196	195	243	284	1,469
	1975[2]	416	63	7	300	175	183	(54)	1,090
	1972[1]	211	11	7	–	123	98	–	450
Hamilton	1977	39,136	2,693	2,839	5,761	3,304	9,133	2,544	65,410
	1976[2]	32,859	2,926	2,661	5,740	1,894	11,078	619	57,877
	1975[2]	30,449	3,092	2,192	5,143	1,591	8,771	(615)	50,623
	1972[1]	22,362	1,094	2,704	–	1,088	5,354	–	32,902
Stoney Creek	1977	2,756	486	55	202	489	597	283	4,968
	1976[2]	2,471	208	54	241	502	614	(157)	3,933
	1975[2]	2,308	178	39	201	457	596	(590)	3,189
	1972[1]	1,020	108	27	–	307	260	–	1,722

MUNICIPAL FINANCE 93

Total area municipalities	1977	46,534	3,731	2,985	6,935	5,072	11,209	2,644	79,110
	1976²	38,858	3,695	2,804	6,833	3,577	13,388	1,176	70,331
	1975²	36,380	3,691	2,277	6,516	2,863	10,848	(1,604)	60,971
	1972¹	25,754	1,399	2,804	-	2,142	6,569	-	38,668
Regional Municipality of Hamilton-Wentworth	1977	41,936	10,975	1,169	15,073	31,205	4,899	98	105,355
	1976²	34,243	8,551	1,351	13,438	23,434	6,241	57	87,315
	1975²	28,986	7,459	1,149	14,191	24,094	4,546	318	80,743
	1972¹	22,300	7,391	-	3,197	11,162	618	-	44,668
Total (all municipalities)	1977	88,470	14,706	4,154	22,008	36,277	16,108	2,742	184,465
	1976	73,101	12,246	4,155	20,271	27,011	19,629	1,233	157,646
	1975	65,366	11,150	3,426	20,707	26,957	15,394	(1,286)	141,714
	1972	48,054	8,790	2,804	3,197	13,304	7,187	-	83,336

¹ 1972 figures have been adjusted to reflect changes in responsibilities up to and including 1977 to afford valid comparisons.
² 1975 and 1976 figures have been adjusted to reflect the 1977 changes in road and transit responsibilities to afford valid comparisons.
SOURCES: 1972, 1975, 1976 figures: Municipal financial statements.
1977 figures: Municipal budgets.

Figure 7.2: Hamilton-Wentworth Revenues by Source 1972, 1975–1977

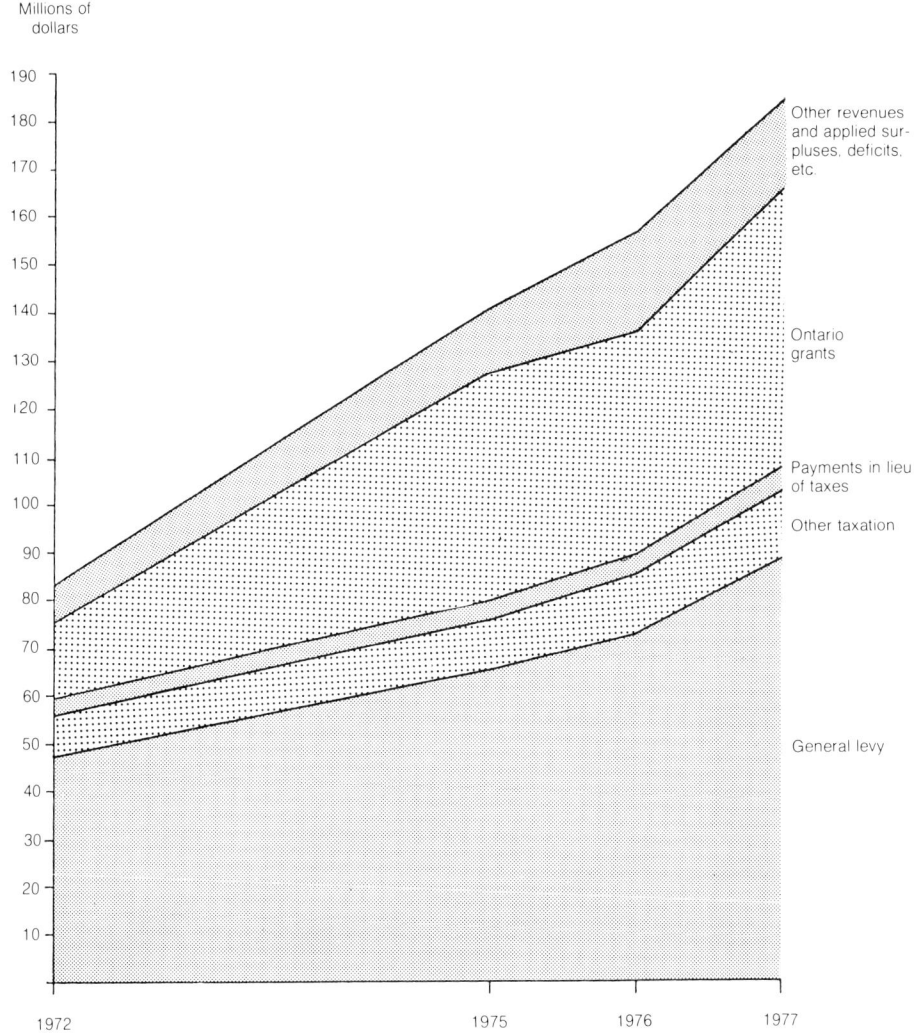

MUNICIPAL FINANCE 95

Table 7.6: Composition of Municipal Revenue Fund Revenues by Types of Municipality

Sources	Hamilton-Wentworth		Metro Toronto		Regional Gov'ts		Cities		Province	
	1975 %	1976 %	1975 %	1976 %	1975 %	1976 %	1975 %	1976 %	1975 %	1976 %
Taxation	53	54	56	56	48	49	51	51	49	49
Ontario grants	34	32	29	28	36	33	36	34	36	34
Other revenues	13	14	15	16	16	18	13	15	15	17
Total	100	100	100	100	100	100	100	100	100	100

SOURCES: See Table 7.2.

Table 7.7: Changes in Residential Mill Rates by Types of Municipality

Area	Municipal		School Boards		Total	
	1976 over 1975 %	1975 over 1974 %	1976 over 1975 %	1975 over 1974 %	1976 over 1975 %	1975 over 1974 %
Hamilton-Wentworth	8	8	28	10	17	9
Metro Toronto	11	12	12	14	12	13
Regional governments	6	13	23	16	14	14
Cities	6	13	27	13	15	13
Province	8	13	21	14	14	14

SOURCES: See Table 7.2.

Table 7.8: Average Gross Residential Property Taxes per Household by Types of Municipality

Area		1975 $	1976 $
Hamilton-Wentworth:	Municipal taxes	245	266
	Municipal charges	50	50
	Subtotal	295	316
	School Taxes	170	218
	Total	465	534
Metro Toronto:	Municipal taxes	280	311
	Municipal charges	7	8
	Subtotal	287	319
	School Taxes	267	299
	Total	554	618
Regional governments:	Municipal taxes	250	266
	Municipal charges	31	35
	Subtotal	281	301
	School Taxes	207	255
	Total	488	556
Cities:	Municipal taxes	234	248
	Municipal charges	18	18
	Subtotal	252	266
	School Taxes	154	195
	Total	406	461
Province:	Municipal taxes	225	242
	Municipal charges	19	21
	Subtotal	244	263
	School Taxes	195	236
	Total	439	499

SOURCES: See Table 7.2.

totalled just over $19 million. The breakdown of these special grants is shown in Table 7.10.

The increased proportion of revenues derived from provincial grants is also a result of different levels of grants for municipalities that have been regionalized than for those that have not. The per-capita grant, the 15 per cent water and sewage system grant, and the density grants are examples of these. Unlike the transitional grants, these grants will not be phased out over time.

MUNICIPAL FINANCE 97

Table 7.9: Average Gross Residential Property Taxes and Incomes per Household in 1976

Area	Average property tax	Average household income[1]	Property tax as % of income	
			1976	1975
Region of Hamilton-Wentworth	$534	$19,700	2.7	2.6
Metro Toronto	618	22,200	2.8	2.8
Regional governments	556	20,500	2.7	2.6
Cities	461	19,000	2.4	2.3
Province	499	19,600	2.5	2.4

[1] Ministry of Treasury, Economics and Intergovernmental Affairs, estimates based on Statistics Canada data.
SOURCES: See Table 7.2.

Table 7.10: Transitional Grants and Special Assistance, 1974-1977

Transitional Grants	
re 1974 restructure	$ 6,134,000
re 1977 transfer of functions:	
Roads	5,051,000
Transit	1,460,000
Special Assistance	
Police, planning	2,600,000
Transit transfer	125,000
Police communication system	774,000
Consolidation of water, sewage charges	2,942,000
Total	$19,086,000

SOURCE: Ministry of Treasury, Economics and Intergovernmental Affairs.

In total, provincial grants in Hamilton-Wentworth provided a lower proportion of revenues in 1976 than they did for other municipalities grouped by type. The main factor in this difference is the lower level of conditional grants for transportation. The Regional Municipality complained to us that insufficient grant monies are being allocated by the Ministry of Transportation and Communications in relation to the needs of the area, and the statistics indicate that a considerably lower allocation for transportation is made to Hamilton-Wentworth than to other regions.

Representatives of the Regional Municipality had a specific complaint about the administration of grants. They stated that, although in general there has been a considerable improvement in the timing of payment of grants, the Ministry of Community and Social Services continues to be extremely tardy in making payments. This situation resulted in a loss of interest to the Region of nearly $250,000 in 1977.

> Recommendation 7.1: The Ministry of Community and Social Services bring its grant payment system into line with those of other ministries.

Capital Expenditures and Financing

Table 7.11 shows capital expenditures and the sources of capital financing for the years 1972, 1975 and 1976. It is difficult to identify clear trends in capital spending over short periods of time, since expenditure levels vary considerably from year to year depending upon special projects and changing provincial incentives. Over half the funds for capital projects are derived from issuing long-term liabilities, a function performed by the Regional Municipality on behalf of all seven municipalities since 1974.

While Table 7.12 indicates that 1975 and 1976 capital expenditures per household in Hamilton-Wentworth are substantially lower than for municipalities in the province as a whole, the proportion of these expenditures financed by provincial grants is less than the provincial average. An analysis of capital fund revenues other than long-term borrowing for 1975 and 1976 shows that, while provincial grant contributions for all municipalities averaged 46 per cent and 45 per cent in the two years, the corresponding figures for Hamilton-Wentworth are only 30 per cent and 23 per cent respectively.

Long-term borrowing to finance capital projects is a necessary and desirable part of public finance, since it allows a public investment in facilities that can be paid for over the life of the assets. Nevertheless, the device must not be used too extensively, since the cumulative total has to be such that the annual carrying charges do not place too heavy a burden on the tax revenues. Table 7.13 shows the long-term debt that has accumulated in the Region per household. The table also shows the breakdown of the total debt for 1976 into the portion that is to be paid for through taxes, and the part financed through user charges, such as water and hydro rates. It may be noted that the level of total debt is greater in Hamilton-Wentworth than in any other class of municipality in Ontario, including Metropolitan Toronto.

Table 7.14 shows the impact the long-term debt has in terms of debt charges that must be met from general tax revenue. It is significant that the residential share of debt charges per household is higher in the Region than in the other classes of municipality shown. In 1976 debt charges averaged 9 per cent of current expenditure for all municipalities in Ontario while the comparable figure for Hamilton-Wentworth is 10 per cent.

These comparisons indicate that the debt burdens for Hamilton-Wentworth are

Table 7.11: Total Capital Expenditures and Financing in Hamilton-Wentworth

Expenditures by function	*(thousands of dollars)* 1972	1975	1976
General government	318	1,811	2,326
Protection to persons and property	592	2,072	6,896
Transportation services	10,813	20,046	11,555
Environmental services	7,025	6,053	5,462
Conservation of health	–	1,382	486
Social and family services	2	89	–
Recreation and cultural services	4,818	3,341	2,633
Planning and development	3,478	3,065	4,703
Other	47	134	1,583
Total general municipal functions	27,093	37,993	35,644
Hydro-electric system	–	165	–
Water supply	3,020	6,899	2,592
Other	1,310	–	–
Total capital expenditures	31,423	45,057	38,236
Reduction of unfinanced capital during the year	2,964	–	–
Totals	34,387	45,057	38,236

Source of capital financing	1972	1975	1976
Long-term liabilities	18,585	27,132	21,497
Contributions from other governments:			
Province of Ontario	6,191	5,491	5,491
Canada	1,134	244	519
Municipal	–	24	132
Reserves and reserve funds	1,018	2,845	7,260
Revenue fund	4,776	7,737	8,010
Other	2,683	2,036	2,621
Total capital funds provided	34,387	45,509	45,530
Excess capital financing during the year	–	(452)	(7,294)
Totals	34,387	45,057	38,236

SOURCE: Municipal Financial Statements.

somewhat higher than for other areas in Ontario, although not excessively so. Comparisons must be tentative, since debt equivalents for some government-financed capital expenditures in other areas are not necessarily reflected in all the statistics.

The Commission's financial consultants conducted a comprehensive review of the borrowing arrangements that have been developed since the Regional

Table 7.12: Municipal Capital Fund Spending per Household by Types of Municipality in 1975 and 1976

Function	Hamilton-Wentworth		Metro		Regional Gov'ts		Cities		Province	
	1975	1976	1975	1976	1975	1976	1975	1976	1975	1976
Transportation	$141	$ 79	$186	$196	$147	$127	$103	$109	$142	$135
Environment	42	37	88	94	107	90	101	103	87	80
Culture and recreation	23	18	69	54	49	42	34	22	49	42
Other	109	127	52	94	96	100	74	91	76	94
Total	315	261	395	438	399	359	312	325	354	351

SOURCES: Ministry of Treasury, Economics and Intergovernmental Affairs, *Local Government Finance in Ontario, 1975 and 1976,* and Municipal Financial Statements.

Table 7.13: Municipalities Net Long Term Debt per Household by Types of Municipality

Area	To be recovered from General revenues	To be recovered from User charges	1976 Total	1975 Total	Total increase 1976 over 1975
Hamilton-Wentworth	$873	$251	$1,124	$1,070	5%
Metro Toronto	892	229	1,121	976	15
Regional governments	722	210	932	805	16
Cities	681	159	840	779	8
Ontario	651	177	828	730	13

SOURCES: See Table 7.12.

Municipality took over the borrowing function on behalf of all the municipalities in the Region. They concluded that no adverse effects had arisen from the change. Policies regarding debt limits were established in the Region in 1975, and these are being adhered to by all the municipalities. The debentures of the Regional Municipality have been given "AA" ratings by both Moody's and Standard and Poor's investor services, a notable achievement.

Capital spending by municipalities is a matter that is subject to close control by the Ontario Municipal Board and may require the consent of the electorate. This consent is ordinarily dispensed with by the board. Prior approval of the board must be obtained before projects requiring capital financing can be undertaken, and no long-term borrowing can be done without board approval. The Commission has considered the procedures to deal with capital expenditures requiring debenture issue. We think that, without reducing the essential function of the Ontario Municipal Board in overseeing municipal financial integrity, and without reducing the role of the electors, the process can be improved.

At present the procedure does not require the municipality, when making its annual application for its capital expenditure quota, to set out in detail the projects it plans to develop. Following the establishment of the quota by the board, the municipality is required to submit applications for individual projects and to go through a procedure to determine whether or not its ratepayers have objections to the proposal. This procedure can be improved, to speed up the process of approvals, and to reduce applications to the board.

Recommendation 7.2: The City of Wentworth be enabled to pass any capital expenditure by-law by means of a vote of council, and no vote of ratepayers be required unless one is ordered by the Ontario Municipal Board.

Table 7.14: Debt Charges for General Municipal Purposes by Types of Municipality

Area	Per household Total		Residential share per household (excluding industrial & commercial share)		As percent of current expenditures	
	1975	1976	1975	1976	1975	1976
Hamilton-Wentworth	$101	$113	$62	$69	10%	10%
Metro Toronto	129	135	61	63	12	12
Regional governments	83	94	49	56	9	9
Cities	94	104	49	54	10	10
Ontario	86	93	46	50	9	9

SOURCES: See Table 7.12.

Recommendation 7.3: The municipality's capital program quota application to the Ontario Municipal Board contain a list of the projects planned for development within the year for which the quota application is made.

Recommendation 7.4: The municipality be required to advertise each project in the normal manner and if no objection is received it be permitted to proceed without seeking approval of the Ontario Municipal Board.

Recommendation 7.5: If objection is received as a result of the advertisement of a proposed capital project, the municipality be then required to apply to the Ontario Municipal Board, which at its discretion may decide whether a hearing is necessary before making its decision.

Recommendation 7.6: Where no objection is received to a proposed capital project, and the project proceeds, an affidavit of the actions of the municipality be submitted to the Ontario Municipal Board.

Recommendation 7.7: A report from the municipality on each year's capital expenditure and borrowing activities accompany its application for the next year's capital expenditure quota.

Causes of Cost and Tax Increases between 1972 and 1977

From the comments of the majority of the people who telephoned and wrote to us, it is clear that the residents of this area believe that the introduction of regional government is the main cause of increased costs and taxes.

Recognizing the importance of determining the extent to which that belief is grounded in fact, the Commission undertook detailed studies to determine the nature and weight of various factors behind the property tax increases between 1972 and 1977. It is our conclusion that the two major causes of increases in taxes within the Region are inflation and the redistribution of responsibilities accompanying reorganization that resulted in shifts of tax burdens.

In Table 7.15, the various factors contributing to tax increases are identified. These components are: inflation; the reforms of local government resulting in shifts of tax burden among people within the Region; area municipality operations; Regional Municipality operations; and school board operations. Also included are reductions due to the special transitional provisions that were introduced to spread out the impact of the redistribution of tax burdens. The final item, "Net actual increase in taxation, 1977 over 1972," shows the actual increase on a typical household. However, the figure before reductions caused by transitional provisions ("Net increase, 1977 over 1972") provides a fairer assessment of the situation, since the reductions are only temporary.

INFLATION

Inflation appears to be the single largest contributor to local cost increases over the period under review. The price indices for municipal expenditure for each year between 1972 and 1977 are shown in Table 7.16. These were derived on the basis of wage and price movements at the national level in each of the main components of municipal expenditures: wages and salaries, and goods and services. From these a composite inflation index for Hamilton-Wentworth was derived. There have been no serious distortions in the relative weighting of the components during this period. Although the inflation index was derived from nation-wide statistics, we have no reason to think that experience in Hamilton-Wentworth has been significantly different from elsewhere in Canada. Accordingly, we assume that inflation accounts for 58 per cent of the rise in municipal and school board expenditures in the Region during the 1972-1977 period. This makes it the major contributor to cost increases.

In nine of the thirteen areas of the Region in this analysis, inflation is the main factor behind tax increases. In the other four areas it was the second highest factor.

SHIFTS IN TAX BURDEN DUE TO REFORM OF GOVERNMENT

In the four areas where inflation was not the highest factor behind tax increases — the part of West Flamborough added to Dundas, Beverly, East Flamborough and

Table 7.15: Factors Contributing to Residential Property Tax Changes, 1972 to 1977

Municipality: Area in municipality: Reason for change	Town of Ancaster (1) Ancaster		(2) Ancaster		Town of Dundas (3) Dundas		(4) West Flamborough	
	Percentage change	Tax increase[1]	Percentage change	Tax increase[1]	Percentage change	Tax increase[1]	Percentage change	Tax increase[1]
Inflation	58.0	$287	58.0	$287	58.0	$348	58.0	$230
Restructuring								
1974 restructure	21.3	105	31.7	158	6.4	38	69.5	275
1977 functional transfers	14.9	74	11.8	58	9.8	59	15.5	61
Local municipality operations:								
Local expenditures	18.0	89	14.4	71	14.4	86	14.4	57
Local revenues (inc. grants)	(18.2)	(90)	(12.5)	(62)	(12.5)	(75)	(12.5)	(49)
Regional Municipality operations:								
Police Commission	6.4	31	6.4	31	6.4	38	6.4	25
Conservation Authorities	(0.1)	–	(0.1)	(1)	(0.1)	(1)	(0.1)	–
Health Board	(0.2)	(1)	(0.2)	(1)	(0.2)	(1)	(0.2)	(1)
Childrens' Aid	(0.9)	(5)	(0.9)	(4)	(0.9)	(5)	(0.9)	(4)
Regionally controlled functions	31.0	154	36.1	179	36.1	217	36.1	143
Total Regional Municipality	36.2	179	41.3	204	41.3	248	41.3	163
Regional revenues (inc. grants)	(54.6)	(270)	(50.3)	(249)	(50.3)	(302)	(50.3)	(199)
School Boards	6.7	33	5.3	26	5.3	32	5.3	21
Assessment growth	(6.7)	(33)	(9.4)	(46)	(9.4)	(56)	(9.4)	(37)
Net increase, 1977 over 1972	75.6	374	90.3	447	63.0	378	131.8	522
1977 reductions due to transitional provisions:								
1974 restructure	(3.1)	(15)	(4.6)	(23)	(1.2)	(7)	(9.7)	(39)
1977 functional transfers	(14.9)	(74)	(11.8)	(58)	(9.8)	(59)	(15.5)	(61)
Net actual increase in taxation, 1977 over 1972	57.6	285	73.9	366	52.0	312	106.6	422

MUNICIPAL FINANCE 105

Table 7.15: Factors Contributing to Residential Property Tax Changes, 1972 to 1977 (cont.)

Municipality:
Area in municipality:

Reason for change	(5) Beverly		(6) E. Flamborough		(7) W. Flamborough		(8) Waterdown	
	Percentage change	Tax increase[1]	Percentage change	Tax increase[1]	Percentage change	Tax increase[1]	Percentage change	Tax increase[1]
Inflation	58.0	$217	58.0	$213	58.0	$230	58.0	$278
Restructuring								
1974 restructure	48.1	180	49.7	182	38.3	152	(3.1)	(15)
1977 functional transfers	13.7	51	14.2	52	13.4	53	9.2	44
Local municipality operations:								
Local expenditures	22.4	83	22.4	82	22.4	89	22.4	107
Local revenues (inc. grants)	(16.4)	(61)	(16.4)	(60)	(16.4)	(65)	(16.4)	(78)
Regional Municipality operations:								
Police Commission	6.4	24	6.4	23	6.4	25	6.4	31
Conservation Authorities	(0.1)	–	(0.1)	–	(0.1)	–	(0.1)	(1)
Health Board	(0.2)	(1)	(0.2)	(1)	(0.2)	(1)	(0.2)	(1)
Childrens' Aid	(0.9)	(3)	(0.9)	(3)	(0.9)	(4)	(0.9)	(4)
Regionally controlled functions	55.7	208	55.7	204	55.7	221	55.7	267
Total Regional Municipality	60.9	228	60.9	223	60.9	241	60.9	292
Regional revenues (inc. grants)	(75.8)	(284)	(75.8)	(278)	(75.8)	(300)	(75.8)	(363)
School Boards	22.2	83	22.2	82	22.2	88	22.2	106
Assessment growth	(23.1)	(86)	(23.1)	(85)	(23.1)	(92)	(23.1)	(111)
Net increase, 1977 over 1972	110.0	411	112.1	411	99.9	396	54.3	260
1977 reductions due to transitional provisions:								
1974 restructure	(7.0)	(26)	(9.3)	(34)	(8.9)	(36)	(3.1)	(15)
1977 functional transfers	(13.7)	(51)	(14.2)	(52)	(13.4)	(53)	(9.2)	(44)
Net actual increase in taxation, 1977 over 1972	89.3	334	88.6	325	77.6	307	42.0	201

Table 7.15: Factors Contributing to Residential Property Tax Changes, 1972 to 1977 (cont.)

Municipality: Area in municipality	(9) Binbrook Township of Glanbrook		(10) Glanford		Hamilton City (11) Hamilton		(12) Saltfleet Town of Stoney Creek		(13) Stoney Creek	
Reason for change	% change	Tax incr.[1]	% change	Tax incr.[1]	% change	Tax incr.[1]	% change	Tax incr.[1]	% change	Tax incr.[1]
Inflation	58.0	$247	58.0	$209	58.0	$306	58.0	$254	58.0	$252
Restructuring										
1974 restructure	24.6	105	49.8	180	(3.5)	(18)	22.6	99	4.2	19
1977 functional transfers	12.3	52	15.1	55	(2.3)	(12)	12.0	53	11.6	51
Local municipality operations:										
Local expenditures	57.8	246	57.8	208	24.8	130	42.7	187	42.7	185
Local revenues (incl. grants)	(38.0)	(162)	(38.0)	(137)	(12.2)	(64)	(35.7)	(156)	(36.1)	(157)
Regional Municipality operations:										
Police Commission	6.4	27	6.4	23	6.4	33	6.4	27	6.4	27
Conservation Authorities	(0.1)	–	(0.1)	(1)	(0.1)	–	(0.1)	–	(0.1)	–
Health Board	(0.2)	(1)	(0.2)	(1)	(0.2)	(1)	(0.2)	(1)	(0.2)	(1)
Children's Aid	(0.9)	(4)	(0.9)	(3)	(0.9)	(5)	(0.9)	(4)	(0.9)	(4)
Regionally controlled functions	46.6	199	46.6	168	12.9	68	58.6	257	60.9	265
Total Regional Municipality	51.8	221	51.8	186	18.1	95	63.8	279	66.1	287
Regional revenues (inc. grants)	(75.9)	(324)	(75.9)	(273)	(27.0)	(142)	(62.6)	(274)	(65.2)	(283)
School Boards	16.2	69	16.2	58	2.4	12	17.0	75	17.0	74
Assessment growth	(14.9)	(63)	(14.9)	(54)	(12.8)	(67)	(29.8)	(131)	(29.8)	(130)
Net increase, 1977 over 1972	91.9	391	119.9	432	45.5	240	88.0	386	68.5	298
1977 reductions due to transitional provisions:										
1974 restructure	(7.1)	(30)	(7.0)	(25)	–	–	(1.7)	(7)	(1.7)	(7)
1977 functional transfers	(12.3)	(52)	(15.1)	(55)	–	–	(12.0)	(53)	(11.6)	(51)
Net actual increase in taxation, 1977 over 1972	72.5	309	97.8	352	45.5	240	74.3	326	55.2	240

( ) = reductions
[1] Tax increases: Typical household represented by a local assessment of $22,000 in the former Town of Stoney Creek (reassessed in 1968) and $5000 in all other areas.

Table 7.16: Price Indices for Municipal Expenditures

Year	Wages and salaries	Non-wage goods and services	Derived composite index for Hamilton-Wentworth
1972	100	100	100
1973	106.7	106.8	106.7
1974	116.0	119.2	117.3
1975	130.6	131.1	130.8
1976	149.8	142.2	146.7
1977[e]	163.3	150.4	158.0

[e] = Estimated
SOURCE: Woods, Gordon & Co., *Finance Research Study,* February 1978.

Glanford — the redistribution of tax burdens caused by the introduction of regional government and the consequent 1974 restructuring and 1977 functional transfers is the main cause of increases. In six of the other areas, it is second only to inflation in pushing up tax levels.

These shifts in tax burden are caused by two aspects of the reforms of 1974: the transfer of certain functions to the region-wide municipality, and the amalgamation of some municipalities, or parts of municipalities, into larger units at the lower-tier level.

Most of the services provided by the Regional Municipality of Hamilton-Wentworth are paid for by a general levy on all property in the Region. The distribution of tax burden is determined according to equalized assessment. Prior to 1974, the municipalities in the former County of Wentworth were already paying for some services on a county-wide basis, and public health and child welfare costs were already regionalized. In 1974, however, certain additional functions such as policing and regional planning were added to those paid for in the general levy at the upper-tier level. In addition, the City of Hamilton was added to the two-tier system, with the result that items such as the city's relatively heavy social service expenditures were thenceforth paid for by all residents in the Region. Some roads and transit expenditures that had been paid for only by city residents were added to tne regional levies in 1977. The main impact of these transfers of functions to the Regional Municipality is to shift tax burdens from the City of Hamilton to the people in the other municipalities. As is shown in Table 7.15, only in the city did the shift in tax burdens caused by the reforms result in a decrease.

The other shift in tax burdens was caused by the amalgamation of formerly separated areas into new area municipalities. This resulted in the costs of functions that remained a responsibility of the area municipalities becoming equalized among

Table 7.17: Financial Effects of the 1974 Reorganization

Area	Internal shift within area municipality ($000's)	External shift between areas ($000's)	Net shift ($000's)
Ancaster	–	230	230
Dundas			
Ancaster	2	3	5
Dundas	(66)	106	40
West Flamborough	64	75	139
Flamborough			
Beverly	(35)	166	131
East Flamborough	60	294	354
West Flamborough	44	307	351
Waterdown	(69)	14	(55)
Glanbrook			
Binbrook	(45)	104	59
Glanford	45	242	287
Hamilton	–	(1,843)	(1,843)
Stoney Creek			
Saltfleet	56	284	340
Stoney Creek	(56)	18	(38)

( ) = Reductions
SOURCE: Ministry of Treasury, Economics and Intergovernmental Affairs.

the areas that had been amalgamated. For example, the residents in those parts of West Flamborough and Ancaster that were added to the former Town of Dundas now found themselves contributing to the costs of the much higher levels of service that had long existed in Dundas.

Table 7.17 shows the relative impacts of these two types of shifts in tax burdens. By far the largest shift is caused by the transfer of burdens from the city to non-city municipalities. Other readjustments — among residents of the same area municipality — resulted in shifts from the former Town of Dundas to the parts of West Flamborough and Ancaster added to it, from Waterdown and Beverly to East and West Flamborough, from Binbrook to Glanford and from Stoney Creek to Saltfleet. These transfers, like those from Hamilton to the rest of the Region, are essentially shifts of tax burdens from urban and suburban properties to rural ones.

The decisions of the Regional Municipality to move from the pre-existing different bases of charge for water to a more uniform basis, and to equalize sewage charges by a surcharge on water charges, have also caused shifts in burdens between and within the area municipalities. The estimated effects, based on 1974

Table 7.18: Estimated Effects of Establishing Uniform Water and Sewage Charges

Area	Increase or decrease ($000's)[1]	
	Water	Sewage
Ancaster	(74)	–
Dundas	(218)	(15)
Flamborough (Waterdown)	(19)	(52)
Hamilton		
non-metered	253	(283)
metered	148	411
Stoney Creek		
non-metered	71	(147)
metered	(161)	86

[1] Based on 1974 operations.
( ) = decrease
SOURCE: Ministry of Treasury, Economics and Intergovernmental Affairs.

figures, are shown in Table 7.18.

These shifts of tax burdens have had a significant impact on taxpayers in the Region. Indeed, the transfer of some of these burdens was one of the reasons for introducing regional governments originally. It was then thought that certain inequitable financing situations existed that allowed some people to have the advantages of a service without paying their full share of the costs. This explained two of the transfers of functions to the Regional Municipality: roads and social services.

Prior to the establishment of regional government the city made some contribution towards roads outside its borders through the Suburban Roads Commission, but this amounted to only $369,940 in 1972. In 1974 its share of regional roads costs, excluding roads within the city, was more than $1.5 million, and rose to more than $2 million in 1976. The effect of the transfer of the costs of regional roads within the city to the Region was to shift about one quarter of those costs to the other municipalities. In the first year, 1977, the Province of Ontario met the additional burden, although this is to be phased down over five years. Table 7.19 shows the effects of these transfers.

Similarly, it was thought that the social responsibility for providing basic welfare services should be shared equally by all people in the Region, and not weigh unduly on those in the city where the majority of recipients tend to live. Also, many of the more urbanized sections outside the city felt that the rural residents, though using facilities such as recreational facilities, were not contributing their fair share.

The total impact of these shifts is not yet being felt by the taxpayers because of transitional provisions which consist of two elements: provincial grants; and the

Table 7.19: Financial Effects of 1977 Transfer of Hamilton Roads and Transit Functions

Area	Increased levy ($000's)
Ancaster	287
Dundas	
Ancaster	1
Dundas	372
West Flamborough	21
Flamborough	
Beverly	111
East Flamborough	141
West Flamborough	145
Waterdown	47
Glanbrook	
Binbrook	80
Glanford	97
Hamilton	(2,063)
Stoney Creek	
Saltfleet	614
Stoney Creek	147

SOURCE: Ministry of Treasury, Economics and Intergovernmental Affairs.

phasing in of shifts between residents in newly formed area municipalities over a five-year period. We think it is important, however, to understand the changes in burden that reorganization has created, and to recognize that the cushioning effect of provincial transitional grants will only temporarily alleviate the full impact for the taxpayers.

SCHOOL BOARD OPERATIONS

In most cases, increases in property taxes for education purposes is the third highest contributor to total increases in tax levels over the 1972-1977 period. After adjustments to allow for inflation, the impact ranged from an increase of 2.4 per cent in Hamilton to 22.2 per cent in the Township of Flamborough. Table 7.15 shows that in every instance school taxes (which are of course net of provincial subsidies) outstripped inflation and, particularly outside the City of Hamilton, made an extensive contribution to total tax increases.

    Several people making submissions to the Commission raised questions about the education system, and some questioned the need for separate continuance of the Hamilton and the County of Wentworth School Boards from an operational and administrative viewpoint. It was also pointed out that for school purposes there is no direct sharing of the benefit of the commercial and industrial assessment existing in the City of Hamilton.

The Commission did not conduct an extensive inquiry into the education system of the Region. We did review education finances generally, however, and found that school taxes in the City of Hamilton are somewhat higher than in the rest of the Region. The Ministry of Education school grant formula strives for common equalized mill rates for secondary and elementary school purposes given generally comparable levels of service. For secondary education, both the Hamilton and Wentworth boards are above those standard levels, Hamilton being higher than Wentworth. For elementary purposes, however, while Hamilton is again above the ministry levels, Wentworth is somewhat below them.

The Commission thinks that the unique structure of two public school boards in the City of Wentworth warrants further consideration by the Government of Ontario.

OPERATIONS OF AREA AND REGIONAL MUNICIPALITIES

The actual expenditures on municipal services, after allowing for inflation, have risen substantially over the period. The lowest percentage increase in area municipal costs is found in Dundas, with 14.4 per cent. Glanbrook experienced an increase of 57.8 per cent, while Stoney Creek was next highest with 42.7 per cent. The share of expenditures on functions performed by the regional government rose from a low of 18.1 per cent in Hamilton to a high of 66.1 per cent in the former Town of Stoney Creek; these figures are affected by growth in assessment.

To be offset against these increases, however, are increases in such revenues as user charges and provincial grants. These revenues increased so markedly that the resulting net expenditure picture, the one that affects tax rates, is substantially different.

Net expenditure increases by the municipalities are actually the lowest contributors to increases in tax levels. Indeed, for everywhere except the Town of Stoney Creek, the constant dollar costs to the local taxpayers for services provided through the Regional Municipality actually decreased between 1972 and 1977. Area municipal net expenditures increased in Glanbrook by 19.8 per cent, but nowhere else was the increase greater than Hamilton's 12.6 per cent. Net expenditures in Ancaster show a fractional decrease.

ASSESSMENT GROWTH

In Table 7.15 a negative percentage is shown under each municipality beside the heading "Assessment growth." This indicates the estimated reduction in the tax burden on each household caused by growth of assessment in each municipality during the period. As a result of this growth the tax burden is spread over a wider base. The figures must be approached with considerable caution, however, since they do not take into account the growth in expenditures that may be directly related to the property developments that lead to increased assessments.

Changes in Taxation Levels

We recognize that for the majority of residents of the Region municipal finance is important mainly for its impact on their residential taxes. Table 7.20 shows the residential mill rate and the dollar amount of residential property taxes on typical households in Hamilton-Wentworth for both 1972 and 1977. These mill rates and tax levels include the levies necessary for both municipal purposes (area and regional operations) and school board purposes. Clearly, it is the residents of the more rural parts of the area who experienced the sharpest increases in tax levels after regional government was introduced in 1974. The sections of Hamilton-Wentworth where residents experienced the highest increases between 1972 and 1977 were, in descending order, the section of West Flamborough added to Dundas in 1974, Glanford, Beverly, East Flamborough, West Flamborough, Saltfleet, the part of Ancaster added to Dundas, and Binbrook. In each of these areas the increase over the period was over 70 per cent; in the part of West Flamborough added to Dundas the increase was 106.6 per cent. These are all the more rural parts of the Region of Hamilton-Wentworth. The more urbanized sections had smaller increases: 42.0 per cent in Waterdown, 45.5 per cent in Hamilton, 52.0 per cent in Dundas, 55.2 per cent in Stoney Creek, and 57.6 per cent in Ancaster, which is the least heavily urbanized of these areas.

Extreme caution should be used in dealing with the actual dollar amounts of the increases shown in the table. Although the assessed value of the residences is considered typical in the various municipalities, differences in assessment practice make it improper to assume that the properties are truly comparable from one municipality to another. It should also be noted that an amount equal to sewer surcharges has been added to the 1977 figures for comparability with 1972. Nonetheless, an examination of the actual dollar amount of residential taxes on typical households further indicates how substantial the shift has been. In 1972, the more rural sections of the Region had the lowest residential property taxes. In 1977, typical homes in the former Town of Stoney Creek and Waterdown — two heavily urbanized areas — had the lowest tax levels. Typical homes in Hamilton had the second highest level in 1972; only Dundas' tax level was higher. In 1977, homes in Dundas, the sections of Ancaster and West Flamborough that were annexed to Dundas, and Ancaster had higher tax levels than did typical residences in Hamilton.

It is important to point out that taxes in the areas outside the City of Hamilton have not risen as rapidly as they would have had the provincial government not paid

Table 7.20: Residential Property Taxes, 1972 and 1977

Area	Residential mill rates 1972	1977	Increase mills	%	Residential property taxes on typical households[1] 1972 $	1977 $	Increase $	%
Ancaster	99.09	156.13	57.04	57.6	496	781	285	57.6
Dundas								
Dundas[2]	120.16	182.63	62.47	52.0	602	914	312	52.0
West Flamborough	79.14	163.50	84.36	106.6	396	818	422	106.6
Ancaster	99.09	172.27	73.18	73.9	495	861	366	73.9
Flamborough								
West Flamborough	79.14	140.59	61.45	77.6	396	703	307	77.6
East Flamborough	73.32	138.30	64.98	88.6	367	692	325	88.6
Beverly	74.47	141.37	66.90	89.3	372	706	334	89.3
Waterdown[2]	95.54	135.68	40.14	42.0	478	679	201	42.0
Glanbrook								
Glanford	71.94	142.33	70.39	97.8	360	712	352	97.8
Binbrook	85.10	146.82	61.72	72.5	425	734	309	72.5
Hamilton[2]	105.29	153.20	47.91	45.5	526	766	240	45.5
Stoney Creek								
Saltfleet	87.70	152.89	65.19	74.3	438	764	326	74.3
Stoney Creek	19.97	30.99	11.02	55.2	440	680	240	55.2

[1] Typical household represented by a local assessment of $22,000 in the former Town of Stoney Creek (reassessed in 1968) and $5,000 in all other areas.
[2] In 1972 the mill rates included sewage expenditures; for comparative purposes, therefore, the 1977 mill rates have been increased by 9.40 mills ($47), the equivalent of the 1977 sewage surcharge.
SOURCE: 1972 and 1977 municipal tax levy by-laws.

transitional grants specifically designed to ease burdens on the non-city municipalities. As these temporary grants are phased out, the residents outside the city will be subjected to additional tax increases. For example, if there had been no transitional grants, the residents of Waterdown who had had the lowest tax increases would have experienced an increase between 1972 and 1977 of 54.3 per cent rather than 42.0 per cent. Taxes paid by the people of West Flamborough annexed to Dundas, which already had the highest percentage increase, would have risen from 106.6 per cent to 131.8 per cent. The taxes of the people in the City of Hamilton, where such assistance is not given, will not be affected by the phasing out of these transitional grants, although those of people in the rest of the Region will increase accordingly.

An Evaluation

From the foregoing analysis we conclude that the overall state of municipal finance in Hamilton-Wentworth is satisfactory. In general terms, the levels of expenditure, taxation and debt are in keeping with those found throughout Ontario in larger municipalities.

Although the introduction of regional government has resulted in some increases in expenditures, these are still being cushioned to a degree by transitional grant provisions. This cushioning will not continue indefinitely, and further effects of the changes in organization will be felt in the form of increased taxes in the future when the grants are phased out.

Another important impact of the reorganization is a shift in the burden of financing certain services from the city to the more rural areas. This has resulted in an uneven pattern of tax increases within the Region.

The rest of this chapter outlines the way that the new City of Wentworth can ensure an equitable distribution of the burden of taxes among the people who benefit from the services provided, without creating the internal shifts of tax burdens that resulted from the previous reorganization.

The Future

Our prime recommendation is that there be only one municipal government in the Region — the City of Wentworth. We are convinced that, in addition to allowing elected representatives to provide better service, this structure of government will encourage financial savings and as a result decrease the demands on the taxpayers of this Region. We think it is possible, too, to ensure that tax burdens are equitably distributed within the Region.

For the purpose of analysing the financial situation of the City of Wentworth we have taken the latest budgeted figures available for the existing municipalities — those for 1977. These estimates have been amended to exclude previous years' adjustments and provincial transitional grants, in order to determine the absolute amount required for the year. From this has been deducted the amount of the estimated increased provincial transfer payments that will result if the Commission's recommendations are adopted. The result is a revised estimated total levy of $93,129,000, which is used in all following calculations to illustrate the financial effects of the proposals. The calculations showing how this sum was determined are shown in Table 7.21. No allowance has been made for the savings in administrative costs we expect to accrue from the recommended reforms.

Effects Without Special Taxation Arrangements

If normal municipal financing practices were followed the expenses of the City of Wentworth to be raised from taxes would be distributed by means of a general levy. The amount to be raised is the total current expenditures of the city, less grants and other current revenues. Because assessment levels vary throughout the area, the

MUNICIPAL FINANCE 115

general levy mill rate would vary to provide equalized taxation throughout the whole city.

Table 7.22 shows the shifts in tax burdens between various parts of the city that would have occurred in 1977 if the City of Wentworth had been established and was operating primarily on such a general levy basis. Table 7.23 illustrates the effects within each part of the city on residential public school taxpayers. The results would have been dramatic. Taxpayers in the City of Hamilton would have had a reduction in taxes for municipal purposes of 7.3 per cent. In all other areas, there would have been an increase in municipal taxes ranging up to approximately $200 on a typical residential household.

Taxation Proposals

Such a redistribution of tax burdens within the city is unacceptable to the Commission. The reforms of local government of 1974 resulted in substantial shifts in tax burdens, as have been outlined in detail in this chapter. Although some of those shifts were justified, we do not think that further shifts should be the result of this reform of local government. Our objective is to keep further redistribution of tax burdens in the Region to a minimum. To achieve this, we recommend two special techniques: an urban-rural tax differential for some services; and area rating for certain other services. This means that the City of Wentworth should raise the revenues from the local people by a combination of levies: an urban-rural differential levy; an area-rated levy; special user charges on benefiting ratepayers; and a general levy. The City of Wentworth is, after all, a unique community comprising a highly urbanized core surrounded by a rural hinterland and its taxing system should reflect this unique composition.

URBAN-RURAL DIFFERENTIAL

People in more densely populated areas require and demand both higher levels of service and different types of service. It is entirely appropriate, therefore, that there should be a differential tax rate between urban and rural taxpayers in the new city to reflect these differences in services. The expenditures on general government (salaries, materials, services and rents), on parks and recreation, on local cultural services, and on major urban improvements (such as Jackson Square) should be allocated on a differential basis. (Those cultural facilities such as the Art Gallery that are now financed by the general regional levy should continue to be handled in that manner.)

For services that are to be financed on this differential basis, rural properties should be taxed at a level no greater than 50 per cent of the rate for the urbanized areas. The new municipality should have the discretion to give a greater amount of

Table 7.21: City of Wentworth — Estimated Total Levy

(thousands of dollars)

	Hamilton	Ancaster	Dundas	Stoney Creek	Flamborough	Glanbrook	Totals
Lower-tier expenditures	65,856	2,011	2,986	4,969	2,400	1,493	79,715
Less: Own account revenues	26,720	1,041	954	2,213	1,122	844	32,894
Area rated charges		77			139	71	287
Net lower-tier general levy	39,136	893	2,032	2,756	1,139	578	46,534
Upper-tier expenditures							94,952
Less: Own account revenues							53,014
Net upper-tier general levy	35,564	776	1,215	2,499	1,424	460	41,938
Actual general municipal levies (including area-rated charges)	74,700	1,746	3,247	5,255	2,702	1,109	88,759
Add: Surplus and (deficit) adjustments applied	1,845	—	(99)	292	32	(53)	2,017
provincial transitional grants	—	388	470	916	899	330	3,003
Revised general levies	76,545	2,134	3,618	6,463	3,633	1,386	93,779
Less: Increased provincial transfer payments expected after consolidation							
Per capita density grant							490
Resource equalization grant							160 650
Revised total estimated general levy and inter-municipal charges.							93,129

SOURCE: 1977 municipal budgets adjusted for contra items, such as debt charges recoverable and inter-municipal charges.

Table 7.22: City of Wentworth — Tax Effects of Consolidation without Special Taxing Arrangements

Existing merged areas	Existing		After consolidation		Increase or (decrease) over existing ($000's)
	Actual levies ($000's)	Distribution %	Revised levies ($000's)	Distribution %	
Ancaster	2,134	2.275	2,878	3.090	744
Dundas					
Dundas	3,410	3.636	3,870	4.156	460
West Flamborough	195	.208	222	.238	27
Ancaster	13	.014	15	.016	2
Flamborough					
Beverly	897	.957	1,324	1.422	427
East Flamborough	1,154	1.231	1,682	1.806	528
West Flamborough	1,185	1.264	1,728	1.855	543
Waterdown	397	.423	558	.599	161
Glanbrook					
Binbrook	624	.665	857	.920	233
Glanford	762	.813	1,038	1.115	276
Hamilton	76,545	81.623	70,938	76.172	(5,607)
Stoney Creek					
Stoney Creek	1,240	1.322	1,538	1.652	298
Saltfleet	5,223	5.569	6,481	6.959	1,258
Totals	93,779	100.000	93,129[1]	100.000	(650)[1]

[1] The $650,000 net decrease represents the total estimated increase in provincial transfer payments after consolidation.

118 CHAPTER 7

Table 7.23: City of Wentworth — Tax Effects on Residential Taxpayers of Consolidation without Special Taxing Arrangements

Area	RESIDENTIAL MILL RATES Gen. municipal[1] Existing	RESIDENTIAL MILL RATES Gen. municipal[1] Revised	Educa. Existing	TOT. MILL RATES Existing	TOT. MILL RATES Revised	RESIDENTIAL PROPERTY TAXES ON TYPICAL HOUSEHOLDS[2] Gen. municipal Existing	Gen. municipal Revised	Educa. Existing	TOTAL TAXES Existing	TOTAL TAXES Revised	% Chge. in Gen. municip. taxes	% chge. in total taxes	$ chge. in total taxation
Ancaster	90.30	121.78	81.69	171.99	203.47	452	609	408	860	1017	+34.7	+18.3	+157
Dundas													
Dundas	108.45	123.08	74.86	183.31	197.94	542	616	374	916	990	+13.7	+ 8.1	+ 74
W. Flamborough	112.15	127.69	81.32	193.47	209.01	561	633	407	968	1045	+13.7	+ 8.0	+ 77
Ancaster	106.87	122.61	82.31	189.18	204.92	534	613	412	946	1025	+14.8	+ 7.7	+ 79
Flamborough													
Beverly	82.46	121.71	81.97	164.43	203.68	412	608	410	822	1018	+47.5	+23.8	+196
E. Flamborough	84.97	123.85	79.33	164.30	203.18	425	619	397	822	1016	+45.6	+23.6	+194
W. Flamborough	87.32	127.35	80.60	167.92	207.95	437	637	403	840	1040	+45.8	+23.8	+200
Waterdown	74.49	104.69	69.96	144.45	174.65	372	523	350	722	873	+40.6	+20.9	+151
Glanbrook													
Binbrook	84.99	116.72	78.04	163.03	194.76	425	584	390	815	974	+37.4	+19.5	+159
Glanford	82.55	112.45	75.80	158.35	188.25	413	562	379	792	941	+36.1	+18.8	+149
Hamilton	87.43	81.03	58.54	145.97	139.57	437	405	293	730	698	- 7.3	- 4.4	- 32
Stoney Creek													
Stoney Creek	19.07	23.65	15.69	34.76	39.34	420	520	345	765	865	+23.8	+13.1	+100
Saltfleet	93.04	115.45	77.00	170.04	192.45	465	577	385	850	962	+24.1	+13.2	+112

[1] Actual 1977 general municipal mill rates adjusted to exclude transitional tax adjustments and surplus applications.
[2] Typical household represented by a local assessment of $22,000 in the former Town of Stoney Creek (reassessed in 1968) and $5,000 in all other areas.

relief to its rural taxpayers if it so chooses.

The area that we propose be defined as "urban" for the purposes of this differential tax rate consists of the present City of Hamilton and the contiguous built-up areas of the present towns of Ancaster, Dundas and Stoney Creek. The urban-rural dividing line is shown on Map 7.1.

The boundary of the urban area will have to be adjusted periodically as development occurs in formerly rural parts of the city. Since development plans are normally known well in advance of building, the boundary adjustment should usually precede development. The boundary should be reviewed annually, and application made to the Ontario Municipal Board for any necessary adjustments.

There may be instances, however, where development was not anticipated, or has occurred earlier than was expected. This problem can be overcome if the city is able to obtain Ontario Municipal Board approval for the designation of certain areas in which property will be given urban status immediately upon the approval of a draft plan of subdivision. The properties covered by the draft plan would then automatically be given urban designation. In such areas the actual designation of the properties for urban status would not need Municipal Board approval, which would have already been given in principle to the designation of the broader area within which the property is located.

The recommendations that follow cover the establishment of the urban-rural differential.

> **Recommendation 7.8:** Legislation provide that the City of Wentworth be divided, for taxation purposes, into an urban area and a rural area and, for purposes of financing the city's net expenditures on general government (salaries, materials, services and rents only), parks, recreation, local cultural services, and urban improvements the properties in the area designated as rural be taxed at 50 per cent of the tax rate for these services in the urban area.
>
> **Recommendation 7.9:** The City of Wentworth be empowered to increase the differential between the rate of tax on properties in the rural and urban areas for the services specified in Recommendation 7.8.
>
> **Recommendation 7.10:** For the purposes of urban-rural differential taxation the portion of the city that is initially designated urban be the following:
> i) the present City of Hamilton;
> ii) two portions of the Town of Stoney Creek:
>   first, the portion of the Town of Stoney Creek that is adjacent to the

120 CHAPTER 7

Map 7.1

CITY OF WENTWORTH

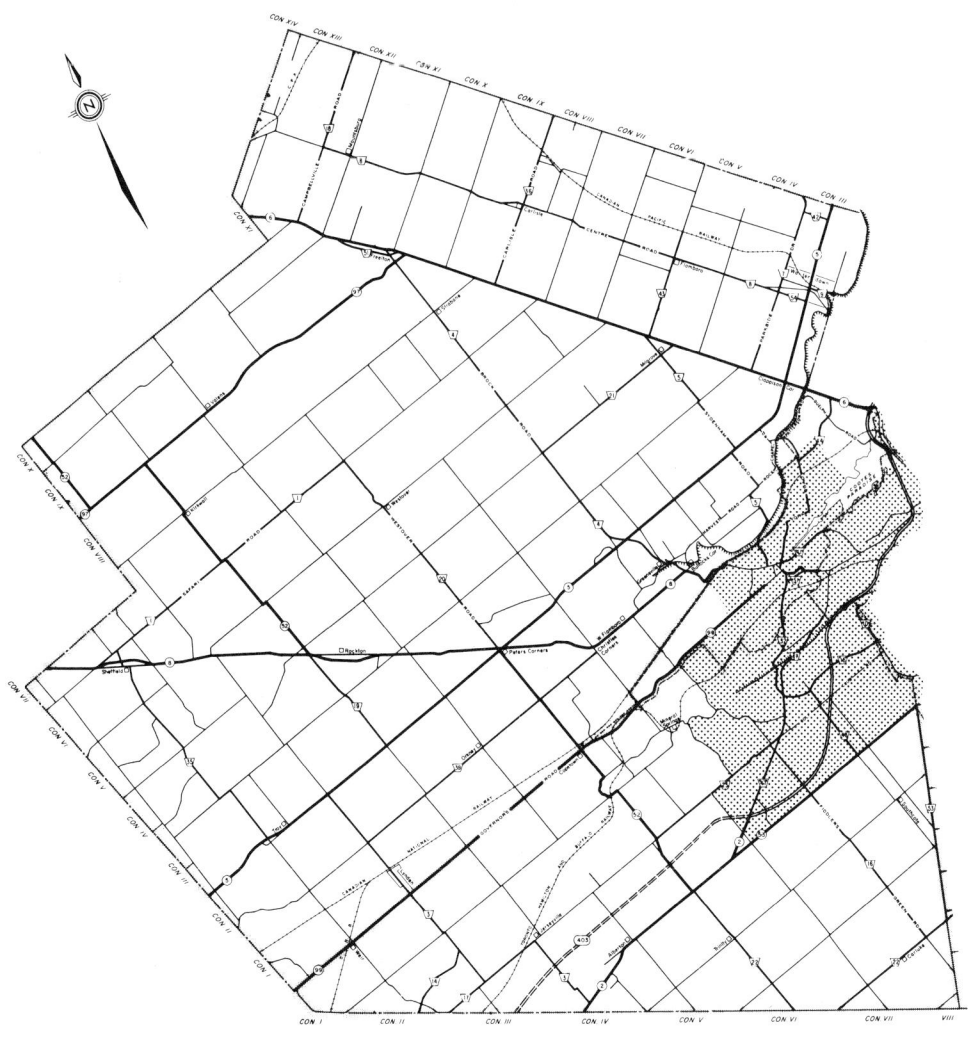

MUNICIPAL FINANCE 121

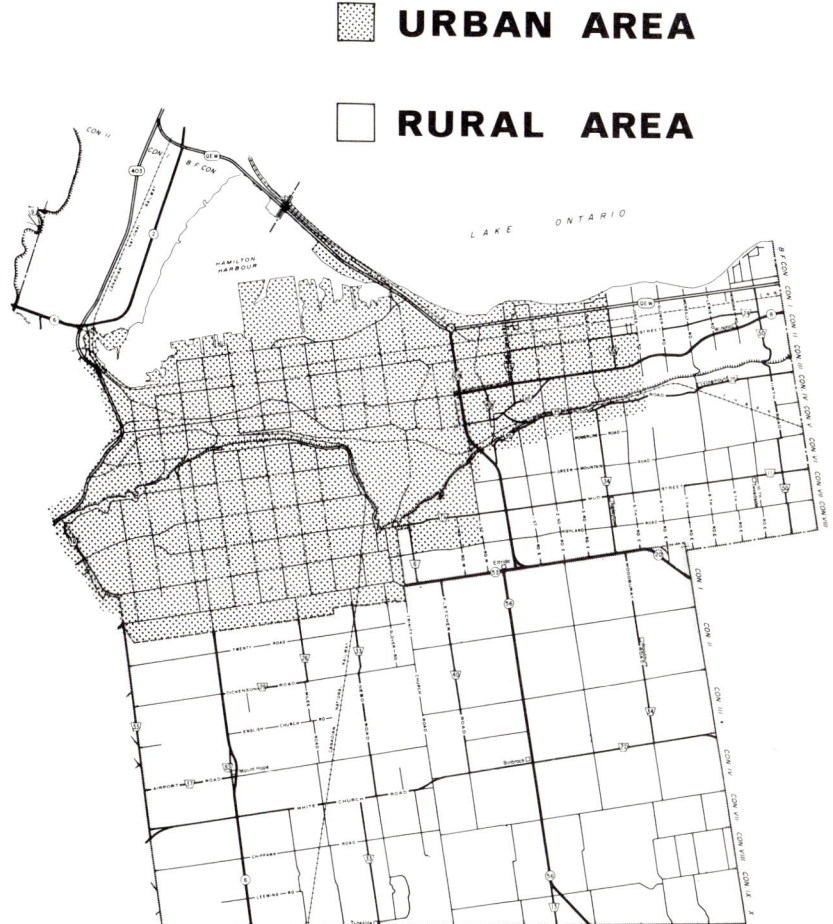

City of Hamilton commencing at the northern boundary of the Town and Fruitland Road; thence southerly along Fruitland Road to Barton Street, thence in an easterly direction along Barton Street to Jones Road; thence in a southerly direction along Jones Road to the Toronto, Hamilton and Buffalo Railway right-of-way; thence in a westerly direction along the railway right-of-way to the City of Hamilton limits; and second, the portion of the Town of Stoney Creek adjacent to the City of Hamilton commencing at Green Mountain Road allowance and the city limits; thence easterly along Green Mountain Road to Second Road West; thence southerly along Second Road West to Mud Street; thence in an easterly direction to First Road West; thence southerly along First Road West to Highland Road; thence in a westerly direction to Mount Albion Road; thence northerly along Mount Albion Road to the city limits;

iii) the portion of the municipality of the Town of Ancaster that is adjacent to the City of Hamilton and the Town of Dundas commencing at King's Highway No. 53 and the City of Hamilton limits; thence in a southwesterly direction along King's Highway No. 53 to Shaver Road; thence in a northwesterly direction along Shaver Road to Jerseyville Road; thence in a northeasterly direction to Marlin Road; thence in a northwesterly direction along Marlin Road to Sulphur Springs Road; thence in a northerly direction to the limits of the Town of Dundas; and

iv) the portion of the Town of Dundas commencing where the Town of Dundas, Town of Ancaster and City of Hamilton limits meet; thence in a southwesterly direction along the limits of the Town of Dundas to the road allowance between the Township of Ancaster and West Flamborough (prior to 1974) on the western boundary of the town; thence in a northeasterly direction along the road allowance to King's Highway No. 99; thence in a northeasterly direction along King's Highway No. 99 to the eastern boundary of lot 11 in the 1st Concession; thence in a northerly direction to the present boundary of the Town of Dundas; thence in a northeasterly direction following the town limits to York Road; thence in a northeasterly and then southerly direction along the former boundary of the Town of Dundas (prior to 1974) to the present town boundary; thence in a southwesterly direction to the place of commencement.

Recommendation 7.11: The City of Wentworth review the urban area boundary at least once a year and be empowered to change that boundary at any time, subject to prior approval by the Ontario Municipal Board.

Recommendation 7.12: The municipality be empowered to apply to the Ontario Municipal Board to approve the designation of an area or areas within which any property for which a draft plan of subdivision is approved shall be automatically included within the urban area at the time of such approval.

AREA RATING

Area rating is a system used by municipalities to allow some residents to assume all the costs of having a higher level of a particular service than the other residents of the municipality demand. Garbage collection, transit and street lighting are services that are area rated within Hamilton-Wentworth at the present time.

Levels of certain services vary substantially within the Region. The Commission thinks that area rating is a very desirable way of allowing people living in certain parts of the new municipality to maintain their higher levels of service without creating pressure from those not now receiving such a service either to have the special service cut out or to have it extended to all residents of the municipality.

The tendency when municipalities are amalgamated to upgrade service in all parts of the new municipality to the highest level is an undesirable consequence of creating larger governmental units. The system of area rating will help avoid this effect in the City of Wentworth, while allowing people in areas where service has traditionally been of a higher level to continue enjoying superior service. Nevertheless the system will permit the aldermen of particular areas to discuss with and recommend to council appropriate levels of service in their areas.

We suggest that the services now area rated continue to be so in the new municipality. Two other major functions in Hamilton-Wentworth now have widely differing levels of service and costs distributed among the existing municipalities. These are the fire and libraries services, and for the reasons indicated in the appropriate chapters their costs are recommended to be area rated to preserve the existing bases of charge. In addition, the cost of roadway improvements to a higher than general standard may be area rated.

The Commission has examined the circumstances relating to all other services and has identified several services where the differences in costs and in benefits received in each area municipality are sufficient to warrant area rating. These services are special tax assistance to the aged, parking, tree-planting and maintenance, weed-control, dental treatment, and neighbourhood improvements.

124 CHAPTER 7

Tax assistance to the aged is provided in three of the six existing municipalities but the programs are not all the same. We have identified substantial costs for the other services in the City of Hamilton and consider that it would be inequitable for any part of these to be transferred to the other areas of the new city.

Where area rating is used in the City of Wentworth, the areas charged for the special level of services should be the same as those now enjoying, and paying for, the services. To ensure that such charges are not inequitably spread over other parts of the city, any changes in the boundaries of the areas used for this purpose should require approval from the Ontario Municipal Board.

> **Recommendation 7.13: The costs of the following services be area rated to preserve the existing basis of charge: transit, subsidization of bus fares for the elderly and students, garbage collection, street lighting, fire, libraries, storm drainage, special roadway work such as a higher level of snow clearance and sidewalks, special tax assistance to the elderly, parking, tree-planting and maintenance, weed control, dental treatment and neighbourhood improvements.**

> **Recommendation 7.14: Changes in the boundaries of the parts of the city to be area rated for certain services require approval of the Ontario Municipal Board.**

USER CHARGES

The existing user charge method of paying for sewage and water should continue, as should direct charges to benefiting landowners such as for local improvements.

GENERAL LEVY

Apart from the services identified in the preceding sections, the net cost of all other services of the City of Wentworth should be financed through a general levy on all properties in the whole area. These will include all existing regional services now generally rated, plus those services now the responsibility of the area municipalities, that have not been mentioned for other treatment.

> **Recommendation 7.15: The net cost of all municipal services provided by the City of Wentworth, apart from those identified for special treatment in Recommendations 7.8, 7.13, 9.1 and 9.2 be financed by a general levy on all property in the city.**

The schedule in Table 7.24 shows the recommended method of financing services in the new city.

Table 7.24: Schedule of Recommended Taxing Arrangements

Generally rated	Area rated	Rated urban/rural
General government (financial expenses, capital contributions, reserves and allowances)	Fire	General government (salaries, wages, materials, services and rents)
Police	Bus fare subsidization for elderly and students	Parks and recreation services (presently local)
Conservation Authority	Transit	Urban improvements
Emergency measures	Special road services	Cultural services (presently local)
Protective inspection and control	Parking	
Roadways: general	Street lighting	
Traffic control	Storm sewers	
Airport	Garbage collection	
Garbage disposal	Library	
Public health services	Elderly assistance tax reductions	
Hospitals	Dental treatment	
Ambulance service	Residential development	
Cemeteries	Tree-planting and maintenance	
General welfare assistance	Weed control	
Assistance to aged persons		
Assistance to children		
Day nurseries		
Parks and recreational services (presently regional)		
Cultural services (presently regional)		
Planning and zoning		
Commercial development		

DISTRIBUTION EFFECTS OF PROPOSALS

One of the impacts of the proposed municipal taxation structure will be an increased sharing of industrial and commercial assessments over the entire Region.

Since more items will be paid for out of the general levy in the new City of Wentworth than are now in the Regional Municipality of Hamilton-Wentworth, residents will receive more equal benefit than they now do from industrial-commercial assessment, regardless of where they live. The urban-rural differential rating will result in some further sharing. In paying for area-rated services, however, the resident of a designated area will not be helped by an industrial or commercial enterprise outside that specific area.

FINANCIAL EFFECTS OF TAXATION PROPOSALS

The proposed tax measures provide substantially different financial impacts than would have occurred if the City of Wentworth financed more services through a general tax levy. Tables 7.25 and 7.26 show the impact that these tax measures will have. At the overall expenditure levels of 1977, the residents of the rural areas will pay less municipal taxes than they do under the existing system. This reduction will be a maximum of almost 20 per cent in the rural part of Ancaster and a minimum of 10 per cent in the former Township of Beverly. In the City of Hamilton, there will be no change in residential taxes for municipal purposes. The urban areas adjacent to the City of Hamilton will experience small tax increases under this system, varying from a high of 6.6 per cent in the urban part of Ancaster to a low of 1.7 per cent in the urban parts of the Town of Stoney Creek. The Commission recommends in Chapter 14 of this report that transitional provisions be introduced to phase in these tax changes.

TRANSITIONAL TAX ADJUSTMENTS 1974 AND 1977

To indicate accurately the effects of these proposals, the taxation figures shown in Tables 7.25 and 7.26 exclude the reductions brought about by existing provincial transitional grants. These were instituted to help phase in the effects of the major reforms of 1974 and the transfer of roads and transit services from the City of Hamilton to the Regional Municipality in 1977. These arrangements should not be disturbed. The estimated tax changes arising from these established transitional arrangements and the effects on typical households are set out in Table 7.27. This table shows that in some areas there will be substantial tax increases in 1979 as the 1974 transitional adjustments largely disappear, and in each year to 1982 as the additional 1977 adjustments are phased out. These effects have nothing to do with changes brought about by this Commission's proposals

> **Recommendation 7.16: The transitional taxation and special financial assistance arrangements initiated by the Government of Ontario in relation to the 1974 restructure and 1977 transfer of functions to the Regional Municipality of Hamilton-Wentworth not be changed.**

EFFECT OF RESTRUCTURE ON PROVINCIAL TRANSFER PAYMENTS

At the start of this chapter we mentioned that all transfer payments used in the calculations for the illustrations in this chapter are of necessity based on the provincial arrangements as they currently stand. The calculations used for Tables 7.22 and 7.25 showing the effects of the proposed restructure, with and without the proposed taxing arrangements, take into account increased provincial grants that will result from the recommendations of this Commission.

MUNICIPAL FINANCE   127

Table 7.25: City of Wentworth — Effects of Consolidation with Proposed Taxing Arrangements

	EXISTING		PROPOSED TAXING ARRANGEMENTS				
	Actual levies ($000's)	Distribution %	Proj. levies ($000's)	Distribution %	Net area rated levy ($000's)	Net urban rural levy ($000's)	Net general levy[1] ($000's)
Urban areas							
City of Hamilton	76,545	81.623	76,518	82.164	29,149	21,992	25,377
Part Town of Ancaster	1,520	1.621	1,623	1.743	254	636	733
Town of Dundas							
Former Town of Dundas	3,410	3.636	3,620	3.887	1,035	1,200	1,385
Part Township of Ancaster	13	.014	14	.015	4	5	5
Town of Stoney Creek							
Former Town of Stoney Creek	1,240	1.322	1,260	1.353	233	477	550
Part Township of Saltfleet	3,957	4.219	4,026	4.323	746	1,523	1,757
Rural areas							
Part Town of Ancaster	614	.654	493	.529	69	128	296
Town of Dundas							
Township of West Flamborough	195	.208	171	.184	58	34	79
Town of Stoney Creek							
Part Township of Saltfleet	1,266	1.350	1,031	1.107	225	244	562
Township of Flamborough							
Township of Beverly	897	.957	802	.861	123	205	474
Township of East Flamborough	1,154	1.231	1,018	1.093	156	261	601
Township of West Flamborough	1,185	1.264	1,047	1.124	161	268	618
Village of Waterdown	397	.423	338	.363	52	86	200
Township of Glanbrook							
Township of Binbrook	624	.665	529	.568	89	133	307
Township of Glanford	762	.813	639	.686	107	161	371
Total levies	93,779	100.000	93,129[3]	100.000	32,461	27,353	33,315
Distribution[2]					34.86%	29.37%	35.77%

[1] After crediting all non-specific grants and revenues, and specific grants and revenues, related to generally rated services.
[2] Distribution according to type of levy.
[3] The $650,000 decrease represents the total estimated increase in provincial transfer payments.

128 CHAPTER 7

Table 7.26: City of Wentworth — Effects on Residential Taxpayers of Consolidation with Proposed Taxing Arrangements

Area	RESIDENTIAL MILL RATES Gen. municipal[1] Existing Proposed		Educa. Existing	TOT. MILL RATES Existing Proposed		RESIDENTIAL PROPERTY TAXES ON A TYPICAL HOUSEHOLD[2] Gen. Municipal Existing Proposed		Educa. Existing	TOTAL TAXES Existing Proposed		% Chge. in Gen. municip. taxes	% chge. in total taxes	$ chge. in total taxation
Urban areas													
City of Hamilton	87.43	87.40	58.54	145.97	145.94	437	437	293	730	730	–	–	–
Part Town of Ancaster	90.30	96.42	81.69	171.99	178.11	452	482	408	860	890	+ 6.6	+ 3.5	+30
Town of Dundas													
Former Town of Dundas	108.45	115.13	74.86	183.31	189.99	542	576	374	916	950	+ 6.3	+ 3.7	+34
Part Twshp. of Ancaster	106.87	113.62	82.31	189.18	195.93	534	568	412	946	979	+ 6.2	+ 3.5	+33
Town of Stoney Creek													
Former Town of Stoney Creek	19.07	19.38	15.69	34.76	35.03	420	427	345	765	772	+ 1.7	+ 0.9	+ 7
Part Twshp. of Saltfleet	93.04	94.66	77.00	170.04	171.66	465	473	385	850	858	+ 1.7	+ 0.9	+ 8
Rural areas													
Part Town of Ancaster	90.30	72.48	81.69	171.99	154.17	452	363	408	860	771	–19.7	–10.3	–89
Town of Dundas													
Twshp. of W. Flamborough	112.15	98.35	81.32	193.47*	179.67	561	491	407	968	898	–12.5	– 7.2	–70
Town of Stoney Creek													
Part Twshp. of Saltfleet	93.04	75.76	77.00	170.04	152.76	465	379	385	850	764	–18.5	–10.1	–86
Township of Flamborough													
Township of Beverly	82.46	73.73	81.97	164.43	155.70	412	369	410	822	779	–10.4	– 5.2	–43
Twshp. E. Flamborough	84.97	74.96	79.33	164.30	154.29	425	375	397	822	772	–11.8	– 6.1	–50
Twshp. W. Flamborough	87.32	77.15	80.60	167.92	157.75	437	386	403	840	789	–11.7	– 6.1	–51
Village of Waterdown	74.49	63.42	69.96	144.45	133.38	372	317	350	722	667	–14.8	– 7.6	–55
Township of Glanbrook													
Township of Binbrook	84.99	72.05	78.04	163.03	150.09	425	360	390	815	750	–15.3	– 8.0	–65
Township of Glanford	82.55	69.23	75.80	158.35	145.03	413	346	379	792	725	–16.2	– 8.5	–67

[1] Actual 1977 general municipal mill rates adjusted to exclude transitional tax adjustments and surplus applications.
[2] Typical household represented by a local assessment of $22,000 in the former Town of Stoney Creek (reassessed in 1968) and $5,000 in all other areas.

MUNICIPAL FINANCE 129

Table 7.27: Benefits for Typical Residential Taxpayers of Existing Transitional Adjustments

Area	1974 Restructuring							1977 Functional Transfers[1]									
	1977 Mills	$	1978 Mills	$	1979 Mills	$	1980 Mills	$	1977 Mills	$	1978 Mills	$	1979 Mills	$	1980 Mills	$	1981 Mills	$	1982 Mills	$
Ancaster	4.27	21	2.21	11	0.15	1	–	–	12.15	61	10.15	51	7.98	40	5.55	28	3.12	16	–	–
Dundas																				
Ancaster	10.27	51	5.20	26	0.15	1	–	–	11.71	59	9.59	48	7.51	38	5.17	26	2.83	14	–	–
Dundas	1.89	9	1.02	5	0.14	1	–	–	11.84	59	9.69	48	7.60	38	5.23	26	2.86	14	–	–
W. Flamborough	18.18	91	9.16	46	0.15	1	–	–	12.25	61	10.02	50	7.86	39	5.41	27	2.96	15	–	–
Flamborough																				
Beverly	8.95	45	3.18	16	0.13	1	–	–	10.24	51	8.69	43	6.52	33	4.47	22	2.43	12	–	–
E. Flamborough	12.88	64	5.13	26	0.13	1	–	–	10.41	52	8.84	44	6.63	33	4.55	23	2.47	12	–	–
W. Flamborough	12.50	62	4.89	24	0.13	1	–	–	10.71	54	9.09	45	6.82	34	4.70	23	2.54	13	–	–
Waterdown	2.64	13	0.21	1	0.11	1	–	–	8.80	44	7.47	37	5.60	28	3.84	19	2.08	10	–	–
Glanbrook																				
Binbrook	9.47	47	4.81	24	0.14	1	–	–	10.84	54	9.17	46	7.51	38	5.34	27	3.18	16	–	–
Glanford	9.14	46	4.64	23	0.14	1	–	–	10.46	52	8.85	44	7.25	36	5.16	26	3.06	15	–	–
Hamilton	–	–	–	–	–	–	–	–	–	–	–	–	–	–	–	–	–	–	–	–
Stoney Creek																				
Saltfleet	2.26	11	1.19	6	0.12	1	–	–	10.93	55	9.17	46	6.79	34	4.61	23	2.42	12	–	–
Stoney Creek	0.46	10	0.24	5	0.02	1	–	–	2.24	49	1.88	41	1.39	31	0.94	21	0.50	11	–	–

[1] Figures for 1979, 1980, and 1981 attributed to 1977 functional transfers are estimated on expected phase-down.

The City of Wentworth should be entitled to a resource equalization grant, as are all the area municipalities now in Hamilton-Wentworth except Stoney Creek. If it is entitled to this grant, the effect of the recommended reforms will be to increase the amount payable to the new city by approximately $160,000, based on 1977 figures, over the total of such grants currently being received in the Region.

Some of the less densely populated area municipalities also receive per capita amounts in relation to the "density grant" element of the unconditional grant. The amount varies according to the ratio of residential properties to acreage. If this formula had been applied to the new city in 1977, it would have produced $490,000 more than the amounts of density grants actually received in the Region.

These increases in unconditional grants would result in the receipt of a total of $650,000 more from the province than was actually received in 1977. All City of Wentworth taxpayers should benefit from provincial unconditional grants.

> **Recommendation 7.17:** The City of Wentworth be deemed to be a lower-tier municipality for the purposes of The Ontario Unconditional Grants Act, 1975, in respect of resource equalization grants.

> **Recommendation 7.18:** The City of Wentworth be deemed to be an area municipality for the purposes of The Ontario Unconditional Grants Act, 1975, in respect of density grants.

> **Recommendation 7.19:** All grants receivable under The Ontario Unconditional Grants Act be credited generally to the benefit of all City of Wentworth taxpayers.

The Commission has not identified any potential losses in specific grants that will arise from the proposed consolidation into a single municipality. Nevertheless, should there be any, protection from losses or special compensation should be given by the province as has been done in other restructured areas.

> **Recommendation 7.20:** Any financial losses in grants arising directly as a result of the creation of the City of Wentworth be compensated for in special assistance arrangements made by the Government of Ontario.

The Future Prospect

The taxing and other financial provisions we recommend for the new City of Wentworth make a unique package, designed for the particular circumstances of this area. We are convinced that the implementation of these recommendations will result in the establishment of the new municipality without any disadvantageous shifting of tax burdens. Indeed, the distribution of taxes under our proposal will be in certain respects more equitable than under the existing arrangements, and should mitigate some of the less satisfactory shifts that have occurred as a result of previous reorganizations.

Under our proposals the new city should be able to provide the same level of service that is available to the residents now, but at a lower cost. The savings will result from the removal of some of the duplications inherent in the present two-tier structure and from a consolidation of the professional management skills already available within the area. We urge the new council to take full advantage of these opportunities.

Although the recommended differential tax system will require skilful calculations and careful administration, we are convinced that the competent municipal staff in the area is entirely capable of handling it with the existing data-processing facilities.

Under a single municipal council, better financial planning will be possible. Combined with the implementation of our suggestions for improved budgeting practices, the financial health of the community can be even more easily assured. Above all, councillors will have an opportunity never before available to plan on the basis of the total needs and desires of the people of this Region.

Finally, the implementation of our proposals will make municipal government more financially accountable to the people than ever before. With responsibility for all municipal functions placed in the hands of a single council, there will be no cause for any confusion in the minds of residents about who is accountable for the services provided and for the resulting levels of expenditure and taxation.

Chapter 8

Planning and Development

The Planning Framework

The municipal planning system is the primary means through which municipalities may influence their own development, and the principal techniques for doing so are those provided by The Planning Act. The Act authorizes the preparation and adoption of official plans as the basis for other municipal planning activity. Within the context of the plan, municipal councils may allocate land uses through zoning by-laws and control development through both development agreements and demolition control. In addition, The Planning Act requires landowners to obtain permission to subdivide their land, whether by the severance of one or two lots or on a larger scale in the form of a plan of subdivision. Decisions on these matters are subject to the final approval of the province, acting through the Minister of Housing or the Ontario Municipal Board.

The common provision of planning services for all of Hamilton-Wentworth dates back to 1949, when the Hamilton-Wentworth Planning Area was established as a joint planning area encompassing the City of Hamilton and the County of Wentworth. The responsibility for preparing an official plan was assigned to an appointed planning board made up of five members representing the county and four city representatives. The City of Hamilton remained a subsidiary planning area with its own appointed planning board, and also retained its own planning department which had been in place since 1948.

While planning for all of the municipalities except Hamilton was carried out by the Hamilton-Wentworth Planning Area Board and its staff, there was no regional or county-wide planning as such. In essence, the staff served as the planning department for each of the municipalities separately. Although there was an official plan for the Hamilton-Wentworth Planning Area, for example, it was merely a composite of plans prepared and adopted at different times for and by the individual municipalities. Despite efforts to make these plans consistent with each other, their focus remained local and not region-wide.

Recognition of the need for planning on a truly region-wide basis was one of the main factors leading to the establishment of regional government in Hamilton-Wentworth in January 1974. Under The Regional Municipality of Hamilton-Wentworth Act, responsibility for planning is now divided between the Region and the area municipalities. The primary regional planning function is the preparation and adoption of a regional official plan to guide overall growth and development. Area municipalities are responsible for the adoption of their own official plans, which must conform with the regional plan, and for zoning and most forms of development control. There is, however, a regional zoning power over lands within 150 feet of regional roads. Whereas before regional government, consents to land severances were obtained from committees of adjustment appointed by the council of each municipality, the Act transferred the authority for granting severances to a land division committee appointed by Regional Council. Committees of adjustment were retained in each area municipality to perform the function of allowing minor variances from zoning by-laws.

Among the most important changes effected by the Regional Act is the abolition of appointed planning boards, thereby substantially enhancing the accountability of the elected local governments. It is the Regional Council itself that is charged with the task of preparing a regional official plan, and the councils of the area municipalities that are responsible for their official plans.

In addition to the planning authority conferred by the Regional Act and in keeping with the provincial policy embodied in recent amendments to The Planning Act, the Regional Council has also been delegated certain of the Minister of Housing's planning approval powers. These include the power to approve plans of subdivision and applications to construct condominiums.

The Role of the Province

The province has a traditional role in setting the ground rules for municipal planning and in exercising final approval over a variety of local planning decisions. Through legislation and regulations it establishes the powers and structures to be used by municipalities in this field. Through the Minister of Housing for official plans, and the Ontario Municipal Board for zoning by-laws, it makes the final decisions on approvals of local proposals. Other local decisions may be referred or appealed to the Ontario Municipal Board, including variances from zoning by-laws, land severances, subdivision approvals, condominium approvals, demolition permits, and development agreements.

In addition to this traditional role, the province has recently been taking a more active part in the planning process. In 1971, the province adopted "Design for Development: The Toronto-Centred Region," a policy statement concerning growth in the area of southern Ontario extending from Brantford and Kitchener-Waterloo on the west to Peterborough and Cobourg-Port Hope on the east. The Toronto-Centred Region development concept was intended to shape the region's metropolitan core along Lake Ontario into a two-tiered structure of cities separated and defined by a parkway belt containing transportation and other services.

The province's most recent official announcement concerning the status of the Toronto-Centred Region, a program statement by the Treasurer to the legislature in 1976, reaffirmed the commitment to the basic Toronto-Centred Region policy. Reviewing planning and growth in the region since 1971, the statement described Hamilton-Wentworth as "the western terminal of the Toronto-Centred Region," and indicated that the "government's policy is to encourage the Regional Municipality to develop as a Regional Centre in its own right, subject to provincial policies relating to preserving prime agricultural land and recreational resources." The work of the regional municipality in connection with a regional official plan has in large part been based on this view of the future of Hamilton-Wentworth. It is, however, a view that, if it is to be fulfilled, requires a streamlined municipal planning system that places no unnecessary obstacles in the way of desirable development.

The strategic physical location of Hamilton-Wentworth has led the area to be involved not only in the general Toronto-Centred Region concept but also in specific provincial plans for the Parkway Belt West and the Niagara Escarpment. Both these plans are now proceeding toward approval by the Lieutenant-Governor-in-Council; once they are approved, all municipal plans must conform with them. The Parkway Belt plan is further advanced, and is in final form awaiting approval, while the Niagara Escarpment Commission has only recently released preliminary proposals for its plan. Whatever this plan's content may be when it finally emerges from the process of consultation and hearings, the twin goals of preserving the Escarpment and maintaining a strong and comprehensible municipal planning structure can best be achieved by incorporating the provisions of the Escarpment plan into municipal plans as expeditiously as possible following its adoption, rather than by establishing it as a separate plan additional to existing municipal plans. Similarly, if the system of development control initiated by the Niagara Escarpment Commission is to continue after the plan's adoption, all necessary steps should be taken to minimize the need for landowners to make multiple applications for development permission. At present, in areas of Escarpment Commission development control, requirements for development permission are superimposed on the normal municipal development requirements, such as consent to the severance of land.

Recommendation 8.1: All relevant aspects of the Niagara Escarpment plan, when it is adopted, be incorporated into the official plan of the City of Wentworth, which shall be authorized to undertake complete

responsibility for the implementation of the Escarpment plan within its boundaries.

The Hamilton Harbour Commissioners

The role of the Hamilton Harbour Commissioners in the regulation of land use in the harbour and its vicinity has been a matter of some dispute between the Harbour Commissioners, who derive their authority from a federal statute, and the City of Hamilton. The parties have now resorted to litigation, and a decision of the Ontario High Court generally favourable to the city's position is presently under appeal to the Court of Appeal.

While the outcome of the litigation depends on the resolution of a constitutional issue as to the division of authority under the British North America Act, it is apparent that, whatever the result, there will continue to be a need for cooperation between the Harbour Commissioners and municipal planning authorities. Given the importance of the harbour to the economy and to recreation in Hamilton-Wentworth, it is vital that the final judicial decision provide a firm basis on which cooperative efforts can proceed.

The Regional Planning Function

To assist Regional Council in carrying out its planning duties, a Regional Planning and Development Committee was struck and a Regional Planning and Development Department formed at the inception of regional government. Initially, the staff of the department was drawn largely from the staff of the former Hamilton-Wentworth Planning Area Board. But when the City of Hamilton decided early in 1974 to contract with the Region for local planning services, the city's planning staff also joined the regional department, which now has a staff of 64, down from 72 in 1974. The department's main activities are the preparation of the regional official plan, local planning, development control and business development. It also provides administrative support to the land division committee.

REGIONAL OFFICIAL PLAN

The legislation establishing regional government requires that the Regional Council, by December 31, 1976, prepare, adopt and forward to the Minister of Housing for approval a regional official plan. As in all regional municipalities where plan preparation has been made mandatory, the timing constraint has proved somewhat unrealistic. Substantial progress has been made, however, and the plan is expected to be submitted to Regional Council for approval by mid-1978.

The preparation of the plan began in 1974 with the undertaking of a series of background studies designed to develop both an inventory of existing conditions and a forecast of future growth and servicing requirements. These studies were followed by the identification of seven alternative regional development patterns, which were then brought before the area municipalities and the public for intensive review. Three final alternatives were selected for further consideration. A choice was offered between two broad growth strategies: the expansion of the central urban area; and the direction of future growth to suburban communities physically separated from the central urban area.

The actual development pattern adopted by Regional Council in September 1977 for inclusion in the draft official plan is in some respects a compromise between these two choices. It contemplates a population increase from the 1976 figure of 409,000 to a total of 550,000 in the year 2001, reflecting an average annual growth rate of approximately 1.2 per cent. Among its most important features are the provision for significant urban settlement areas in Binbrook, Greensville and Winona and suburban expansion in Ancaster, all physically separate from the existing urban area; the designation of areas of industrial development in all area municipalities but Dundas, where no appropriate land remains; and an emphasis on the need to encourage a strong central business district in Hamilton.

The goals this development pattern seeks to accomplish are several, and include the provision of a wide choice of urban, suburban and rural living places and the fulfilment of the role of Hamilton-Wentworth as the western terminus of the Toronto-Centred Region. It also "recognizes the importance of a diversified assessment base for each municipality" and, responding to the submissions of the area municipalities concerning the plan, distributes growth to each. The need to allocate growth in this way is almost certain to be felt in a two-tier municipality where the continuing financial strength of the lower-tier municipalities depends in large part on their ability to attract new assessment.

The second major component of the regional official plan is to be a set of policies designed to achieve and complement the preferred regional development pattern. Draft policies have been prepared dealing with such areas as economic growth, housing, land severances and regional services; these are being circulated for public comment before presentation to Regional Council.

LOCAL PLANNING

The City of Hamilton and the Town of Dundas have both contracted with the Region for local planning services. These services are provided by a separate division of the Regional Planning and Development Department.

DEVELOPMENT CONTROL

This aspect of the department's work includes processing subdivision and condominium applications and reviewing local zoning by-laws and land severance applications, all on behalf of the Region, and reporting on development applications for Hamilton and Dundas.

Final approval of plans of subdivision is now granted by Regional Council rather than the Minister of Housing, and this has resulted in a speeding up of the previous rather cumbersome process. Because responsibility for municipal services is now divided between the Region and area municipalities, however, it is necessary for an applicant to enter into two subdivision agreements, rather than the one required before regionalization, as a condition to approval. Similarly, once construction of the subdivision begins, inspections must be made for compliance with both regional and area requirements. In practice, the two levels are cooperating to some extent so that often one inspector inspects for both, but this is not always possible. Where it is not possible, it has given rise to occasional, and quite understandable, complaints.

BUSINESS DEVELOPMENT

The important functions of business and industrial promotion for Hamilton-Wentworth as a whole are the responsibility of the Planning and Development Department. The Region also maintains a relatively active industrial land acquisition program. As the Commission was preparing its report, Regional Council was considering a proposal that would see the Planning and Development Department assume the tourist and convention promotion activity now undertaken by the Hamilton Visitors and Convention Bureau, in order to integrate and strengthen the total promotion effort of the Region.

LAND DIVISION COMMITTEE

Prior to the establishment of regional government and the land division committee, the number of severances granted in rural areas led to a considerable amount of unplanned development. The attendant problems were several: good agricultural land was no longer farmed; ribbon development created traffic problems; the physical characteristics of the area deteriorated; and demands were created for costly urban services. The land division committee, applying a policy developed with the assistance of the Regional Planning and Development Department, has adopted a more restrictive attitude towards severances. The percentage of applications granted has decreased markedly, and the problems they create have begun to be contained.

Planning in the Area Municipalities

With the dissolution of the Hamilton-Wentworth Planning Area Board at the formation of regional government, it was necessary for the area municipalities to make staffing arrangements to carry out their planning responsibilities. The City of Hamilton and the Town of Dundas chose to contract for services with the Region; the other municipalities opted to retain consultants. More recently, three of the area municipalities that originally retained consultants — all except Glanbrook — have established their own planning departments, however small, principally for reasons of cost and accessibility of advice.

At the time of regionalization, there were official plans and zoning by-laws in effect in each of the area municipalities though many of these were badly out of date. Since the Regional Act contains a requirement that on the adoption of a regional official plan, the plans of the area municipalities be amended "forthwith" to conform, one of the main planning activities of the area municipalities has been the preparation of new official plans or the updating of older plans. A new plan has been submitted for provincial approval by Glanbrook; plans are nearing completion in Ancaster and Flamborough; and the City of Hamilton is proceeding with a new official plan component by component. A consolidation of the Dundas official plan is under way as well.

Since regionalization, there has also been an increased emphasis on the preparation of neighbourhood or secondary plans. The City of Hamilton has continued its well-established neighbourhood planning program, and the other area municipalities have either extended or begun their own.

As Table 8.1 demonstrates, the total costs of planning services in the Region rose significantly from 1972, before regional government, to 1977. A substantial proportion of the increase is attributable to new planning programs undertaken to meet the terms of the Regional Act and to bring existing planning instruments up to date, though provincial grants have offset some of these costs to the area municipalities. The Region has also incurred costs in connection with carrying out the approval and commenting functions delegated by the province.

In 1974, the province included an element of 20 cents in an increase in the unconditional per capita grant to all regional municipalities to recognize their increased planning responsibilities. These were credited to the Region's general revenues, as were the special assistance grants made toward the cost of preparing the regional official plan.

Housing in Hamilton-Wentworth

The primary direct responsibility of municipalities in the provision of housing lies in facilitating the availability of serviced land to the private housing industry. There are also a number of housing programs available to or through municipalities. Through the Ontario Housing Action Program, begun in 1973 in response to the housing shortage then perceived, the municipalities in Hamilton-Wentworth have all

Table 8.1: Planning Expenditures

	1972	1975	1976	1977 (est.)
Hamilton-Wentworth Planning Area Board	$ 206,412			
Regional Municipality of Hamilton-Wentworth		$ 739,385	$ 834,070	$ 894,880
City of Hamilton	620,000	611,155	726,241	732,440
Town of Ancaster		59,707	65,368	70,182
Town of Dundas		17,283	20,021	21,000
Town of Stoney Creek		89,876	106,378	105,559
Township of Flamborough		65,692	69,229	79,256
Township of Glanbrook		68,804	69,330	59,685
TOTAL	826,412	1,651,902	1,890,637	1,963,002

SOURCE: The Region and area municipalities. Costs reported for the area municipalities are net of grants and other recovered costs; those shown for the Region are not, since planning-related grants have been credited to general revenues. In 1972, the then existing municipalities other than Hamilton incurred minor administrative costs in connection with planning.

received provincial grants to assist with official plan preparation. There have, in addition, been grants to offset possible increases in municipal taxes due to new residential development, and interest-free loans to assist in the funding of roads, water supply and sewerage. Because the housing shortage is thought to have abated, this program is scheduled for termination in 1978.

All of the area municipalities have also participated in programs for the repair and improvement of the existing housing stock and the amenities in older neighbourhoods. While the bulk of the funding for these programs comes from the federal and provincial governments, the municipalities contribute as well, and are responsible for administration and inspection.

Municipalities may also play an important role in the conservation of existing housing through the enactment of property standards by-laws. These by-laws are authorized by The Planning Act and prescribe standards for the maintenance and occupancy of property, prohibit the occupancy of property that fails to meet the standards, and require that substandard buildings be either repaired or demolished.

The effectiveness of by-laws depends on the availability of municipal staff to enforce them. Only Dundas, Glanbrook and Hamilton have passed property standards by-laws. The other three area municipalities, each faced with the prospect of hiring its own enforcement staff, have considered that the costs of administration outweigh the possible benefits. It is unfortunate that the two-tier system in Hamilton-Wentworth has resulted in some parts of the Region not benefiting from the enforcement of such by-laws.

Assisted housing in the Region for senior citizens and low-income families is provided by the Ontario Housing Corporation on the invitation of the area municipalities, who also contribute a portion of the cost. The attitudes of area councils toward assisted housing for their communities can thus be a serious constraint on the availability of a choice of living space for those who require this type of accommodation. A report on future housing requirements in the Region prepared in 1976 in connection with the regional official plan pointed out that the Region's supply of assisted units, with the exception of some senior citizen units in Stoney Creek, was to be found almost exclusively in Hamilton.

In the short time since that housing report was prepared, the situation has been corrected by the construction of new senior citizen units in Ancaster and Dundas and new family units in Dundas and Stoney Creek. In addition, a recent survey concludes that there is no longer any significant demand for assisted units in Glanbrook.

Assisted housing units built by the Ontario Housing Corporation in the Region are managed and maintained by the Hamilton-Wentworth Housing Authority, whose nine-member board is made up of three appointees each from the federal, provincial and regional governments. The Regional Housing Requirements Study recommends that the municipality not assume the function of providing and managing assisted units itself, in view of the operational complexities and the availability of these units through existing government programs. The Commission sees no reason to differ from this conclusion.

We recognize, however, the close connection that does and should exist between assisted housing and municipally provided social services. Residents of assisted housing units often rely in some measure on social services, and these services ought to be readily available where such housing is located. On the establishment of the recommended municipal structure, coordination should be assured between the Housing Authority and the city's Social Services and Health Committee.

Recommendation 8.2: The Social Services and Health Committee of the City of Wentworth take appropriate steps to ensure that the provision of social services and assisted housing is coordinated.

Another housing problem identified by the Housing Requirements Study is the lack of diversity in the type and cost of housing in parts of the Region; in many areas single, detached dwellings predominate. This, too, is a matter that largely depends on the receptiveness of councils to different types of development, but there appears to be a growing willingness to see a variety of housing types constructed.

In general, contrary to the situation just a few years ago, there can no longer be said to be a "housing crisis" in Hamilton-Wentworth.

A New Planning Structure

The planning structure for the new City of Wentworth must have a number of characteristics. It must provide for political accountability for planning decisions, since such decisions involve important choices concerning the future of the municipality. It must recognize the community of interest that exists throughout the present Hamilton-Wentworth, for while its different parts may have some different concerns, they are all components of an interdependent community that shares common services, common commercial, recreational and cultural facilities, and a common orientation toward the urban core.

The new planning structure must be efficient. There must be no duplication of effort and no unnecessary delays, not only to minimize costs to the taxpayers and to protect rights of interested parties, but also to encourage desirable development. In an increasingly competitive economic environment, the planning system must not act as a barrier to the diversification of the municipal economy. At the same time, it must be large enough and strong enough to carry out essential planning programs with the requisite degree of sophistication. In addition, planning must be responsive to the needs of local communities within the municipality. Finally, planning services must be accessible to individual residents of the municipality who must be able conveniently to seek advice and to apply for and receive whatever permissions are required.

The Commission is convinced that a unified planning structure will best be able to achieve this range of purposes. Regionalization in 1974 yielded substantial benefits for planning in Hamilton-Wentworth: planning from a truly regional perspective was made possible for the first time; and responsibility for planning decisions was transferred from appointed boards to elected councils. The end of the old county system acted as a spur to undertake new programs required by good planning practice in the light of changed circumstances. A unified planning structure will enable the municipality to build upon these changes while offering significant improvements as well.

Under the proposed structure the capacity for region-wide planning will be enhanced. Freed from the need to direct a share of growth to each area municipality in order to maintain its assessment base relative to the others, the municipality will be able to avoid the possible distortion of other planning goals. The approval of plans of subdivision will require only a single, comprehensive municipal subdivision agreement, thus streamlining the approval process to bring more housing on to the market. There will also no longer be a need for two sets of municipal inspections once construction of subdivisions begins.

There are also cost considerations. There are certain fixed costs of establishing separate planning departments, as Hamilton and Dundas recognized when, primarily to minimize costs, they opted to contract with the Region for local planning services. These will no longer be incurred, and equally importantly, the expertise acquired by the existing planning departments will be pooled for the common benefit of the municipality. In addition, the proposed new municipality will be able to enact and enforce desirable property standards by-laws, something that hitherto has been impractical in the less populous area municipalities.

An extensive review of municipal planning in Ontario was recently undertaken by the Planning Act Review Committee, whose report was submitted to the Minister of Housing in April, 1977. The recommendations of that committee, which would work significant changes in the planning system, are currently under consideration by the province. Rather than itself embark upon new directions not contemplated by the existing Planning Act, the Commission has chosen to focus on improving the provision of planning services in Hamilton-Wentworth within the present framework, with the confidence that the new city will be able in the future to derive the benefits that more general changes will bring.

The question whether planning should be the responsibility of an appointed planning board or the elected council caused the Commission little difficulty. Every restructuring of local government carried out in Ontario during the past several years has concluded that it is anomalous to leave important decisions concerning the future of a community to be made in the first instance by an appointed body unaccountable to the electorate. And because planning issues pervade municipal decision-making, it would be unwise to remove them from the purview of the council that decides on other municipal services.

Recommendation 8.3: The council of the City of Wentworth be assigned all the powers of a planning board under The Planning Act.

Under The Planning Act, decisions on two types of matters remain to be made in the first instance by bodies other than council: applications for minor variances from zoning by-laws, and applications for land severances. The Act provides for the appointment by the council of each municipality of a committee of adjustment to deal with variances. In some municipalities, these committees also decide on severances, but the policy of the province has for some time been to transfer this responsibility to land division committees appointed by county or regional councils in order to ensure that consents to severances are granted only after taking into account their broader implications for municipal planning and servicing. This policy has been implemented in Hamilton-Wentworth.

In the proposed City of Wentworth, of course, there will be no need to separate the two functions to achieve this wider perspective. The Commission is concerned, however, about the workload that the citizens appointed to a committee with dual responsibility would have to bear. The present regional land division committee has heard an average of more than six hundred applications annually for the past several years, and even this number is exceeded by the total number of variance applications made each year to the six existing committees of adjustment in the area municipalities. To avoid overburdening committee members and to ensure that applications will be heard without unreasonable delay, the Commission suggests that two separate committees be established. There would not appear, however, to be any need for separate staffing of the two committees, since their methods of operation and functions would be similar.

Recommendation 8.4: The council of the City of Wentworth be authorized to appoint both a committee of adjustment and a land division committee, the two committees to be served by the same municipal staff.

At present, the regional land division committee meets exclusively in the courthouse in Hamilton, while meetings of committees of adjustment take place in their respective municipal buildings. As a means of maintaining and increasing accessibility to the decision-making process, it would be appropriate for both the land division committee and the committee of adjustment of the City of Wentworth to consider meeting, where it is warranted, in the district offices to be established by the city discussed in Chapter 4.

Recommendation 8.5: The land division committee and the committee of adjustment of the City of Wentworth hold meetings in the district offices, whenever appropriate.

The authority of the Minister of Housing to approve plans of subdivision has, since June 1975, been exercised by Regional Council, in keeping with the province's policy of delegating planning approval powers. The results of this arrangement have been positive: the approval process has been speeded up, and decisions on subdivisions have been taken by a locally accountable body able to apply its knowledge of local circumstances. The Commission is anxious that these benefits not be lost when the new planning structure is established. Since the provincial policy extends to delegating subdivision approval powers to councils of regional municipalities where planning is exclusively an upper-tier function, there seems no sound reason for withholding this power from the council of the new city.

Recommendation 8.6: The council of the City of Wentworth be delegated the power of the Minister of Housing to approve plans of subdivision.

The question of an official plan for the new city also deserves consideration. The Commission recognizes that considerable time and resources have been devoted to the preparation of new regional and area official plans during the past several years, and does not want to see these efforts rendered futile. Moreover, the status of existing official plans must clearly be preserved pending any future changes.

The present two-tier planning structure actually contemplates three levels of plans: the regional official plan, containing general policies for growth and development; the area official plans, containing more detailed policies consistent with the regional plan; and secondary plans, containing policies of still greater detail and usually focusing on individual neighbourhoods. In the new planning structure, there will no longer be a need to maintain the first two of these levels separately. The appropriate course will be for the council of the new city to build upon the work already undertaken toward a draft regional plan and integrate into it the desirable features of existing and proposed area plans. Council will, of course, be free to make what changes it sees fit in policies at both levels of generality, but when a plan is finally adopted and submitted for provincial approval, it should comprise a complete and self-contained official plan.

> **Recommendation 8.7:** The City of Wentworth adopt a single, comprehensive official plan for the municipality, which, on its approval, will supersede all existing plans; and pending its approval, existing plans remain in full effect.

In the Commission's view, it would not be wise to require in legislation that such a plan be adopted by a specified date. Attempts to do so have in the past proved unrealistic, and it is unlikely that the council of the city will require prompting to be impressed with the urgency of proceeding with an official plan.

In Chapter 4 of this report, the Commission recommends that the new city establish district offices to ensure that its services, including planning-related services, are accessible to residents in all parts of the municipality. The Commission foresees, for example, that through planning staff located at these offices, residents will be able to obtain basic planning assistance and to make applications for planning permits and approvals. In addition, we trust that the new council will place an emphasis upon involving citizens in each community in the various planning activities.

> **Recommendation 8.8:** The council of the City of Wentworth give careful consideration to the placing of planning staff in district offices to provide basic planning assistance, to receive and process applications for planning permits and approvals, and to provide liaison with other municipal departments.

Chapter 9

Physical Services

This chapter deals with certain physical services provided by municipal government in Hamilton-Wentworth: water supply and treatment, sewerage and sewage treatment, storm drainage, and solid waste management.

Water

Water supply system design is dependent on factors unrelated to area municipal boundaries, such as topography and population distribution. Therefore, under The Regional Municipality of Hamilton-Wentworth Act, the Region was made solely responsible for the supply and distribution of water. As of January 1, 1974, the Region was required to assume and to operate all water supply and treatment facilities, pumping stations, storage facilities, and trunk and distribution water mains. It exercises its responsibilities through the Regional Engineering Department, and new water facilities are planned in close cooperation with the Regional Planning and Development Department.

Prior to the formation of the Region, each municipality was responsible for the provision of water within its borders. The City of Hamilton operated a water supply system that treated water drawn from Lake Ontario and delivered it to customers in the city and also, by intermunicipal agreements, in Dundas, Stoney Creek, Saltfleet and part of Ancaster. A system of municipal wells served the remainder of Ancaster, and a number of isolated well systems provided water to communities in Flamborough. Agreements with the Town of Burlington (since assumed by Halton Region) and the Town of Grimsby (since assumed by Niagara Region) provided for supply to portions of Flamborough and Stoney Creek respectively.

These were the supply facilities assumed by the Region. The city system became the major component of the regional system, and the most significant immediate changes effected by regionalization were the removal of intermunicipal meters and the abandonment of the agreements that had made them necessary. Since 1974, an extensive program of capital improvements has been undertaken to upgrade and extend the system in accordance with a long-range regional waterworks plan. Areas which had little likelihood of service prior to 1974 are now being opened up for development, and communities with water problems are scheduled to receive adequate quantities of potable water. The regional water system now serves some 376,000 customers.

Charges for water services were determined in a variety of ways before the establishment of regional government. In Hamilton, industrial and commercial customers purchased water on a metered basis, while residential charges were related to assessment. Dundas and Ancaster were entirely metered, while Stoney Creek and Flamborough had both metered and flat rate services. These variations, together with the rate-setting provisions of intermunicipal agreements, resulted in significant disparities in charges for identical services in different parts of the present Region.

One of the important accomplishments of regional government has been the equalization of water rates throughout the Region on a user-pay basis. The waterworks system operates as a utility, and all costs associated with capital construction, operation and maintenance (except capital costs for new developments and local improvements, which are supported by lot levies and improvement assessments) are recovered through water rates. Only those connected to the system pay for the services, with charges determined by actual meter readings where they are available or, in the unmetered portions of Hamilton and Stoney Creek, on a fixed schedule based on charges paid for homes with similar assessments. All commercial, industrial and institutional customers are metered, as are all new residential services. Costs required to be paid by users are reduced through a number of federal and provincial grant and subsidy programs, and water

Table 9.1: Annual Water Costs for an Average Household

Municipality	1972	1977
Hamilton - metered	$48.44	$44.56
- flat rate ($5,000 assessment)	33.00	46.74
Ancaster	55.20	44.56
Dundas	72.66	45.33
Stoney Creek - metered	31.92	44.56
- flat rate ($5,000 assessment)	24.00	46.74
Flamborough-East Flamborough	67.08	44.56
- Waterdown	37.20	44.56

SOURCE: The Region and area municipalities

rates in Hamilton-Wentworth compare favourably with those in neighbouring municipalities.

Table 9.1 sets out the annual cost of water to an average household in the Region in 1972 and 1977, based upon a consumption of 50,400 gallons per year.

The transfer of responsibility for water services to the proposed City of Wentworth will permit their rational, municipality-wide planning and operation to continue. The Commission thinks that the present system of user-pay charges for water is an equitable one, and ought to be retained.

Recommendation 9.1: Water services in the City of Wentworth be provided on a common, user-pay basis.

In Chapter 4, the Commission recommends the establishment of district offices to serve the citizens of Wentworth; among their functions in connection with water services could be to deal with complaints and to receive requests for inspections and repairs. The availability of their assistance could significantly improve citizen access to what is now a centrally administered service.

Sanitary Sewers

Responsibility for the collection and treatment of sewage is vested in the Region by The Regional Municipality of Hamilton-Wentworth Act. The design of sewerage systems, like that of water supply systems, is primarily influenced by topography and population densities. In addition, account must be taken of the availability of an adequate receiving body of water for disposal of treatment plant effluent. None of these factors has any necessary correlation with area municipal boundaries.

At the time of the formation of the Region, most built-up areas in the City of Hamilton and certain portions of the County of Wentworth were serviced by sanitary sewers, while the remaining areas used septic tanks or holding tanks. No sanitary sewers existed in Ancaster, but the Ministry of Environment had initiated a construction program to provide the town with a complete sewer system connecting with treatment facilities in Hamilton. There were three principal sewage treatment facilities, located in Hamilton, Dundas and Waterdown. A major expansion program was under way at the Hamilton plant; the Dundas plant had exceeded capacity, and development in that town had been curtailed as a result; and the Waterdown plant was operating at capacity.

Charges for sewer services and methods of charging varied considerably before 1974. Sewage costs in Hamilton and Dundas were included in the general tax levy. The former Town of Stoney Creek employed a flat rate, while Waterdown and Saltfleet used surcharges of different percentages on water bills.

As of January 1, 1974, the Region assumed all existing sanitary sewers, as well as the Waterdown and Dundas treatment plants. The Ancaster sewer system is now operated by the Region although ownership remains with the province. Because of a contractual dispute concerning expansion of the Hamilton plant, it too has yet to be assumed in full by the Region, though the Region operates the complete facility.

In the few years since regionalization, the Region has been able to utilize its broader financial base and planning perspective to improve the availability and quality of sewage services. For example, expansion programs are under way at both the Dundas and Waterdown treatment plants, which will permit new development in the areas they serve, and trunk sewers are approaching the boundaries of the present Township of Glanbrook, permitting sewer service to begin where none was previously available.

Just as with water rates, the Region has equalized sewer charges throughout the municipality on a user-pay basis, in this instance by means of a surcharge on water bills. At present the surcharge is 100 per cent and consists of two elements — a 45 per cent capital cost surcharge, and a 55 per cent operating cost surcharge.

Table 9.2 indicates the annual cost of sewage services to an average household in the Region in 1972 and 1977, based on water consumption of 50,400 gallons per year and an assessment of $5,000.

Table 9.2: Annual Sewage Costs for an Average Serviced Household

Municipality	1972	1977
Hamilton - metered water	$39.96	$44.56
- flat rate	39.96	46.74
Ancaster	69.00	44.56
Dundas	26.10	45.33
Stoney Creek - former town	15.00	44.56
- former township	21.84	44.56
Flamborough	78.38	44.56

SOURCE: The Region and area municipalities

The increased charges in Hamilton reflect the improved degree of treatment now provided by the expanded Hamilton treatment plant. It is significant that sewage costs in Dundas had been scheduled to rise to approximately $86.00 per household annually on the assumption that the Dundas plant would, on completion of its expansion program, remain under the ownership of the town. In general terms, the costs of sewage treatment have accelerated during the past decade, in part because provincial pollution control requirements have become more stringent, requiring a higher quality of effluent, and in part because costs of treatment materials have escalated.

The Commission has concluded that the present user-pay charge structure is both equitable and appropriate, and ought to be continued.

> **Recommendation 9.2: Sewage services in the City of Wentworth be provided on a common, user-pay basis.**

Storm Drainage

On the formation of the Regional Municipality of Hamilton-Wentworth in 1974, the Region was charged with responsibility for the drainage of storm water from regional roads and surrounding tributary lands. The operation and maintenance of all remaining drainage systems, including storm sewers, ditches and culverts on local roads, were left with the area municipalities. The Region was also empowered by by-law to assume any portion of an area municipality's system, and because the majority of sewers in the City of Hamilton were combined sewers carrying both storm water and sanitary sewage, the Region's responsibility for sanitary sewage required that it assume the entire Hamilton system.

The four Conservation Authorities with jurisdiction within the Region — the Grand River, Halton Region, Hamilton Region and Niagara Peninsula Conservation Authorities — also play an important part in the management of storm drainage. Conservation Authorities are established by the province on a watershed basis, and are authorized to pass regulations prohibiting building in areas susceptible to flooding and to undertake stream protection measures. They also provide comments on the drainage implications of proposed development, and cooperate with the municipalities on the planning of drainage programs.

The drainage facilities within the Region are, for the most part, those that were developed in individual systems by the municipalities existing prior to regionalization. The type and capability of drainage systems largely depend on land use; in rural areas, roadside drainage ditches discharging into watercourses predominate, while storm sewers (or, where the system is an older one, combined storm and sanitary sewers) are usual in urbanized areas.

The costs of storm drainage are recovered by area municipalities as part of their general tax levy, and costs associated with roadside drainage are normally included with the costs of the roads themselves. In the City of Hamilton, because of its combined sewer system, the Region designs and maintains storm drainage facilities and charges the costs back to the city; in the other area municipalities, drainage works are supervised by their engineering staff.

Table 9.3 shows the costs incurred in 1976 and 1977 by the area municipalities for operating and maintaining storm sewers.

When land is developed by plan of subdivision, area municipalities normally require provisions concerning drainage facilities to be included in subdivision agreements. The municipalities have not developed a common approach to

Table 9.3: Storm Sewer Maintenance and Operating Costs

Municipality	1976 Actual	1977 Budgeted
City of Hamilton	2,575,000	2,839,000
Town of Dundas	11,500*	15,000*
Town of Ancaster	972*	5,679*
Town of Stoney Creek	43,376	58,900
Township of Flamborough	N/A	N/A
Township of Glanbrook	N/A	N/A

    Storm sewers are defined as enclosed sewers to facilitate surface drainage and not open ditches forming part of the roadway system.
    *Municipalities that incorporate storm sewers as part of their roadway operations (i.e., not budgeted on a separate functional basis).
N/A — Municipalities not having storm sewers within urban sectors of their municipality. This has been confirmed with representatives of the municipality.
SOURCE: The Region and area municipalities.

servicing requirements, however, and substantial differences exist between the various requirements.

When storm water runoff occurs, the pattern of land drainage is determined by topographical features that bear no relation to existing area municipal boundaries. Assumption of control over the entire land drainage function will enable the proposed City of Wentworth to develop a coordinated storm management policy for the whole municipality, and to establish uniform design criteria. But because the nature and sophistication of storm drainage facilities actually required in a particular area vary with the degree of urbanization, the Commission suggests that the operating costs of storm drainage should be borne on the basis of area rating.

Recommendation 9.3: The costs attributable to operating storm drainage facilities in the City of Wentworth be area rated.

Solid Waste Management

Solid waste management includes the storage, collection, transportation, processing, reduction and final disposal of garbage. Responsibility for this function is divided under the Regional Act: the Region provides and operates disposal facilities, while the area municipalities collect and transport garbage to the Region's disposal sites.

Prior to regionalization, each of the existing municipalities was responsible for both collection and disposal. In the urban areas, municipal household collection was provided, while rural areas were served by private contractors or by individual delivery to disposal sites. Each local municipality operated its own disposal facilities; most were semi-sanitary landfill sites which failed to comply with provincial standards established by the Ministry of the Environment. While those inadequacies were recognized, the acquisition of new sanitary landfill facilities was beyond the means of any individual municipality.

At present the residents of all urban and most rural areas are provided with weekly collection services. Rural residents of Flamborough may elect whether or not to receive these services, while in Ancaster rural residents are obliged to make individual arrangements for collection with a private hauler. Collection is carried out in Hamilton and Dundas by municipal employees; in the other area municipalities it is done by private firms on contract with the municipality. Collection costs are included in the tax billings of those ratepayers who receive the service.

Since bidding for private garbage collection contracts is at present quite competitive, and since residents of the municipalities letting these contracts seem quite satisfied with the services provided, the Commission thinks that the council of the proposed City of Wentworth would be wise to maintain the system of private contracting for waste collection. Unlike disposal, there are few economies to be achieved by larger scale collection operations.

Recommendation 9.4: The council of the City of Wentworth continue the use of private contracting for solid waste collection, where appropriate.

Of the ten land disposal sites operating before 1974, only three are still accepting municipal refuse. One of these, a small facility in Flamborough, is scheduled to close in the near future. The Upper Ottawa Street site in Hamilton has been virtually full for some time, and the Jerseyville site in Ancaster, regarded by the Ministry of the Environment as the only acceptable existing landfill operation, will be full within two years at present rates. Apart from land disposal sites, the other major disposal facility assumed by the Region was the Solid Waste Reduction Unit, a waste incinerator constructed by the City of Hamilton. Because of certain design problems, this facility has been unable to approach its anticipated disposal capacity despite substantial modifications.

In recognition of the strains on existing disposal facilities, the Region recently initiated action to acquire property in the Township of Glanbrook for a sanitary landfill site of substantial size, which must be approved by the provincial Environmental Assessment Board. Because of opposition by the residents of Glanbrook to the establishment of the site, an Ontario Municipal Board hearing may also be required under the terms of The Municipal Act before the project can proceed.

Subject to provincial approval, Regional Council has, in addition, entered into an agreement with a private firm to operate a complete solid waste disposal system to serve the Region for the next twenty years. Among the terms of the agreement are provisions for the operation of three transfer stations where collection vehicles can conveniently discharge waste for transportation to the Glanbrook site by high capacity transfer trucks, and for the operation of the Solid Waste Reduction Unit at a guaranteed capacity. Under the proposed system, disposal costs would increase by approximately $3.00 per ton to some $12.00. A substantial portion of this and other cost increases associated with solid waste management is attributable to the necessity to comply with stricter provincial standards.

Disposal costs for solid waste are currently included in the general regional levy. Since waste disposal facilities serve the entire community equally, the Commission suggests that disposal costs should continue to be borne equally by all the residents of the municipality, and that they should be generally rated. By contrast, different levels of collection service are now provided in the area municipalities, and those differences will, unless the ratepayers request otherwise, continue to be appropriate in the City of Wentworth. In sum, the present system for funding solid waste management services should remain.

Recommendation 9.5: The costs of solid waste disposal be generally rated, but costs of solid waste collection be area rated on the basis of existing area municipal boundaries.

Chapter 10

Transportation

This chapter deals with the municipal role in the provision of transportation services: roads, public transit, parking, the airport, and taxicabs.

Roads

Responsibility for roads encompasses the following functions: planning, design, construction, maintenance (including cleaning, patching and snow removal) and traffic control through signals, pavement markings and signing. The road system in Hamilton-Wentworth is now a shared responsibility between the province, which administers the provincial highway network, and the regional and area municipal governments.

Prior to regionalization, local roads were under the jurisdiction of the eleven former municipalities. In the municipalities other than the City of Hamilton, responsibility for arterial and major collector roads was divided between the County of Wentworth and the Hamilton-Wentworth Suburban Roads Commission, depending on the function of the road in question. Suburban roads under the control of the Commission (those that connected the city with the surrounding area) were funded one-half by the province and one-quarter each by the County of Wentworth and the City of Hamilton. The city itself had complete responsibility for all arterials within its territory.

Under The Regional Act, some 190 miles of roads that had constituted the county and suburban systems were transferred to the Region as of January 1, 1974, to become the regional road system. Regional Council is also empowered to add other roads to the system, and through this means, 135 miles of City of Hamilton arterial roads and 2 miles in the Town of Dundas were transferred to the Region in May 1977. The transfer was not effected until then because of concerns about the associated outstanding debt. The change was facilitated, however, when the province agreed to provide a grant to the Region amounting to $5.1 million. This sum is being used by the Region to phase in over five years the additional costs of the transferred roads, including debenture charges, that would otherwise be borne by taxpayers of the area municipalities other than Hamilton. The full additional costs were relieved in 1977 and reducing credits will be allowed each year until 1981, the final year. All public roads apart from those comprising the regional system and provincial highways are now the responsibility of the area municipalities.

Maintenance and engineering services on roads other than regional roads are all provided by the area municipalities. While the Region maintains the portion of the regional road system outside the City of Hamilton through a number of service depots, it has contracted with the city for maintenance of regional roads within Hamilton. The city also provides traffic control services on all regional roads by contract with the Region.

A substantial portion of the construction and maintenance costs of municipal roads, with the exception of sidewalk costs, is assumed by the province under a variety of grant programs. Maintenance subsidies amount to approximately 50 per cent of total costs, and are higher for roads that form connecting links with the provincial highway network. The effect of these grants is that the province plays an important role in the determination of municipal roads priorities, since a municipal decision to construct or maintain roads not eligible for subsidy will be relatively very costly to the municipality.

Table 10.1 shows road costs in Hamilton-Wentworth since 1972.

Several factors contribute to the increase in costs of roads: inflation, particularly in labour costs; a need to accelerate the purchase of equipment to comply with more stringent provincial requirements; increased levels of service in response to public demand (for example, for more frequent snow plowing); and the need to undertake projects ineligible for subsidy.

Our examination of this function leads us to conclude that road-related services can most effectively and efficiently be provided throughout the proposed City of Wentworth by a single governmental unit. The need for a Suburban Roads Commission prior to 1974 demonstrated the integrated nature of the road system even before regionalization, and an integrated system requires overall planning and coordination. Similarly, traffic control must be taken into account in designing the complete transportation network, and must be centrally directed.

Because roads serve the transportation needs of the entire municipality, we suggest that the costs associated with roads should, for the most part, be borne generally without area rating. With respect to certain services ancillary to roads, such as snow clearing, street lighting and sidewalks, desirable levels of service may, however, differ from one part of the municipality to another. Some residents may wish their local roads plowed more quickly after a snowfall than is normally done; and sidewalks may serve a general function (to provide for a safe route to school, for

TRANSPORTATION   155

Table 10.1: Road Expenditures, 1972-1978
(In thousands of dollars)

Area Municipality	Year	Gross Costs						Subsidy	Net cost
		Construction		Maintenance	Traffic	Overhead and Misc.	Total		
		Capital to be debentured	Capital out of current						
Town of Ancaster	1972	—	119	176	4	44	343	174	169
	1976	171	0	423	29	31	483	246	237
	1978	N/A	N/A	N/A	N/A	N/A	N/A	N/A	N/A
Town of Dundas	1972	—	108	breakdown not available		—	406	206	200
	1976	171	233			—	844	292	552
	1978	N/A	N/A			N/A	N/A	N/A	N/A
Township Flamborough	1972	—	137	229	8	125	499	229	270
	1976	—	164	394	7	304	869	272	597
	1978	N/A	N/A	N/A	N/A	(land purch.) N/A	N/A	N/A	N/A
Township of Glanbrook	1972	—	74	147	1	66	288	138	150
	1976	—	20	467	11	126	624	308	316
	1978	N/A	N/A	N/A	N/A	N/A	N/A	N/A	N/A
City of Hamilton	1972	N/A	8,875	5,468	571	—	14,914	5,964	8,950
	1976	N/A	9,389	7,976	949	—	18,314	6,700	11,614
	1978	N/A	9,609	4,749	499	—	14,857	5,822	9,035
Town of Stoney Creek	1972	N/A	N/A	N/A	N/A	N/A	N/A	N/A	N/A
	1976	—	188	466	155	104	913	384	529
	1978	N/A	N/A	N/A	N/A	N/A	N/A	N/A	N/A
County and Suburban Roads Commission	1972	—	658	442	59	574	1,733	842	891
Region of Hamilton-Wentworth	1976	—	1553	965	179	761	3,458	1,724	1,734
	1978	—	3578	3,389	975	1706	9,647	4,563	5,084

1 Maintenance costs include debt repayment and debt servicing costs.
2 Total does not include those capital costs debentured for the year in question.
N/A Not available.

SOURCE: IBI Group — Research Report for Hamilton-Wentworth Review Commission.

example) or be primarily for the residents of a particular street. When justifiable demands are made for increased services in parts of the municipality, the council of the city should of course feel free to respond to them, but it is only fair that the beneficiaries should bear the additional costs.

> **Recommendation 10.1:** The costs of roads be generally rated throughout the municipality; but where higher than normal levels of service are provided with respect to snow clearing or sidewalks (where not financed as local improvements), council be authorized to provide for area rating of the consequent additional costs.

There are wide disparities in levels of service and costs of street lighting. Already some municipalities area rate this service and the Commission thinks this practice should be extended to recognize these differentials.

> **Recommendation 10.2:** The costs of street lighting be area rated to preserve the existing basis of charge.

Road maintenance services are now provided through a number of depots in different parts of the Region, some operated by the Region and some by the area municipalities. Since decentralized operations are both more efficient and more responsive to varying needs, we think it will be advantageous to integrate the existing system of regional and area road maintenance depots into a single, decentralized system for maintaining the roads of the new municipality.

> **Recommendation 10.3:** Road maintenance be provided on a decentralized basis by integrating existing regional and area municipal maintenance facilities.

Public Transit

Public transit became an exclusive regional responsibility in January 1977. Originally, transit services were provided in Hamilton-Wentworth by a private company, the Hamilton Street Railway, and its wholly owned subsidiary, Canada Coach Lines. These companies were purchased by the City of Hamilton in 1960 and operated by the Hamilton Transit Commission until 1977, when they were acquired from the city by the Region as authorized by amendments to the Regional Act.

Formally, it is still the two companies that operate transit services, under the control of the Regional Municipality of Hamilton-Wentworth Transit Commission. The Hamilton Street Railway provides urban transit service to the City of Hamilton and to several of the area municipalities, and also connects with Burlington, while Canada Coach Lines provides inter-urban service to points both within and beyond the Region. Functionally, since the Commission consists of ten members of Regional Council appointed by Regional Council, the companies comprise a regional transit department under the control of a Regional Council committee. The transit amendments to the Regional Act provide for the dissolution of the Commission as of December 31, 1979, after which Regional Council is to continue to appoint the directors of the companies from among its own members.

Beginning in 1973, the province has provided operating subsidies to transit systems in Ontario amounting to approximately 15 to 20 per cent of total operating costs. Prior to regionalization, and until the Region assumed control of transit in 1977, the City of Hamilton was responsible for the remaining deficits, after fares and other revenues, on all routes, including those extending into neighbouring municipalities.

Regional control has changed this funding arrangement and rendered it more equitable. Pursuant to the amendments to the Regional Act, the Region is now divided into three areas for purposes of transit operation and subsidy. Within the Urban Transit Area — which is now defined as the City of Hamilton but may be enlarged by the Treasurer of Ontario on the application of Regional Council — deficits may be recovered from the area municipalities on an equalized assessment basis. This means that at present the deficits on Hamilton Street Railway routes within the city are borne by the city's residents.

In area municipalities outside the Urban Transit Area, transit services are provided at the request of the municipal council and on terms as to level of service and fare structure agreed to with the Region. Any deficits arising from operations in an area municipality are assumed by that municipality. However, for transit operations within the Urban Transit Service Area — which is a defined area larger than the Urban Transit Area and encompasses urban settlements outside the city — provincial subsidies are available. Subsidies are not normally available for operating deficits on routes within area municipalities but outside the Urban Transit Service Area. Transitional grants are being paid by the province, however, over the five years from 1977 to phase in the impact of the transfer of the transit function to the Region.

Deficits incurred on routes outside the Region — the Hamilton Street Railway service to Burlington and Canada Coach Lines inter-urban service — are paid for by the Region. Until the early 1970s, Canada Coach Lines did not in fact incur a deficit, but by 1976 the deficit had become substantial, and the province in that year began to subsidize a limited number of routes between Hamilton and other municipalities outside this Region. The majority, however, remain unsubsidized.

During the period 1973 to 1977, transit costs per bus mile and per passenger increased roughly in the same proportion as the rate of inflation, and total operating costs increased in an amount corresponding to a combination of inflation and increased levels of service. Comparisons undertaken for the Review Commission indicate that transit operations in Hamilton-Wentworth are at least as efficient as those in other Ontario municipalities of comparable size. Yet, as indicated by Table 10.2, deficits have continued to increase, as has the share of the deficits required to be borne by municipalities.

Table 10.2: Public Transit Deficits
(In thousands of dollars)

	Net operating deficit	Provincial subsidy	Municipal share
Hamilton Street Railway			
1973	3,181	1,140	2,041
1975	5,444	2,684	2,760
1976	6,279	2,766	3,513
1977 (est.)	8,439	2,875	5,564
Canada Coach Lines			
1973	48	-	48
1975	525	-	525
1976	455	102	353
1977 (est.)	704	103	601

SOURCE: See Table 10.1.

The increases are in large part reflections of provincial policy decisions. The province's public transit policy of 1973 proposed higher levels of provincial assistance if proper service levels were maintained at low fare rates. Since that time, however, it has been decided to allow municipalities to bear a greater proportion of the transit burden.

In our view, the existing system for the provision of transit services should, in general, continue under the proposed municipal structure. As currently constituted, the system enables transit planning and operations to be carried out efficiently for all of Hamilton-Wentworth, while permitting the level of service to be tailored to the needs of the residents of different parts of the municipality and to their willingness to pay for it. The major existing obstacle to comprehensive transit policy-making and implementation — that Regional Council is unable to provide a transit service it believes desirable beyond the Urban Transit Area without agreement of the area council concerned — will disappear under the unified municipal structure. It will be important, however, that decisions take careful account of the need for, and the costs of, any extension of service.

It is our belief that the council of the City of Wentworth should be authorized to alter the boundaries of the Urban Transit Area without provincial approval. This would enable council to decide that the basic transit service for the urban core of the municipality extends to an area larger than the present city, and that all residents within that larger area should bear its costs. Since the level of provincial subsidy is the same whether a route is inside or outside the Urban Transit Area, provided it is within the Urban Transit Service Area, and since it will no longer be necessary to protect the right of area councils to determine the nature of transit service beyond the Urban Transit Area, the Commission is of the view that no significant provincial interests will be at stake in decisions to alter Urban Transit Area boundaries. Where service is provided outside the Urban Transit Area, council will be able to area rate its costs in a manner that more closely conforms to the area benefited by the service, without regard for pre-existing area municipal boundaries.

Recommendation 10.4: The costs of transit service within the Urban Transit Area continue to be borne by the ratepayers living within it, and the costs of service outside the Urban Transit Area be area rated according to the area benefiting from the service. Council should be authorized to alter the boundaries of the Urban Transit Area without provincial approval, provided the change is connected with a change of service to the area affected.

The position of the inter-urban transit services now provided primarily through Canada Coach Lines — but also in the case of Burlington through the Hamilton Street Railway — requires separate mention. In many respects, these services are the equivalent in the area centred on Hamilton to the services provided by GO Transit in the Toronto area. Yet GO Transit deficits are funded 100 per cent by the province, while despite some provincial assistance, the residents of Hamilton-Wentworth continue to pay for the majority of the deficits incurred in the Hamilton area services. At the same time, provincial transportation regulations administered through the Ontario Highway Transport Board preclude the termination of unprofitable routes. Even if these routes could be terminated, it would not necessarily be wise to do so, since the maintenance of an extensive public transportation network oriented to Wentworth is essential to enhancing its role as the strong western pole of the Toronto-Centred Region.

In the Commission's view, it is only fair that the principles supporting provincial assumption of the GO Transit deficit be applied to Hamilton-Wentworth also.

Recommendation 10.5: The province subsidize on the same basis as GO Transit the analogous inter-urban and commuter services provided by the City of Wentworth.

As has already been explained in this chapter, some Canada Coach Line services to areas within the Region are not eligible for the provincial subsidy that other transit services receive. The amounts involved are not very great, but the Commission thinks, on principle, this anomaly should be corrected.

Recommendation 10.6: All municipally owned transit operations servicing the Region be eligible for provincial subsidy.

Transit policy should be regarded as part of an overall municipal transportation policy and, as for other transportation services, direct responsibility for transit should be vested in the council of the City of Wentworth. The existing Regional Transit Commission is an interim body scheduled for dissolution by 1980, and in practice operates as a committee of Regional Council.

Recommendation 10.7: The council of the City of Wentworth be assigned direct responsibility for the provision of transit services.

The appropriate committee structure for the new council is discussed in Chapter 6, where we recommend that transit be included among the services to be dealt with by the Physical Services Committee.

Because the Hamilton Street Railway Company and the Canada Coach Lines now exist merely as corporate shells through which municipal services are provided, the Commission has considered whether they should be wound up once transit responsibility is vested in the new city. This would no doubt be desirable as a means of clarifying operating relationships; however, we are concerned that there be no adverse tax or legal consequences to the citizens of Wentworth from the formal dissolution of these two private companies.

Recommendation 10.8: The council of the City of Wentworth take the appropriate steps to wind up the Hamilton Street Railway Company and Canada Coach Lines Limited, providing that there will be no adverse consequences of the dissolutions.

Parking

Parking facilities are of two basic types: on-street; and off-street, including both private and municipal lots. Responsibility for on-street parking ordinarily accompanies responsibility for the roads themselves. At present, therefore, responsibility is divided, the Region determining parking policy and regulations on regional roads and where transit operations are concerned, and the area municipalities parking by-laws governing the roads within their own jurisdiction. The area municipalities control all off-street parking.

Enforcement of parking regulations is now the responsibility of the area municipalities and the Regional Police. In the City of Hamilton, enforcement is primarily handled by a by-law enforcement unit established in 1974 to relieve the police of the necessity of dealing with non-moving violations. The unit is funded from parking meter and parking fine revenues. The only area municipality with a significant amount of off-street parking, Hamilton has placed responsibility for administering its off-street parking facilities in the hands of an appointed parking authority.

In the proposed City of Wentworth, there will be no question of divided authority over parking; the city will acquire complete municipal jurisdiction. The only organizational matter to be decided is whether a parking authority should be created or whether council should assume full responsibility.

In our view, the latter course should be followed. It has recently become recognized that parking is an important element of a total transportation system, and that parking policy can be used to complement other transportation policies. Thus, for example, both the Region and the City of Hamilton have adopted the policy of prohibiting parking on major arterial roads, particularly during peak hours, to increase road capacity and defer the need for road improvements. It is also possible to vary parking charges to make the use of private vehicles less attractive when compared to the costs of using public transit. The council of the City of Wentworth should be in a position to coordinate parking policies with policies for roads, transportation and land use, and should not divest itself of this opportunity by establishing an independent parking authority.

Recommendation 10.9: The power to establish a parking authority be abolished, and parking be the responsibility of council and of the Physical Services Committee.

Because the existing off-street parking facilities have been purchased at different times to meet the needs in individual area municipalities, we think that the residents of the communities that benefit should continue to pay any deficit from those operations, or to benefit from any surplus.

Recommendation 10.10: Any net cost relating to parking facilities in any existing area municipality be rated to that area, or any surplus credited.

Hamilton Civic Airport

Hamilton Civic Airport is owned by the federal government but leased and managed by the City of Hamilton. The Ministry of Transport is responsible for the staffing and operation of the control tower and for major capital expenditures such as runway extensions and new buildings. Policing on the airport grounds is provided by the Regional Police. All remaining maintenance functions are carried out by City of Hamilton personnel at the direction of an airport manager who reports to the Airport Committee of city council. The federal Ministry of Transport subsidizes 100 per cent of the operating deficit, which amounted to some $498,000 in 1977. The residents of Hamilton do not therefore bear any financial burden for airport operations.

The airport provided only general aviation services until the early 1970s, when Nordair initiated limited scheduled and charter service. Following a protracted period of discussion and study concerning the future role of the airport, in particular its possible expansion or relocation from its Mount Hope site, the federal government recently announced a major program of expansion and improvement at its present location. There will no doubt be significant short- and long-term economic benefits to the municipality from the expansion program, but in the meantime new roads and other municipal services will have to be provided.

Another consequence of the expansion may well be that the federal government will take over direct responsibility for airport operations, just as it has in other major airports in Canada. Until that comes about, we suggest that the proposed City of Wentworth assume the operating responsibilities now undertaken by the City of Hamilton, subject to the same arrangement concerning federal subsidies. Even before the expansion plans were announced, the airport served an area far larger than Hamilton, and if it is to be managed by a municipality it is appropriate that the municipality be one that represents a wider constituency. The new council should assign airport matters to the Physical Services Committee.

Recommendation 10.11: The City of Wentworth assume the operating responsibilities for Hamilton Civic Airport now undertaken by the City of Hamilton.

Taxicabs

Taxi services in the Region are provided by private operators under licences granted by the area municipalities. In 1976, the most recent year for which data are available, there were 220 licensed taxicabs in the City of Hamilton, 21 in Dundas, 10 in Stoney Creek, 2 in Flamborough, and none in either Ancaster or Glanbrook. Generally, only taxis licensed to operate within a particular municipality may both pick up and deliver fares within that municipality. Trips may either begin or end, however, in a municipality for which a taxi is not licensed.

Prior to regionalization, taxi licences were issued by the then existing municipalities, and licensing by-laws were enforced by local police departments. Since the formation of regional government and the transfer of the policing function to the Region, the responsibility for enforcement has, for the most part, remained with the area municipalities, although the Regional Police undertook by-law enforcement during the transitional period and still occasionally perform meter inspections. In the area municipalities other than Hamilton, by-law enforcement is normally only a part-time responsibility of one or more municipal employees, and the enforcement of taxicab by-laws is largely ineffective.

In Chapter 6, the Commission recommends that licensing in the City of Wentworth be a direct responsibility of a committee of council rather than a licensing commission; taxicab licences are among those that should be dealt with in this way.

There are, however, two particular concerns with respect to taxi licences. The first is that there be some means of ensuring that taxi services are available in all parts of the city, and that operators do not concentrate solely in the central urban area at the expense of the more outlying areas. The second is that there be fair treatment of both existing Hamilton operators and applicants for new Hamilton licences who have been placed on the waiting list. It has been reported to the Commission that progress through the waiting list now takes approximately five years: a Hamilton taxi licence is a very valuable asset. If, after the City of Wentworth is established, licensees of the existing area municipalities are free to operate in the present City of Hamilton, they will receive a windfall from the effective transformation of their licences into Hamilton licences, and those who have waited for years for Hamilton licences will have done so for no reason.

The Commission suggests that these concerns can be accommodated by providing that existing taxi licences continue to be effective only for the territory for which they were issued, and by authorizing the City of Wentworth to attach territorial restrictions to licence renewals and new licences.

Recommendation 10.12: Existing taxicab licences continue to be effective only for the territory for which they were issued, and the City of Wentworth be authorized to attach territorial restrictions to licence renewals and to new licences.

Chapter 11

Public Safety Services

The protection of its citizens and their property is an inescapable and essential function of government. National defence, policing, fire protection, and emergency measures planning are all part of this broad function. In all but national defence, local government plays a significant part. This chapter deals with these services as they are carried out in Hamilton-Wentworth.

Another program sometimes considered under the heading of public safety is ambulance service. In Hamilton-Wentworth, as in most parts of Ontario, this is a provincial responsibility, undertaken by the Ministry of Health. Apart from a contractual arrangement whereby the Fire Department of Ancaster provides service in that community, this service has no direct impact on local government.

Policing

The police function is shared by the federal, provincial and local governments. The federal force, the Royal Canadian Mounted Police, concentrates its attention on enforcement of certain federal statutes. Accordingly, it is concerned with investigations and prosecutions in such fields as drugs, customs and excise, immigration, commercial crime, income tax evasion, weights and measures, and explosives. It also has a security function and investigates possible violations of the Aeronautics Act.

In Ontario, policing comes under the jurisdiction of the provincial Solicitor General, who is the minister responsible for the Ontario Police Commission and the Ontario Provincial Police. Under the terms of The Police Act, the Ontario Police Commission has overall supervisory responsibility for police services in the province. Among its functions are the following:

— maintaining statistics on criminal occurrences and other policing matters
— consulting with and providing assistance to local police authorities
— visiting local police forces
— operating the Ontario Police College

PUBLIC SAFETY SERVICES

- coordinating the activities of local police forces
- carrying out investigations under The Police Act
- hearing and deciding appeals by members of police forces
- arranging for police services in any municipality that does not maintain its own police force.

The Ontario Provincial Police have a general responsibility for patrolling King's Highways in the Region. As directed by the provincial Solicitor General, they also conduct certain criminal investigations, including possible frauds against the provincial government. In addition, the Special Services Division is available to local police forces to assist in any of their investigations. Such assistance may be provided on the request of the Crown Attorney or the local Chief of Police, or on the direction of the Solicitor General.

In Hamilton-Wentworth local policing is provided by the Hamilton Harbour Police, the McMaster University security force and the Hamilton-Wentworth Regional Police. The first of these operates under the Hamilton Harbour Commissioners, and is confined to providing security in the property owned and operated by them. The McMaster force, as its name implies, provides security services on University property.

HAMILTON—WENTWORTH REGIONAL POLICE

The Hamilton-Wentworth Regional Police force was created in 1974 at the time of the creation of regional government. It combined the existing police departments of Hamilton, Stoney Creek, Saltfleet, Dundas and Ancaster under the supervision and control of a Hamilton-Wentworth Regional Board of Commissioners of Police.

Prior to regionalization the area was policed by the forces mentioned above, with the Ontario Provincial Police providing service free of charge in the remaining county municipalities — the Village of Waterdown, and the townships of Beverly, Binbrook, East Flamborough, West Flamborough and Glanford. After the formation of the regional force, the Ontario Provincial Police continued to serve Glanbrook and Flamborough until April 3, 1977. At that time, the Hamilton-Wentworth Regional Police assumed responsibility for policing the entire Region. By contractual agreement with the federal government, the force also polices the Mount Hope airport.

The Hamilton-Wentworth Regional Police is divided into two bureaus, an Operations Bureau and an Administration Bureau. Each is under the direction of a Deputy Chief of Police reporting to the Chief. The Operations Bureau has a platoon command division, a patrol division for each of the three areas into which the Region is divided for policing, a Traffic Division, a Criminal Investigation Division and a

Special Services Division. The Administration Bureau handles such functions as personnel, transportation, finance, communications, building maintenance, internal security, complaints, training and other specialized staff functions. It also includes the Youth Division, comprising the Safety Branch, the School Traffic Branch and the Juvenile Branch.

The force currently operates out of nine buildings in the Region, and has a total of 172 vehicles, of which 144 are cruisers.

The most important and most expensive resource of a police force is its personnel. The Hamilton-Wentworth Regional Police has a complement of 662 police and 177 civilians. Table 11.1 shows the numbers of personnel in three consecutive years. The large increase in uniformed staff is in large part the result of adding personnel to take over the policing function in Glanbrook and Flamborough that formerly had been the responsibility of the Ontario Provincial Police.

It can be seen from the table that the intensity of policing service has remained virtually constant over the period. The overall costs of policing in the Region are substantial, and have been increasing in recent years.

Table 11.1: Complement Data, Hamilton-Wentworth Regional Police, 1975-1977

	1975	1976	1977
Police officers[1]	607	660	666[2]
Civilian employees[3]	107	108	124
Ratio of civilians to police	1/5.67	1/6.11	1/5.37
Police per 1,000 people	1.62	1.61	1.62

[1] Includes 4 officers at Mount Hope airport paid by the Government of Canada.
[2] Includes 2 officers seconded to Ontario Police Commission.
[3] Includes full-time staff only; part-time personnel total 7.
SOURCE: Calculated from data received from the Hamilton-Wentworth Regional Police and the Regional Planning and Development Department.

Table 11.2 shows total costs of the Hamilton-Wentworth Regional Police for selected years. The breakdown in expenditures in Table 11.3 shows the areas in which costs have increased. Clearly the areas that have experienced large increases are salaries, benefits, the deficiency payments for the Hamilton Municipal Retirement Fund, and building costs resulting largely from the construction of new facilities.

It may be noted here that the province gives an unconditional per capita grant to all municipalities that have their own police forces. The amount given to Hamilton-Wentworth, as to all municipalities with regional police forces, is $15.00 per capita. The money need not be earmarked for the police function, and is not intended by

PUBLIC SAFETY SERVICES 167

Table 11.2: Municipal Policing Costs in Hamilton-Wentworth, 1972, 1975-1977

Municipality	1972	1975	1976	1977
Ancaster	$ 214,868			
Dundas	363,026			
Hamilton	8,631,101			
Saltfleet	407,716			
Stoney Creek	144,527			
Regional Total	$9,761,238	$15,367,437	$19,371,306[1]	$23,023,910[2]

[1] Includes cost ($142,917) of setting up process for assuming responsibility for policing in Flamborough and Glanbrook.
[2] Includes cost ($901,923 est.) of policing in Flamborough and Glanbrook.
SOURCES: (1) Hamilton Burlington Wentworth Local Government Review Data Book; (2) Information provided by Hamilton-Wentworth Regional Finance Department; (3) Information provided by Ontario Provincial Police; (4) Information provided by the Hamilton-Wentworth Regional Police.

CHAPTER 11

Table 11.3: Analysis of Costs of Hamilton-Wentworth Regional Police, 1974–1977

	1974 Actual	1975 Actual	1976 Actual	1977 Estimate	% increase 1974-77
Police Commission	$ 15,246	$ 24,242	$ 20,657	$ 20,000	31.2
Salaries	9,925,082	12,073,747	13,559,968	15,294,370	54.1
Benefits	1,292,131	1,712,704	2,221,408	2,638,760	104.2
HMRF deficiency	—	—	840,878	2,549,699	—
Building costs	232,207	238,038	1,274,078[1]	1,757,380[2]	656.8
Motor vehicle operations	683,995	743,268	737,725	1,081,800	58.2
Uniforms, clothing and accessories	181,578	237,127	244,935	349,620	92.5
Communications system	103,837	155,280	258,351	374,310	260.5
Other operating costs	188,291	235,086	269,775	401,470	113.2
Court officer's salaries	32,537	37,039	45,596	46,000	41.4
Beach rescue unit	4,000	4,000	11,500	5,200	30.0
Total gross cost	12,658,904	15,460,531	19,484,871	24,518,609	93.7

[1] Approximately $1,000,000 was debenture costs, and $274,078 operating costs.
[2] Approximately $1,325,000 was debenture costs, and $432,380 operating costs.
The debenture costs in 1976 and 1977 reflect the costs of the new regional police building.

SOURCE: Hamilton-Wentworth Regional Police.

the province to cover the entire costs of that service. In 1977, the amount of the grant to Hamilton-Wentworth was $6,139,965, which is approximately one quarter of the costs of the Hamilton-Wentworth Regional Police.

The Commission is satisfied that the Hamilton-Wentworth Regional Police provides a high level of service to the Region and that it operates with an acceptable degree of efficiency. Comparisons we have made with the police forces of other comparable regions in the province support this view. Perhaps the most common criticism about the force that was voiced to us is that the rotation system used prevents officers on duty in the rural areas from being sufficiently familiar with those areas. We suggest that the Police Commission give due weight to this comment, and take it into account in reviewing its policies concerning allocation of personnel. We also commend to their attention the matter of the siting of divisional headquarters from the point of view of service to both urban and rural areas. The location of the police station is important not only for efficient police operation, but also for access by the public. As policing is the major twenty-four-hour public service operated by local government, it is vital that the convenience of the public be given appropriate consideration in decisions about location of stations.

Since the force now serves the entire study area, and is a service of the regional municipality, our recommendation to move to a single-tier administration should have no significant impact on the operation of the Hamilton-Wentworth Regional Police.

HAMILTON-WENTWORTH REGIONAL BOARD OF COMMISSIONERS OF POLICE

Under the provisions of The Regional Municipality of Hamilton-Wentworth Act the Hamilton-Wentworth Regional Board of Commissioners of Police comprises five members. Three, including a county court judge, are appointed by the province; the other two members are regional councillors, appointed by council. The Act is silent on the questions of who is chairman of the board, and whether one of the Regional Council representatives should be the regional chairman.

The board is the governing authority of the regional police force and has responsibility for policing and the maintenance of law and order in the Region. It has a dual reporting relationship: to the Regional Council, and to the provincial government through the Ontario Police Commission. Under The Police Act the Board has the authority to make regulations regarding the operation of the police force, including the appointment of personnel.

Policing costs are borne by the regional municipality, although, as previously mentioned, there is a grant provided because the police force exists. The Police Commission prepares its own budget which it submits to the Region. In the event of a dispute on budget between the Police Commission and the Region, the matter is referred to the Ontario Police Commission to be settled.

It has often been claimed that one of the prime reasons for the generally excellent performance of the police in Ontario is the organizational arrangement for the direction of the service: the Ontario Police Commission and the local Boards of Police Commissioners. In light of the broad satisfaction with the operation of the policing function in Hamilton-Wentworth, we see no reason to suggest any major revisions in the current system. We offer, however, two proposals that will help to ensure that the policing function is coordinated as closely as possible with the other services provided in the municipality.

One suggestion is that one of the municipal representatives on the Police Commission be the head of council. This is the practice in municipalities in Ontario, and indeed is required by statute for the majority. Since policing is such a vital local function, and since it has an impact on, and is affected by, so many other local services, we think it is appropriate that the mayor of the City of Wentworth be one of the two council appointees to the Police Commission. For similar reasons, and to give the police function the representation it deserves in council considerations, we suggest that the second municipal representative on the Police Commission be made a member of the Policy and Finance Committee of Council.

These two changes should ensure the greatest possible coordination (if not integration) of policing policy with other local government policy, without jeopardizing the independence of the Police Commission and the advantages that accrue from it.

> **Recommendation 11.1:** The mayor of the City of Wentworth be a member of the Board of Commissioners of Police, and the second municipal representative on the Board be made a member of the Policy and Finance Committee of Council.

Fire Services

Fire protection can be thought to comprise two functions: fire fighting, and fire prevention. In reality, fire departments also provide a number of other emergency services that do not involve actual or possible conflagrations.

Although there are no provincial mandatory standards for fire protection, the province does play a role in the provision of this service. Under The Fire Marshal's Act the Ontario Fire Marshal in the Solicitor General's ministry is given the following powers and duties:

— investigation of suspected arson, fires involving losses of more than $250,000, fatal fires and gas explosions;

— providing training services to municipal fire fighters, which is done primarily

through the Ontario Fire College;
- keeping records of fires, fire deaths, injuries and fire losses throughout Ontario;
- setting standards for such equipment as hydrants and hose couplings to ensure intermunicipal compatability;
- providing a fire prevention information service and disseminating relevant information; and
- advising and assisting municipal fire departments in providing effective service to their communities.

The Fire Departments Act regulates working conditions for full-time firemen in Ontario. Apart from these constraints, municipalities are free to provide fire services in whatever way they see fit.

The Regional Municipality of Hamilton-Wentworth Act assigns responsibility for fire services to the area municipalities, and provides for the position of Regional Fire Coordinator, who is to be appointed by the Regional Council and is responsible for the establishment of an emergency fire service program and plan for the regional area. This position is currently held by the Fire Chief of the City of Hamilton.

The area municipalities of Hamilton-Wentworth have adopted no single pattern for the provision of fire services. The City of Hamilton has the largest department, staffed entirely by full-time personnel. Stoney Creek, Dundas and Ancaster each has a single department staffed in part by full-time personnel and in part by part-time volunteers. Glanbrook has two fire departments comprised entirely of volunteers, and Flamborough has five, also all volunteer. Regionalization had little impact on this service, apart from some quite minor boundary adjustments, and in the main, the fire services operate much as they did before the establishment of the Region.

All fire chiefs report to a standing committee of council of the relevant area municipality, with the exception of the Ancaster chief, who reports to the committee-of-the-whole. The full-time chiefs are treated as full department heads, and are accordingly given that status in the local administration. A similar status is not formally accorded to the part-time chiefs in Flamborough and Glanbrook. The most important implication of this is that the fire department is not automatically consulted on building and development proposals in the townships as they are elsewhere.

The total number of firefighters in the Region now amounts to 468 full-time and 283 part-time, a moderate increase from the 442 full-time and 258 part-time personnel in the Region in 1972. Table 11.4 shows the distribution of the firefighters among the area municipalities, and the fire department budgets.

Our research indicates that all fire departments are capable of satisfactory performance in terms of time taken to respond to fire alarms; the average time falls

Table 11.4: Municipal Net Operating Budgets for Fire Services in Hamilton-Wentworth Region, 1977

Municipality	Population	Fire Fighters full-time	Fire Fighters volunteer	Fire stations	Fire budget
Ancaster	14,118	8	16	1	$ 129,534
Dundas	19,328	16	20	1	465,394
Flamborough	23,867	—	123	5	194,045
Glanbrook	10,039	—	49	2	53,850
Hamilton	311,907	437	—	10[1]	10,724,986
Stoney Creek	32,099	7	75	3	371,800
Regional Total	411,358	468	283	22	11,939,609

[1] Includes facility at Mount Hope Airport.

SOURCES:
1. Andre Bernard et al., *Profile: Hamilton-Wentworth*, (Ottawa: Information Canada, 1975)
2. Hamilton-Wentworth Regional Planning and Development Department.
3. Regional budget documents.
4. Officers and fire chiefs of the area municipalities.
5. Municipal operating budgets for 1977.

well within the norm accepted for such services. It is clear, however, that the smaller volunteer departments are not as able as others to provide preventive services such as inspections. Though all departments in the Region do some prevention work, the obvious restrictions of manpower in the smaller departments do not allow for major programs of this kind. There is, however, no evidence that the fire losses experienced in the municipalities are directly related to the relative intensity of such preventive services.

Mention has been made of the non-fire functions of fire departments. The number of non-fire calls in the Region has been growing steadily over the years. In 1977, of a total of 5,524 calls responded to by the departments in the Region, fully 4,658 (or 84 per cent) were non-fire calls. It is clear, therefore, that the role of fire departments in providing other community safety services, such as answering calls for rescue work and for inhalators, is a large and important one.

Effective firefighting depends not only on ensuring that the men and equipment get to the scene as quickly as possible, but also that they know what to do when they arrive. Training, therefore, is an essential part of the program of every fire department. As might be expected, the training program of the full-time department in Hamilton is much more intensive than those of the volunteer departments. Nonetheless, regular training programs, under the direction of the Chief or Deputy Chief, are carried on in all departments. The fire personnel also periodically take advantage of courses offered by the Ontario Fire Marshal. There is as yet no integration of training programs or facilities in the Region.

EFFECT OF THE PROPOSAL TO RESTRUCTURE

Our recommendation to restructure local government into a single jurisdiction in the Region will have a substantial effect on the formal organization of fire services. We think, however, that the formation of a single department, reporting to the City of Wentworth council, can offer distinct advantages, and need not unduly disrupt current arrangements, or result in substantial increases in costs. Benefits will accrue from service rationalization, joint use of training facilities and coordinated allocation of equipment.

In our view, there should be a single department, under the direction of a chief who reports to the Planning and Development Committee of Council. Under such an arrangement the Fire Chief will work closely with the councillors and other department heads who deal with matters on which fire considerations are most important.

We suggest that there be district chiefs for the several areas now served by their own departments, ensuring continuity of direction and service. Our studies indicate that some consolidation may be advantageous in the services of present Glanbrook and Flamborough, and that is something to which the new administration will have to direct its attention.

We are impressed with the effectiveness and dedication of the volunteer firefighters in the Region, and strongly recommend that the use of volunteers continue under the new organization. Indeed, it may well be that in certain parts of the present City of Hamilton a role could be found for volunteers. Experience in three of the area municipalities has shown that full-time and volunteer firefighters can work together closely and effectively, and we would like to see this type of collaboration expanded. At the same time, the formation of a single department will bring to areas that now are served entirely by volunteers the advantage of drawing on the expertise of full-time specialists, who can act as a resource for the entire Region.

It would not be appropriate, in our view, to try to provide a common standard of service throughout the City of Wentworth. The demands of fire service in rural areas are not such as to require the full-time staff needed in urban Hamilton. The cost implications of such differentials in service are obvious, and should be taken into account through differential mill rates. This is one service for which, as indicated in Chapter 7 of this report, the councillors from the areas affected should be consulted before budget decisions are taken that will result in an increase in mill rates for the residents. Any new capital expenditures that benefit residents in more than one area, or indeed any operating expenditures that have the same effect, should be pro-rated over the benefiting areas.

> Recommendation 11.2: Fire services in the Region be combined into a single department that will continue to use an appropriate combination of full-time and volunteer personnel, the cost of whose services will be area rated to take account of continuing and acceptable differentials in level of service.

Emergency Measures

Formal emergency measures services began with the establishment of the Emergency Measures Organization within the Privy Council Office of the federal government in 1957. A program was instituted to involve all three levels of government, with the bulk of the finances provided by the federal and provincial governments. In Ottawa, the Emergency Measures Organization was replaced by the National Emergency Planning Establishment in 1974.

The provincial response to the federal initiative was to establish an Emergency Measures Branch, most recently located in the Ministry of the Solicitor General. The branch had the responsibility for coordinating provincial government activities in this field, and assisting municipalities in drafting plans for dealing with local emergencies. The branch and program were phased out by the end of 1975, and were replaced by a system whereby individual ministries are responsible for planning for, and dealing with, the specific types of emergencies that fall within their jurisdiction. Municipalities now gain assistance from several ministries, depending on the nature of the problem addressed. The provincial government does not normally provide any funds of its own to municipalities for this purpose, but will pass on funds made available by Ottawa.

Responsibility for responding to, and planning for, emergencies at the local level falls to the Regional Council. It has produced a number of documents in this regard, including a Disaster Procedures Manual, a Vital Services Directory, a Wartime Emergency Plan, and a Peacetime Emergency Plan.

An important part of maintaining continuing readiness is the function of on-going coordination with other organizations involved. Such groups include various departments of governments of all levels, fire departments, school boards, various volunteer groups, and other regional governments nearby. This work is performed by the Emergency Measures Planning Officer, who now acts part-time in this capacity. Total regional expenditures in 1977 are estimated to be approximately $37,000, of which half is recovered from senior levels of government.

In general terms, the Region seems to be fulfilling its responsibilities for emergency measures preparedness in a satisfactory manner. Areas of weakness are currently the subject of active study by appropriate groups, and the necessary lines of communication and coordination seem well established and effective. Since the situation in regard to this service seems satisfactory, we do not make any suggestions for changes. Bringing fire under a single integrating jurisdiction should expedite emergency measures planning.

Chapter 12

Social Services and Health

Among the services that most influence the quality of life in a community are the health and social services delivered locally. Both these fields are characterized by the involvement of all levels of government and also of the private sector. Local government in Hamilton-Wentworth, as in other parts of the province, has an important, though not a leading, role to play in providing these services.

Both fields of service suffer to some extent from a lack of overall coordination, though attempts are being made by the province to remedy this in certain respects. At the local level, for the municipally provided services, coordination can be achieved through the proposed Social Services and Health Committee of Council.

This chapter describes the health and social services at present provided and makes suggestions for improvements in the way that municipal responsibilities for them may be discharged.

Social Services

The term "social services" is used to describe a wide range of payments, programs and services that are provided in many different ways by private organizations and by governments. Nearly all of the social services that involve payments to or on behalf of individuals are provided by government, and are designed to provide a basic level of income for people who have no other support or who have insufficient incomes of their own. Other social services, which provide helping services to people or groups in need of such assistance, are offered by both governments and private organizations. The following section gives a brief description of the range of such services available in Hamilton-Wentworth.

FEDERAL GOVERNMENT PROGRAMS
The federal government provides direct payments to individuals through the following programs:

— Canada Pension Plan

— Old Age Security
— Guaranteed Income Supplement
— Veterans' Allowances
— Native People's Entitlements
— Unemployment Insurance
— Family and Youth Allowances.

The federal government also provides what are sometimes considered social services through a variety of programs such as the employment counselling, job-finding, and vocational training programs of Canada Manpower. Several community employment schemes have been embarked upon over the years, some of which have lasted, while others have not. Through a recent federal initiative, an attempt is being made to develop a community employment strategy for the region, involving federal, provincial and local officials as well as representatives from industry and labour. Special assistance of various kinds is made available by the federal government to veterans, native peoples and immigrants.

Large amounts of federal funds are transferred to the provincial government through cost-sharing programs, the single most important of which in the social service field is the Canada Assistance Plan. By its choice of projects it will subsidize, the federal government exerts a powerful influence on the services that are provided in the province. In addition to the Canada Assistance Plan, cost-sharing covers certain programs designed to assist blind and disabled people.

PROVINCIAL GOVERNMENT PROGRAMS

The provincial government provides direct financial aid to individuals through the following programs:

— Family Benefits (for long-term, unemployable people, and for deserted mothers)
— vocational rehabilitation training grants
— Guaranteed Annual Income System (income support for the elderly)
— Workmen's Compensation
— tax credits (geared-to-income tax reductions for the elderly, and in respect of property and sales taxes)
— Legal Aid (for people whose circumstances qualify them for this kind of help).

Provincial government helping services include counselling, referral and information services to Family Benefits recipients; training and rehabilitation programs for the handicapped; certain support services associated with the family court; assistance to former inmates of provincial penal institutions; and some community development services.

In addition to the programs it operates itself, the provincial government supports, through financial subsidy and through setting standards and inspection, a number of programs that are provided by the municipalities and private organizations. Provincial cost-sharing with municipalities includes the payments made for welfare, special assistance and supplementary aid under The General Welfare Assistance Act; homemakers and nurses services; day care for children whose parents qualify for subsidy; homes for the aged and elderly persons centres; and a variety of activities such as community development, information centres and leadership training. Certain facilities, such as day care and community centres, and certain services, such as homemakers and nurses, are licensed and inspected by the provincial government, though the actual programs are contracted for by the municipality. In addition, the province supervises the work of the Children's Aid Societies, and provides a subsidy of 80 per cent of their approved operating costs.

REGIONAL GOVERNMENT PROGRAMS

Under provincial government supervision, and under the terms of provincial statutes, the Regional Municipality of Hamilton-Wentworth administers several mandatory and discretionary programs. It makes direct payments to or on behalf of individuals for:

— General Welfare Assistance (short-term financial assistance)
— special assistance to recipients of general welfare
— supplementary aid to recipients of assistance from other government programs
— burial for indigents
— shelter in residential and nursing homes
— costs of mental examinations ordered by the court.

The Region also provides direct helping services through programs of counselling, day care, employment training, and operation of two homes for the aged.

In addition to providing services directly, the Region purchases services from a number of private community organizations. These include counselling, day care, and visiting homemakers and nursing services. The Region also gives direct grant support to a variety of local social service agencies, including information services, crisis services, neighbourhood services, and the like. The Region is responsible for raising 20 per cent of the operating budget of the Children's Aid Societies, and appoints four of its councillors to the board and executive committee of each Society.

SOCIAL SERVICES DEPARTMENT OF HAMILTON-WENTWORTH

Most of the Regional Council's responsibilities for welfare and social services are discharged by the Social Services Department, headed by a commissioner who reports to the Social Services Committee of Council. The department is the product of a long history of social service work in the area.

Prior to regionalization there were two social service administrations in the area: one operated by the county, and one by the city. The county administration had been formed in 1963, with the encouragement of the province, taking over responsibility from the constituent municipalities. Of the two departments, Hamilton's was by far the larger, with a staff of 96, compared to 9 in the county office. Understandably, the city department offered a wider range of services —such as day nurseries — than did the county.

Regionalization occurred at a time when, largely because of a prolonged strike, the Hamilton department was in a disordered and demoralized state. The opportunity was taken to reorganize completely the delivery of social services; with the strong support of Regional Council, a new and vital department has been developed from the units transferred from the city and county. New staff and programs have been added, and today the department provides a level of service to the entire Region that is the equal of any in the province.

The Social Services Department operates under the provisions of the following provincial statutes:

— The General Welfare Assistance Act, R.S.O. 1970, Chapter 192
— The Homemakers and Nurses Act, R.S.O. 1970, Chapter 203
— The Day Nurseries Act, R.S.O. 1970, Chapter 104.

The municipality recovers from 50 to 80 per cent of the program costs of its Social Services Department from the province, and 100 per cent when payments are made to non-residents of Ontario or to Indians. Table 12.1 shows the total departmental expenditures for selected years, and the net local cost after deducting the provincial subsidy.

Table 12.1: Total Expenditures and Net Cost to Municipalities of Social Services Department Expenditures

	City of Hamilton and Wentworth County 1972	1975	Regional Municipality 1976	1977
Total expenditure	$11,099,644	$18,805,206	$17,189,308	$19,237,668
Net municipal cost	2,488,684	4,254,077	4,417,997	4,676,308

SOURCE: Social Services Department of Hamilton-Wentworth.

The increase since 1972 is accounted for by several factors. Among the most important are increases in staff, salary revisions, the introduction of new programs, the provision of service to areas not formerly covered, and an increase in the level of payments as directed by the province. General inflation has, of course, contributed to a rise in many of the operating costs. The downturn of expenditure experienced in 1976 was in good part attributed to the restraints imposed by the provincial government.

An 8 per cent increase in benefits and a 30 per cent increase in welfare caseloads during 1977 caused that year's total expenditures to rise. The municipal cost — that portion not reimbursed through provincial grants — rose gradually over the period, reflecting a continuing rise in administration and other costs that are not so highly subsidized by the province.

By far the largest program is the administration of General Welfare Assistance. This is the income-support program administered by municipalities in Ontario to people who are otherwise without support and do not qualify for other governmental programs such as the provincial Family Benefits. Of the department's total staff of 142, 75 are involved full-time in the administration of General Welfare Assistance. Table 12.2 shows expenditures under this program and the numbers of people served.

Table 12.2: Payments Made, Municipal Cost, and People Served through Basic General Welfare Payments

	1972[1]	1975	1976	1977
1. (a) Payments 80% cost-shared with province	$ 7,880,706	$12,849,851	$11,027,566	$11,319,539
(b) Net municipal cost	1,576,141	2,569,970	2,205,513	2,238,160
(c) Persons served	130,569	131,097	100,521	105,826
2. (a) Payments 100% recoverable from province	456,781	434,414	417,227	721,613
(b) Persons served	3,358	4,288	4,032	5,680

[1] City of Hamilton only. Comparable figures for Wentworth County were not available.
SOURCE: See Table 12.1.

A separate staff of seven administers special assistance and supplementary aid under the terms of The General Welfare Assistance Act. These are payments to people in receipt of some government income support (and in a few cases to people who are otherwise self-sufficient) for needs over and above those provided for in the payments they are already receiving. Over 90 per cent of the applications for this kind of extra assistance come to the department on behalf of people who are already recipients of provincial Family Benefits. Table 12.3 shows the amounts paid under these programs, the net cost to the municipality, and the number of cheques issued.

Table 12.3: Payments Made, Municipal Cost, and Number of Cheques Issued for Supplementary Aid and Special Assistance

	City of Hamilton 1972	Regional Municipality of Hamilton-Wentworth		
		1975	1976	1977
1. Supplementary aid (80% recoverable)				
(a) Payments	$636,138	$678,426	$727,982	$937,570
(b) Net municipal cost	$127,228	$135,685	$147,596	$194,714
(c) Cheques issued	39,106	25,463	26,615	33,370
2. Supplementary aid (100% recoverable)				
(a) Payments	NIL	$ 268	$ 20	$ 4,055
(b) Cheques issued	—	4	1	201
3. Special Assistance (50% recoverable)				
(a) Payments	$438,662	$590,515	$642,309	$829,259
(b) Net municipal cost	$219,331	$295,258	$321,155	$414,630
(c) Cheques issued	32,374	23,206	26,569	28,703
4. Special Assistance (100% recoverable)				
(a) Payments	$ 105	$ 16,486	$ 17,914	$ 8,096
(b) Cheques issued	N/A	947	1,051	470

Note: Comparable figures for the County of Wentworth are not available.
SOURCE: See Table 12.1.

Because such a large proportion of the people who receive this extra assistance are already in receipt of Family Benefits, and because there is a close connection between the provincial and municipal programs — people who apply for provincial assistance are usually required to rely on municipal welfare for a period of three months before being transferred to the longer-term program — there have been suggestions that the administration of the two systems be combined. It has been argued that such a change would simplify the system from the client's point of view, since only one administration would have to be approached for all requirements.

We recognize that such a change would involve a substantial shift in provincial policy, and could be undertaken only after careful study of the policy and administrative implications. Because of the benefits that could result, and the simplification of what is now a confusing system to those who are dependent on it, we think that the attempt should be made, at least on a trial basis. We suggest that the experiment be made in the City of Wentworth, since this Region already has a good social services administration.

Because it is the municipal administration that has the most frequent dealings with the clients, and because they have the experience of dealing with the more difficult short-term cases, we think that any such combined administrative responsibility should be given to the municipal level. We think it would be quite inappropriate for the provincial administration to increase its staff to deal with those cases that are now a municipal responsibility.

If the municipality is to take over administrative responsibility for what are now provincial clients, there should be a revision of the financing formula so that local taxpayers are not burdened by the change. The cost-sharing formula should take into account not only the amount of actual benefits paid, but also the costs of administration involved in looking after the enlarged caseload.

A pilot project such as is suggested would give an excellent opportunity for the development of service and administrative standards and guidelines, now generally lacking throughout the system in Ontario.

Recommendation 12.1: The Ministry of Community and Social Services give serious consideration to using the City of Wentworth for a pilot project to combine the administration of Family Benefits and General Welfare Assistance under the local Social Services Department, and full compensation be made to the municipality for the added costs that it will thereby incur.

Subsidized day care is provided by the department to the children of parents whose financial circumstances qualify them for the service. In the main, these services are purchased by the department from more than fifty private day care centres in the region, and from private home day care operators. In addition, the department operates one large centre of its own, the Red Hill facility, with a staff of 20. This municipally operated centre specializes in children with difficulties such as mental, emotional or physical handicaps. The department has divested itself of the other day care centres that it used to operate directly. Table 12.4 shows cost and service figures for subsidized day care in the Region.

A separate division of the department, with a staff of 14, is responsible for providing counselling, homemaker and nursing services to people in need of them. In most instances, these services are purchased under contractual arrangements with such organizations as the Victorian Order of Nurses, the Visiting Homemakers Association, and Family Services of Hamilton-Wentworth, Inc. In addition, the

Table 12.4: Municipal Day Care Expenditures and Children Served

Program	1973	1975	1976	1977
1. (a) Purchase from private nurseries	$ 618,990	$1,325,131	$1,147,018	$1,172,790
(b) Municipal cost	123,798	265,026	229,404	234,558
2. (a) PHDC*		239,304	263,941	301,755
(b) Municipal cost		47,861	52,788	60,351
3. Municipal centres	8,133	20,683	59,816	214,714
(b) Municipal cost	1,627	4,137	11,963	42,943
Children served				
1. Purchase from private nurseries	1,268	1,850	1,571	1,396
2. PHDC	—	498	395	487
3. Municipal centres	61	73	117	201

*Private home day care
SOURCE: See Table 12.1.

Table 12.5: Expenditures, Net Municipal Cost and Caseloads for Homemakers and Nurses Services

	City of Hamilton 1972	Regional Municipality		
		1975	1976	1977
1. Homemakers and nurses services				
(a) Total expenditures	$287,956			
(b) Net municipal cost	$ 57,591			
(c) Number of visits	11,909			
2. Homemaker services				
(a) Total expenditures		$463,284	$339,369	$300,896
(b) Net municipal cost		$ 92,557	$ 67,874	$ 60,179
(c) Hours of service		166,654	117,957	119,504
3. Nursing service				
(a) Total expenditures		$161,563	$ 9,280	$ 5,609
(b) Net municipal cost		$ 32,313	$ 1,756	$ 1,122
(c) Number of visits		15,372	864	501

Note: Comparable figures for the County of Wentworth are unavailable.
SOURCE: 1972 figures from Social Services Department of Region of Hamilton-Wentworth, 1975-77 figures from Ministry of Community and Social Services; 1977 figures comprise 10 months actual and 12 months estimated.

division has a staff of 4 counsellors who provide direct service to General Welfare Assistance recipients. This division is also responsible for a work-training program designed to teach regular work habits and skills to people with unsuccessful work experience. Table 12.5 shows expenditures and caseloads for the homemakers and nurses services.

The large drop in nursing expenditures and visits is the direct result of a Ministry of Health home nursing project instituted in the Region, which has taken over many of the cases that would otherwise have been provided for by the department.

In addition to these major programs, the department is also active in co-ordinating its programs with those of Canada Manpower, the courts, and the other social service providers in the Region. Members of the staff of the department serve on a variety of committees dealing with specific and broad matters of social problems and policies.

It is the consensus that provision of municipal social services has improved substantially since regionalization, and that the Region is an entirely appropriate area for this service.

MUNICIPAL HOMES FOR THE AGED

The Regional Municipality of Hamilton-Wentworth operates two homes for the aged: Macassa Lodge, and Wentworth Lodge. Before regionalization, these homes were operated by the City of Hamilton and the County of Wentworth respectively.

The homes do not, as is common in other parts of the province, report through the Commissioner of Social Services: administrative responsibility falls to the Chief Administrative Officer. Each home has a management committee, which is a subcommittee of the Social Services Committee of Regional Council. There are four members on each subcommittee, and they meet monthly to oversee the management of the homes.

Each home offers a range of care for residents, from purely residential to quite intensive nursing care. Applicants are assessed on the basis of their need for the type of care offered by the homes, and are admitted on a first-come-first-served basis. Residents are charged for their accommodation and services, but if an individual cannot support these charges, the home uses the old age pension of the resident after passing on a small "comfort allowance" for personal needs. The operating deficits of the homes are financed 30 per cent by the Region and 70 per cent by the province, which recovers 50 per cent of the total deficit from the federal government.

Both homes are involved to some extent in services to the elderly in the community. These services include meals-on-wheels, wheels-to-meals, and vacation care, which is subject to the availability of beds at specific times. Some private home care is also provided.

Table 12.6 shows total operating costs and the municipal share of the deficit for the two homes.

In our view, the present administrative organization is unduly cumbersome. It is inappropriate that the Chief Administrative Officer and his staff should have to look

Table 12.6: Total Expenditures and Municipal Cost of Homes for Aged

	1972	1975	1976	1977
Macassa Lodge				
Total expenditures	$1,608,033	$2,629,913	$2,911,650	$3,159,731
Municipal cost	257,753	338,338	231,942	401,779
Wentworth Lodge				
Total expenditures	594,400	1,141,581	1,301,784	1,440,492
Municipal cost	9,830	101,094	98,528	124,192

SOURCE: See Table 12.1.

after the administrative needs of the homes. Such duties can only detract from the work of overall guidance of the municipal administration. This difficulty could easily be overcome, as it is in most other parts of Ontario, by having the homes report through the Commissioner of Social Services. Similarly, we question the necessity for management committees for these homes, especially in view of the time demands on the councillors. We think it would be sufficient for the Social Services and Health Committee to deal with the policy issues raised by both homes in the normal course of its work.

Recommendation 12.2: Wentworth Lodge and Macassa Lodge report to the Social Services and Health Committee of Council through the Commissioner of Social Services and the two management committees be discontinued.

AREA MUNICIPALITY PROGRAMS

The constituent area municipalities of the Hamilton-Wentworth Region do not play a major role in the provision of social services, though they do have a place in the system.

Under the provisions of The Elderly Municipal Residents Act the area municipalities are empowered to allow tax relief to senior citizens. Three of the area municipalities — Hamilton, Stoney Creek and Dundas — take advantage of this opportunity and provide relief in amounts of $75 or $100 per annum on the property tax. Other programs available are the provision of grants to Elderly Persons Centres, and the subsidization of transit fares for seniors and students. Table 12.7 shows the expenditures made in 1976 on these programs.

As noted, these payments are completely optional on the part of the municipalities making them. Since the existing programs are by no means uniform, and the Commission would like them to continue under the City of Wentworth, they should be financed by a special levy on the benefiting areas.

Recommendation 12.3: The cost of programs of tax relief for elderly

people and municipal subsidization of bus fares for the elderly and students be area rated.

Table 12.7: Expenditures by Area Municipalities for Services to Aged Persons and Services to Children, 1976

	Services to aged persons	Services to children
City of Hamilton	$1,430,739	$930,549
Town of Stoney Creek	49,538	—
Town of Dundas	25,919*	—
Town of Ancaster	6,900	—
Township of Flamborough	—	—
Township of Glanbrook	—	—

*Does not include $1,825 spent from a trust fund to subsidize local bus fares for seniors.
SOURCE: Information supplied to Commission by individual municipalities.

In addition, all of the municipalities except for Glanbrook have adopted the provisions of The Municipal and School Tax Credit Assistance Act and allow tax credits to elderly taxpayers equivalent to one half of municipal taxes up to a maximum of $150 per year. Since the credits are reimbursed to the municipalities by the Treasurer of Ontario and become a lien on each property, there is no cost borne by the municipalities except for administration.

THE PRIVATE, OR VOLUNTEER, SECTOR

There are literally dozens of private organizations that contribute in one way or another to the social service fabric of Hamilton-Wentworth. Some of these are large, such as the Family Service Agency, and others are very small. Some operate entirely with volunteer help, others employ fully qualified professionals. Most are non-profit, though a few are business enterprises. There is a wide range of services provided, including day care, debt counselling, drop-in centres and social research. Many of the agencies receive financial support from the United Way; grants and purchase-of-service arrangements with the Region and other levels of government, as well as private donations, provide other funds.

Among the private agencies, the Children's Aid Societies hold a special place. Operating under The Child Welfare Act, they have wide powers and responsibilities in keeping with their mandate to protect children.

Hamilton-Wentworth is one of only three areas of Ontario that has two Children's Aid Societies; Metropolitan Toronto and Essex are the others. Until 1954 there was one Children's Aid Society serving the City of Hamilton, and one serving the County of Wentworth. In 1954 a Catholic Children's Aid Society of Hamilton was formed with a mandate to serve the Catholic population of the city. In 1966 the Hamilton Children's Aid Society amalgamated with the Children's Aid Society of Wentworth County to serve the area that was later to become the Region of Hamilton-Wentworth, and the Catholic Society was simultaneously given responsibility for the same area.

Children's Aid Societies are given broad statutory responsibility for the care and protection of children who are neglected, abused or in jeopardy. They also have a mandate for adoption and protection of the interests of the newborn children of unmarried mothers. The work of the Societies involves them in investigating reports of child neglect or abuse, counselling, finding, funding and occasionally operating foster and group homes, and finding suitable adoptive parents. Both Societies employ professional staff for their many programs, and also call on the services of a large number of volunteers.

The boards of directors of the Children's Aid Societies are elected from among the members of the Societies. By statute, each board must have four councillors of the municipal government (in this case the Regional Council) who are also automatically members of the executive committees of the boards. In Hamilton-Wentworth, the councillors chosen are members of the Social Services Committee of Council.

Costs of the operations of the Societies are borne 80 per cent by the province and 20 per cent by the Region. The budgets of the Societies are presented to the Finance Committee of Council for approval, and thence submitted to the province. In the event of a dispute between the Society and council, a Child Welfare Review Board may be established to resolve the matter. In recent years there has been agreement between the Societies and council concerning budgets, and the cutbacks ordered have come from the provincial Ministry of Community and Social Services.

Table 12.8 shows expenditures of the two Children's Aid Societies in the Region and the net municipal cost.

Table 12.8: Expenditures of the Hamilton-Wentworth Children's Aid Society and the Catholic Children's Aid Society of Hamilton-Wentworth

	1972	1975	1976
CAS Total expenditures	$2,209,540	$3,212,780	$3,438,170
Municipal cost	674,296	642,700	687,634
CCAS Total expenditures	896,138	1,295,652	1,506,400
Municipal cost	239,375	247,891	301,280

SOURCE: Annual reports of the CAS of Hamilton-Wentworth and the CCAS of Hamilton-Wentworth.

The Ministry of Community and Social Services has recently announced far-reaching changes to be made in the organization of the provision of services to children. As yet it is too early to assess just how these changes will affect the system in the City of Wentworth; undoubtedly they will have a major impact on the Children's Aid Societies. In the light of this uncertainty, and in view of the general satisfaction expressed with the current relationships between the Societies and the municipal government, we do not make any suggestions for changes in this area.

Health Services

As with social services, health services in Ontario are provided by a complex combination of programs and services operated by all levels of government and by the private sector. In the health field, however, the role of the municipal level of government is not as large as in the provision of social services, and the role of the private sector is more important.

FEDERAL GOVERNMENT SERVICES

The federal government is involved in a number of aspects of health services. For example, through the programs of the Medical Research Council, the National Research Council and the Defence Research Board, the government finances — and thus influences priorities in — medical research. Another important activity is the work of the Food and Drug Directorate, which is responsible for the control, inspection and setting of standards for food, cosmetics, drugs and medical devices.

Undoubtedly, the most significant role of the federal government in the health field is its financial participation in the medical and hospital insurance programs. By providing half of the funds necessary for these programs, and by determining the requirements that must be met before payment will be made, the government has a strong influence on the design and conditions of these provincial programs. As a result of this federal involvement, the ten provincial health insurance schemes are roughly comparable, and the benefits are transferrable anywhere within the country.

PROVINCIAL GOVERNMENT PROGRAMS

The prime responsibility for health services and the regulation of the health field is given to the provincial governments under the British North America Act. In keeping with these powers, the province has undertaken the following responsibilities:

- universal compulsory medical and hospital insurance
- funding of all operating and most capital costs of hospitals
- establishing standards and regulations for such institutions as nursing homes

— funding home care services
— providing substantial funding for public health units operated at the municipal level
— regulating health practitioners
— providing grants to voluntary health agencies and organizations
— establishing and funding district health councils
— doing research and providing treatment and counselling in the field of drug and alcohol addiction.

The Ministry of Health is the department of the provincial government responsible for these activities. Through the operation of these programs, and through the passage of statutes and regulations, the province establishes the type and nature of health care services that are available in Ontario and delegates to the municipalities the responsibility for their implementation.

DISTRICT HEALTH COUNCIL

In keeping with provincial policy to seek local involvement in the design and operation of the health system, the Hamilton-Wentworth District Health Council was established in 1976, with the following responsibilities:

— identifying the health needs of the people of the area and considering alternative means of meeting those needs;
— planning a comprehensive health care program and establishing short-term priorities consistent with long-term goals; and
— coordinating all health activities to ensure a balanced, effective and economical service.

The District Health Council is entirely funded by the province and serves in an advisory capacity to that government. In addition, it has taken on the actual operation of a vocational/social rehabilitation program for ex-psychiatric patients, and an assessment and placement service for senior citizens and disabled persons who require some form of institutional or home care.

There is little doubt that, with the existence of the Regional Planning Department to provide consistent, area-wide information, the planning work of the Health Council has been facilitated by the existence of the regional government.

The Regional Council appoints three of its members to the District Health Council, which has a total membership of nineteen. To ensure the greatest possible coordination in planning health services, it would be useful if the municipal appointees to the Health Council were members of the committee of council dealing with local health services.

Recommendation 12.4: Municipal appointments to the District Health

Council be chosen from members of the Social Services and Health Committee of Council.

HAMILTON-WENTWORTH BOARD OF HEALTH

Under the terms of The Public Health Act, an appointed Board of Health is responsible for the provision of public health services in the Region. The board is composed of seven regional councillors and two citizens appointed by the provincial government. The actual services are delivered by the Regional Health Unit, whose chief executive officer is the Medical Officer of Health.

Of the total full-time Health Unit staff of 158, 84 are nurses and nursing supervisors. Among their many functions, one of the most important is making home visits to aged and disabled people, to parents of newborn infants and to ex-psychiatric patients. A total of 30,844 such visits were made in 1976. They also undertake school visits, and teach at pre-natal classes and venereal disease clinics.

Public health inspection is another major function of the Health Unit. Under a large number of provincial statutes and regional by-laws, the 17 inspectors check food-handling establishments, monitor septic tank installations and are generally responsible for abating public health nuisances and controlling communicable diseases and pests. In 1976 a total of 34,935 public health inspections were made.

The Dentistry Service, with a staff of 17, is responsible for teaching and encouraging preventive dental measures throughout the Region, and particularly in the schools. Dental clinics are also held in the City of Hamilton, for which the city pays the Health Unit. In 1976, 8,313 patients were served in the dental clinics.

The Unit also operates a psychiatric clinic, giving consultation and out-patient treatment to children and adolescents in the Region.

Prior to 1968, there were two boards of health in the area, one serving the city, and one the county. In that year, with the encouragement of the provincial government, the two were amalgamated to form a single unit, with representation of both city and county on the board. Effectively, therefore, public health services have been provided on a regional basis for ten years, and the impact of the creation of the Region has been minimal. Appointments of local councillors to the Board of Health are now made by one municipal council, not two, and budget approvals are similarly now needed from only one municipal council. In addition, the Health Unit is now provided with certain administrative services by the Region, rather than by the city. Apart from these minor changes, the public health function has been unaffected by the reorganization of local government in Hamilton-Wentworth.

The costs of the Health Unit are, in the main, underwritten 75 per cent by the province, with the Region paying the remainder. Some programs, such as the Child and Adolescent Centre, and the planned parenthood service, are fully financed by the province. To establish its budget, the Board of Health presents its estimates to the Regional Council. If approved, the estimates are then submitted to the Ministry of Health, which indicates the amount of the proposed services it is prepared to recognize as approved for cost-sharing purposes. Any proposed expenditures not approved by the Ministry must be either fully financed by the Region — hence needing council approval — or abandoned. Table 12.9 shows the Health Unit expenditures, and the local cost.

Table 12.9: Total Expenditures and Local Cost of Health Unit

	1972	1975	1976	1977
Total expenditures	$2,058,563	$2,901,445	$3,285,616	$3,219,939
Municipal cost	459,620	569,190	651,337	657,519

SOURCE: Annual reports of the Hamilton-Wentworth Regional Health Unit.

A substantial portion of the increase in the costs of the Health Unit are attributable to increases in the salary levels of the professional staff, especially the nurses who negotiated contracts during this period that made sizeable revisions to the salary scales. A concerted effort has been made to keep costs in line, as demonstrated by the decrease in the full-time staff of the Unit shown in Table 12.10.

Our studies, and the opinions we have solicited, indicate that the Health Unit is functioning effectively and providing an excellent service to the people of the Region. There is general agreement, too, that the present area and population of Hamilton-Wentworth are quite appropriate for the delivery of these public health services.

Table 12.10: Full-time Staff of the Hamilton-Wentworth Regional Health Unit

	1972	1975	1976	1977
Nursing (including administration and supervisory)	86	81	82	84
Inspectors	19	17	17	17
Dental	13	15	14	17
Mental health	12	16	15	15
Clerical/administrative	31	27	27	24
All other	6	4	4	1
Total	167	160	159	158

SOURCE: Annual reports of the Hamilton-Wentworth Regional Health Unit.

Among the concerns expressed to the Commission is one that suggests that as a special purpose body, the Board of Health is not fully and appropriately accountable to the municipal council. In fact, the board operates very much like a committee of council, since seven of its nine members are regional councillors. Nonetheless, we are concerned that the lines of accountability be completely clear. We think that the time has come to integrate the health service with the other functions of local government in the area. It is our view that the council is quite capable of handling this responsibility on its own, and no longer needs the device of a separate board. The functions of the Board of Health should be taken over by the Social Services and Health Committee of Council. Such a change would have the added advantage of bringing the Medical Officer of Health into full status as a member of the senior management team of the municipality.

Recommendation 12.5: The Board of Health be abolished, and its duties and functions assumed by the Social Services and Health Committee of Council.

INSTITUTIONAL SERVICES

Hamilton-Wentworth is well served by a variety of institutions capable of providing a range of care. Indeed, the hospitals serve a considerably larger community than just the Region itself. There are one teaching hospital, two civic hospitals, three public hospitals, one psychiatric hospital, three children's mental health centres, and eighteen nursing homes in the Region. At the beginning of 1977, the institutions in the Region had the following capacities:

- active treatment beds — 1,969
- chronic care beds — 407
- psychiatric active care beds — 115
- psychiatric chronic care beds — 505
- general rehabilitation beds — 95
- special rehabilitation beds — 77
- nursing home beds — 1,226
- children's mental health centres beds — 71

The operating costs of the hospitals are met from provincial funds, while nursing homes are privately operated, and receive their funds from fees and contractual arrangements. The municipal role in funding hospitals is confined to a discretionary one of assisting with the capital costs of new plant and equipment, and renovations. Table 12.11 shows the contributions that have been made in this regard.

In addition to making contributions for capital purposes, the Region also makes appointments to the Board of Governors of the civic hospitals. The Region appoints three councillors to the board and eight private citizens. In addition, the mayor of

Hamilton, or his designate, sits on the board. The Region also appoints one of its councillors to the board of the Joseph Brant Hospital in Burlington, and to the West Lincoln Memorial Hospital Board in Grimsby. These appointments are quite appropriate and should continue. In all instances where councillors are appointed, they should, whenever possible, be members of the Social Services and Health Committee.

Table 12.11: Contributions of Local Government to Capital Costs of Hospitals

	1972	1975	1976	1977
City of Hamilton	$855,969	$75,190	$56,670	$61,280
Wentworth County	118,173			
Regional Municipality		939,057	1,069,141	1,101,120

SOURCE: Budget documents of the municipalities.

Recommendation 12.6: Councillors appointed to the boards of public hospitals be chosen from the Social Services and Health Committee of Council.

PRIVATE PRACTITIONER SERVICES

As with hospitals, Hamilton-Wentworth is well provided with private medical practitioners. Table 12.12 shows the number of doctors in the Region, and in the province as a whole. The relatively high number of specialists is undoubtedly the result of the presence of the high quality of institutional facilities found in the hospitals of the Region. As with hospitals, the physicians serve a larger area than just the Region.

Local government has no part to play in the payment of private practitioners for their services.

Table 12.12: Doctors in the Hamilton-Wentworth Region and in the Province of Ontario

	Hamilton-Wentworth	Number per 1,000 population	Province of Ontario	Number per 1,000 population
General practitioners	277	.67	5,568	.68
Specialists	335	.80	5,420	.66
Total	612	1.47	10,998	1.34

SOURCE: Ontario Ministry of Health, 1976.

VOLUNTARY AGENCIES

There are many private agencies in Hamilton-Wentworth whose services relate to the health field. Though their expenditures are relatively small in comparison to the other sectors, these agencies provide valuable services.

Some of the agencies, like the Migraine Foundation, specialize in providing information to the public about access to various services. Others, such as the Society for Crippled Children, provide direct service and act as advocates for people with specific disabilities or diseases. Each has a role, and each finds funds through some combination of government assistance, fees for service, United Way, or private donations. The variety and activity of these groups is a tribute to the community spirit of the Region.

Chapter 13

Parks, Recreation, Libraries and Cultural Facilities

This chapter deals with those local services that are designed to enrich the private lives and leisure-time activities of residents of the Region: parks, recreation, libraries, and a variety of special purpose bodies of a cultural and recreational nature. Because of close similarities in administration, and because of some present instances of joint administration, we also deal with cemeteries in this chapter.

Parks and Recreation

Although parks and recreation are not identical in purpose and have substantial differences in administration, we deal with both subjects under this heading. The prime reason is that the actual administration in some of the municipalities is combined, and it has been impossible to separate them entirely for purposes of analysis.

As is common in so many fields, more than one level of government has an interest in parks and recreation. The federal government has a nation-wide system of parks, though none is found in the Hamilton-Wentworth Region. Federal recreation programs in the area are not so visible, although assistance is given to a variety of activities through grant programs, and through the dissemination of information.

The province, too, has programs in this field. Provincial parks are maintained throughout Ontario, though the closest one to the Region is Bronte Park, in Halton. The Conservation Authorities, joint provincial-municipal bodies, provide substantial parkland, and are dealt with in a following section of this chapter. Provincial recreation programs are fostered primarily by the Ministry of Culture and Recreation. Probably the most important of its programs from the local point of view is the assistance in training, information and financial support given to local recreation departments. Financial assistance is also available through such programs as those supporting community centres and elderly persons centres. Similarly, municipalities may benefit from grants provided through the Ontario Arts Council and

Wintario. Though provincial grants usually have standards that must be met in order to qualify, there are no overall provincial regulations setting down what municipalities must provide in the way of parks or recreational facilities and services.

EXISTING LOCAL SERVICES

Under The Regional Municipality of Hamilton-Wentworth Act the area municipalities are responsible for providing parks and recreation facilities and programs. The municipalities discharge their responsibilities in this regard in different ways. They have been little influenced by regionalization, though the Regional Act does call for the dissolution of all boards of recreation, parks and community centres that formerly had responsibility for operating facilities; the local councils now assume direct responsibility themselves. It may be that, with certain of their former functions transferred to the regional level, the area municipalities now give a higher priority to these programs than previously. Certainly, they are spending more on these services than before regionalization.

There is no common pattern to the way that the area municipalities have organized themselves to provide parks and recreation services. Ancaster has a separate recreation department with four full-time staff. It operates a variety of programs such as a swimming pool, two arenas, senior citizens programs, community centres, and a variety of other programs. The town's eighteen parks are managed by the Works Department, using a full-time staff of five for that purpose. There are also three full-time arena employees who are part of the Works Department.

The Town of Dundas has a Recreation Department with a staff of nineteen, and a Parks Department with a staff of nine, of whom two also serve in the Recreation Department on a seasonal basis. At the time of regionalization the Parks and Cemeteries departments were combined. Both departments report to the same committee of council, and are assisted by a citizens' advisory committee.

The Township of Flamborough has a unique organization for providing its parks and recreation services. The council has a Recreation Committee made up of the mayor, five councillors, and three citizens. This committee oversees the work of nine local recreation subcommittees, each comprising a councillor and five citizens who serve without remuneration. These subcommittees are responsible for recreation activity in the various communities making up the township. The three arenas are governed by an Arena Board of Management made up of the mayor, five councillors and three citizens; the eleven arena employees (five of whom work on recreation activities only in the winter months) are the only full-time staff employed by the municipality for recreation purposes. As can be seen, a very heavy reliance is placed on volunteer citizen activity to foster and carry out the recreational programs of Flamborough. Although the township provides the recreation subcommittees with a small budget, they are responsible for raising most of the money they need to operate, including the costs of maintaining the parks in their communities, and often of improving their facilities.

In the Township of Glanbrook parks and recreation activities are operated by a Recreation Department of five full-time employees, which reports to the Recreation Committee of Council. Since regionalization there has been a marked increase in recreational expenditures, and the municipality has employed a full-time, qualified Director of Recreation to oversee all the programs.

The City of Hamilton has a Parks and Recreation Committee, which is also responsible for cemeteries and historic sites. This committee is assisted in its work by a citizens' advisory committee. Administratively, there are separate Parks and Recreation departments, with 136 and 105 full-time staff, respectively. As is to be expected in a large urban centre, a wide variety of programs is offered, and a wide range of facilities provided. Members of the Recreation Department, like their counterparts in the other area municipalities, work very closely with a number of community groups, and assist them in conducting their programs.

Stoney Creek has a Recreation and Parks Department that reports to the Recreation and Parks Committee of Council. Its responsibilities also include looking after the municipal cemeteries, which occupies three of the twenty-two full-time employees of the department. Twelve staff are involved in the maintenance and upkeep of the various facilities, and the remainder are concerned with providing programs and services.

Table 13.1: Parks and Recreation Departmental Budgets, 1977

Municipality	Population	Budget	Budget per capita
Ancaster	14,118	$ 351,700	$24.80
Dundas	19,328	704,406	36.66
Flamborough	23,867	504,300	21.22
Glanbrook	10,039	296,409	29.50
Hamilton	311,907	6,622,990	21.21
Stoney Creek	32,049	843,250	27.76

SOURCE: The Region and area municipalities.

Unfortunately, because of different and changing accounting practices, it has has not been possible to derive fully comparable figures for parks and recreation activity. In Table 13.1, however, we present information about the services as they stood in 1976. The expenditure figures are gross, and do not take into account the revenues that the recreation activities generate. From the table it is obvious that the different municipalities put varying emphases on their recreational and parks activities.

Private facilities and programs are also very important in assessing a community's recreational and open-space services. Hamilton-Wentworth has a rich variety of private facilities and organizations for almost every kind of pursuit imaginable, including flying, flamenco dancing, singing and swimming.

PROPOSED ORGANIZATION

Strong arguments are made for the provision of municipal recreation services on a very local basis, and for the need to encourage volunteers into the management and operation of the programs. Our recommendation of a single municipal jurisdiction for the area means that there will be a single recreation department for the entire Region. To maintain sensitivity to local wishes, therefore, it will be necessary to ensure that the new Recreation Department provides programs on a decentralized basis. Elsewhere we recommend that some of the staff of the new city be located in the offices now occupied by the area municipal administration. We think it would be advantageous to have recreation staff among those located in what will become the decentralized district offices. Such an arrangement will ensure that local volunteers, and citizens interested in local recreation programs, will not be isolated from the officials responsible for providing the administrative back-up. It will also provide for all citizens to have access to local representatives of the department, and through them, to the expertise of the headquarters staff.

Good use is currently made by some of the area municipalities of citizen advisory committees, and we think the device should be incorporated into the organizational planning for the new department. Local committees could be established for each of the district offices, thereby enabling local needs and considerations to be taken into account in the development and operation of programs.

The acquisition and maintenance of parks is not a function that requires the same degree of local involvement as recreation, though some of the area municipalities have demonstrated that volunteer committees can do an excellent job of looking after local park facilities. Our studies indicate that there are administrative advantages to be gained by having all the parks of the Region handled by a single department, and that definite economies may be expected from such an amalgamation. In our view, there is every reason to expect that a consolidated Parks Department of the City of Wentworth can provide the necessary service while still maintaining a sensitivity to the varying needs of different parts of the municipality.

Recognizing the differences in approach and administrative techniques between parks and recreation, we suggest that separate departments be established for each function in the City of Wentworth. But since there are many points of contact between the two functions, and because in many instances their programs must be carefully coordinated at the administrative level, we suggest that in the interests of both efficiency and economy there be a single Commissioner of Parks and Recreation reporting to council through the Parks, Recreation and Culture Committee.

We also recognize that the total expenditures for parks and recreation are significantly higher for urban populations than for rural. Accordingly, we suggest that the costs of these two services be allocated on a differential urban-rural basis for taxing purposes.

> Recommendation 13.1: A Recreation Department be created for the City of Wentworth, reporting to the Parks, Recreation and Culture Committee of Council through the Commissioner of Parks and Recreation, and that it have staff located in the district offices assisted by local citizens' advisory councils for recreation.
>
> Recommendation 13.2: A Parks Department be created for the City of Wentworth, reporting to the Parks, Recreation and Culture Committee of Council through the Commissioner of Parks and Recreation.
>
> Recommendation 13.3: Expenditures of the Parks and Recreation departments be allocated throughout the municipality on a differential urban-rural basis.

Cemeteries

Under The Cemeteries Act, municipalities are responsible for administering municipally owned cemeteries and any other cemeteries that are declared abandoned. In Hamilton-Wentworth this function falls to the area municipalities.

Different arrangements have been made by the municipalities to look after this responsibility. The City of Hamilton, for example, has a separate Cemeteries Department, while in Dundas and Stoney Creek it is looked after by the Parks Department and Parks and Recreation Department respectively. Ancaster has a separate Cemetery Board made up of private citizens. Flamborough has three such boards, and Glanbrook has two. Throughout the Region there are also a number of private, often church-related, cemeteries that do not fall under municipal administration.

Hamilton is the only municipality that spends a significant amount on cemeteries; in 1977 its budget for this function was $1,057,500. Hamilton has a policy of charging a higher rate for use of its cemeteries to non-residents of the city than to residents.

Our recommendation for a single-tier municipality will bring all local responsibilities for cemeteries under a single jurisdiction, affording an opportunity to abolish the differential charges currently levied by Hamilton. We think that there is merit in the approach that has been taken by Dundas and Stoney Creek which assigns the maintenance of the cemeteries to the Parks Department. While not all the problems of cemetery maintenance are similar to those of parks, there is much in common. The proposed new Parks Department will, for example, be able to employ specialists in the care of trees and shrubs, whose skills could be used by the cemeteries as well as all the parks in the area. Properly handled, we think that there is a good chance for economies to accrue through the advantageous allocation of staff and equipment. This should result in a decrease in the present costs of maintaining both parks and cemeteries.

There are matters of cemetery administration quite separate from grounds maintenance. While this is admittedly a specialized task, we do not think that it is so substantial a function as to require a separate department in the civic administration. A separate unit in the Parks Department could be established to look after such matters.

> Recommendation 13.4: Responsibility for municipal cemeteries be consolidated in the proposed Parks Department of the City of Wentworth, with a separate unit established within that department to look after matters of cemetery administration other than maintenance.

Libraries

EXISTING SERVICES

In Ontario, municipalities are given authority to establish public libraries by provincial statute. There are three public library systems in Hamilton-Wentworth: Dundas, Hamilton and Wentworth.

Both the Hamilton and Dundas libraries are established under the provisions of The Public Libraries Act. Accordingly, each has a library board comprising the mayor of the municipality, three citizens appointed by council, three by the Board of Education, and two by the Separate School Board. Although the province provides a small grant to each, the main source of funds for these libraries is the municipality, which incorporates library needs in its local tax levy after approving the library board budget.

Each of these libraries offers services in a wide range of materials including records, talking books and films. While the Dundas Library operates from a single building, Hamilton has its central library, nine branch libraries, an extension service that provides books for people in nursing homes and senior citizens' apartments, and a library service in St. Peter's Hospital and Geriatric Centre. Neither of these libraries has been significantly affected by the introduction of regional government in the area.

The Wentworth Library, serving those parts of Hamilton-Wentworth outside the City of Hamilton and the Town of Dundas, is significantly different from its two counterparts in several respects. Its history can be traced to the formation of the Wentworth County Public Library Cooperative in 1947. By 1966 the Wentworth County Public Library was formed, and gradually but steadily spread its services throughout the area it served. In 1974 it was amalgamated with the Stoney Creek Public Library to form the Wentworth Library as it now exists.

The special circumstances of adapting the terms of The Public Libraries Act to a library that serves several but not all the area municipalities of a region resulted in The Regional Municipality of Hamilton-Wentworth Act giving the Treasurer and Minister of Economics and Intergovernmental Affairs the power to do whatever he found necessary to provide library services to that part of the Region not served by the Hamilton and Dundas boards. As a result, the Wentworth Library Board was established by Ministerial Order, which also charged the Regional Municipality to pass a by-law to operate and maintain the board. A by-law of the Regional Municipality appoints a seven-member board composed of three regional councillors and four citizens, each from a different area municipality.

To accommodate the special circumstances of the composition of the library board, a unique procedure has been established for approving its budget. The board first submits its budget to the Regional Finance Committee. Approval by that body is followed by referral to the area municipal councils for comment. Any comments are then taken into account by the Finance Committee, which forwards the budget with its recommendations to the Regional Council. Although the system offers an opportunity for any one of the affected area municipalities to impede budget approval, such obstruction has not in fact occurred, and the whole process has been characterized by a spirit of cooperation. The appointment to the board of locally elected representatives may account to a large extent for the smoothness with which budget matters are handled.

To serve the widespread area within its jurisdiction, the Wentworth Library has fifteen libraries and six book centres. These book centres, formerly called deposit stations, are collections of books located in private homes, stores and community centres, with no set hours of operation, and no specifically designed library facilities. Materials available include records, films, projectors and cassette tape players.

Although the three library systems in the Region are quite separate and independent, there are several cooperative arrangements that make them, in concert, into what is effectively a coordinated library system for the Hamilton-Wentworth Region. Inter-library loan arrangements make it possible for patrons of any branch of the three libraries to have access to material held by any library in the Region. Similarly, patrons of one library may use any other library, as the cards are honoured throughout the Region.

All three libraries are members of the South Central Regional Library, composed of all public libraries in the Regional Municipalities of Halton and Hamilton-Wentworth and the County of Brant. Each of the nine member libraries appoints a representative to the board, which under the terms of The Public Libraries Act has responsibility to improve standards by providing a plan for coordinating and developing library service.

These existing cooperative arrangements appear to work well, and it is questionable whether, from a service point of view, an amalgamation would in fact bring benefits to members of the public using the libraries.

PERFORMANCE

There are substantial differences in the operating performance of the three libraries. Table 13.2 provides information on population served, operating costs, and units of service. For purposes of comparison, we also show performance figures for the Ottawa Public Library, which serves the Ontario city most comparable in size to Hamilton.

Several points deserve comment. Utilization of the Dundas Library, and its costs per capita, are much higher than the others, indicating a distinct difference in the importance placed on this service by people in that community. Significant, too,

Table 13.2: Comparative Statistics on Libraries

	Dundas	Wentworth	Hamilton	Ottawa
Population served	19,212	77,957	312,162	302,124
Gross expenditures	$293,904	$522,910	$3,787,725	$3,398,365
Circulation	243,404	502,810	1,963,587	2,157,406
Expenditure per unit of service	$ 1.25	$ 1.04	$ 1.93	$ 1.58
Expenditure/capita	$ 15.29	$ 6.70	$ 12.14	$ 11.24
Units of service/capita	12.2	6.45	6.29	7.14
Salaries as a per cent of total expenditures	54	61	66	61
Library materials as a per cent of total expenditure	17	23	10	15

SOURCE: Ontario Library Review, December, 1977. Data based on 1976 figures.

is the fact that the Wentworth board, despite the large geographical area it must serve, is able to support a utilization rate slightly higher than Hamilton's at a cost per unit of service just slightly over half that experienced by the city board. The proportion of budget devoted to salaries and to library materials shows that the Hamilton board uses a larger portion for salaries and a smaller portion for materials than any of the others. By all these measures, the performance of the Hamilton board appears to be least efficient.

Comparison of Hamilton with Ottawa demonstrates that the former's performance is not completely the result of diseconomies of scale. On every indicator of performance the Ottawa Library, which provides services bilingually, outperforms Hamilton. With a total budget now in the neighbourhood of $4 million, the cost implications of poor library performance should not be ignored. We suggest that the Hamilton Library concentrate on improving its management and service delivery, and that note be made of need for improvement in this regard by municipal councillors.

Recommendation 13.5: Immediate attention be given to improving the administrative efficiency of the present Hamilton library system.

PROPOSED ORGANIZATION

Our proposal for a single municipality for the entire Region would ordinarily lead to the conclusion that a single library board be established for the area. We recognize, however, that the people of Dundas have for years placed much greater emphasis on this service than have the residents of other communities in the Region, and have developed a library that meets their local preferences. We note also that inter-library cooperation places the entire library resources of the Region at the disposal of all residents, and conclude that no appreciable improvement in actual service to patrons would be likely to result from unification of the libraries. In addition, we can foresee no administrative advantage to amalgamation and, indeed, suspect that the relatively low-cost service provided by the two smaller libraries might suffer if they were to be consolidated with the larger Hamilton system. Accordingly, we conclude that the three existing library systems should continue under the City of Wentworth. It may be that some time in the future the residents of the new city may decide that amalgamation would be advantageous. At present, however, we do not think that circumstances warrant such a change.

We think that the time has come to make the libraries more directly accountable to the municipal council. The Wentworth Library has clearly demonstrated that a library board composed in large part of elected officials can not only provide service of a high level at low cost, but can also overcome any potentially difficult matters of accountability to a variety of municipal councils. We also think that there may be advantages to having the same people who are responsible for the two smaller library services placed in charge of the Hamilton Library, where improvements in performance are clearly needed.

We suggest, therefore, that each of the three chief librarians report directly to the Parks, Recreation and Culture Committee of Council of the City of Wentworth. That committee should have the authority to create whatever advisory bodies it thinks might be helpful to it in discharging its responsibilities. It could, for example, create an advisory committee for each of the three libraries, and consult the school boards in the matter of appointments. In our view it is important, however, that responsibility and accountability for this service be clearly established and given to the elected municipal councillors.

As long as there are three libraries serving different parts of the area, the costs of this service should be distributed on an area rated basis. Indeed, area rating should continue as long as complete amalgamation of the service is not achieved.

> Recommendation 13.6: The three present library systems continue, and the chief librarians report directly to the Parks, Recreation and Culture Committee of Council, which shall be authorized to appoint whatever advisory committees it thinks might be able to assist in fulfilling its responsibility.

> Recommendation 13.7: Costs of library services be area rated to preserve the existing basis of charge so long as there is more than one library system in existence.

Special Purpose Bodies

Local government in Hamilton-Wentworth also makes a contribution toward the costs of several other organizations that provide recreational and cultural services in the area. The very variety of purpose and of organizational arrangements displayed by these bodies attests to the vitality of the Hamilton-Wentworth Region.

CONSERVATION AUTHORITIES

There are four conservation authorities operating within the boundaries of the Regional Municipality: Hamilton Region, Halton Region, Niagara Peninsula, and Grand River. These bodies, established under the terms of The Conservation Authorities Act, have a responsibility for flood and erosion control, flood plain acquisition, and the provision of public access to the open space they purchase in the course of discharging their other responsibilities. As a result, one of their most publicly visible activities is the provision of parkland and related facilities and programs. They are established on the basis of watersheds, and hence their boundaries do not often coincide with those of local government. Since Hamilton-

Wentworth is part of four separate watershed systems, it is represented on four conservation authorities.

The Regional Municipality of Hamilton-Wentworth appoints fifteen of the nineteen members of the Hamilton Region Conservation Authority; one is appointed by the Puslinch Township Council and three by the province. Two representatives are appointed by the Region to each of the Halton Region and Grand River Authorities and four to the Niagara Peninsula Conservation Authority. In each of these last three, the nominations are made by the appropriate councils of the area municipalities, and ratified by Regional Council.

Conservation authorities are financed through a combination of provincial funds and a levy on the participating municipalities designed to reflect the relative benefit that each municipality receives from the work that is being financed. The total contributions to all four authorities made by Hamilton-Wentworth in 1977 were $1,310,727.

ROYAL BOTANICAL GARDENS

The Royal Botanical Gardens are situated on two thousand acres mainly in Hamilton-Wentworth, but partly in Halton Region. As well as being a popular recreation site it also serves as a scientific, educational and cultural institution. It has a highly qualified staff who are active not only within the immediate area, but provincially, nationally and internationally as well.

The Regional Council appoints three of its own members and three citizens to the board of the Gardens, whose total membership is nineteen. Funding is provided by the municipalities concerned and by the provincial Ministry of Culture and Recreation. The municipal contributions are for operation and maintenance only; the development, scientific and educational programs are financed entirely by the province. For 1977, Hamilton-Wentworth Region contributed $458,300, Halton Region $26,200, Burlington $77,500, and the province $621,000.

HAMILTON PHILHARMONIC ORCHESTRA

In addition to its concert performances at Hamilton Place, the Hamilton Philharmonic Orchestra gives a large number of other concerts and clinics, many of which are in the schools, hospitals, senior citizens' homes and libraries of the Region. The members of the Hamilton Philharmonic Society, Inc. elect twenty-four members to the board of directors, to which the Hamilton City Council and the Regional Council each appoint one member.

The orchestra derives revenue from ticket sales, fees for performances, and private and corporate donations and sponsorship. The remainder of its funds come from grants provided by the Canada Council, the Ontario Arts Council, and the

Regional Council. The amount budgeted for the Region's contribution in 1977-78 is $107,000, or 10 per cent of the orchestra's total revenue.

ART GALLERY OF HAMILTON

The Art Gallery of Hamilton, greatly aided by the larger facilities into which it moved in the summer of 1977, provides a variety of services to the community, in addition to its art displays, including lectures, workshops, art rental, film showings and concerts, and an outreach and educational program that works closely with the schools. The members of the gallery elect twenty-four members to a board of management, which is augmented by two appointees of the City of Hamilton.

Memberships and donations raised by the gallery itself account for only a small portion of its budget: $88,000 (18 per cent) of a total of $495,893 in 1977. The remainder is obtained by government grants, of which that coming from the regional government is the largest, $243,900. The others are: Canada Council, $30,000; National Museums, $21,900; Ontario Arts Council, $57,625; and Wintario, $54,468.

HAMILTON PLACE

The Hamilton Performing Arts Corporation, Inc. was established under The City of Hamilton Act, 1972, to manage the affairs of Hamilton Place, which opened its doors in 1973. The building has two theatres, one seating 2,100 people, the other 400, as well as a number of meeting rooms available for rental. The management of Hamilton Place rents its facilities and also acts as impresario, doing its own bookings to bring a variety of entertainment that might not otherwise come to the area. The board of the corporation comprises four City of Hamilton councillors and five citizens, all appointed by Hamilton City Council.

Hamilton Place currently runs at a substantial deficit. Of a total budget for 1977 of $1,500,000, box office sales and all other earned revenue amounted to only $575,000, or 38 per cent. The deficit is funded by the City of Hamilton.

CANUSA GAMES COMMITTEE

The Canusa Games Committee is an independent volunteer organization that operates the Hamilton side of an exchange program with Flint, Michigan. The exchange takes the form of summer athletic competitions, involving some twenty-four teams. The games alternate between Flint and Hamilton, with athletes staying in the homes of their hosts. When they are held in Hamilton, the city provides most of the facilities, on a complimentary basis. In addition to providing facilities when needed, the city also gives an operating grant to the committee, an amount of $32,000 in 1977.

WENTWORTH PIONEER VILLAGE

Wentworth Pioneer Village, formerly called Westfield Village, is located on a thirty-seven-acre site in Flamborough and serves as an agricultural museum and pioneer village. Founded originally by a group of private citizens, it was purchased by the County of Wentworth in 1968. At the time of regionalization, it became a responsibility of the regional government, and is provided with administrative services through the Clerk's department.

The Pioneer Village is operated by a committee composed of four citizen volunteers and chaired by a regional councillor. All appointments are made by the Regional Council. The operating deficit of the village is funded by the Region, and involved an expenditure of $49,358 in 1977.

CANADIAN FOOTBALL HALL OF FAME

The Canadian Football Hall of Fame is a joint undertaking by the Canadian Football League and the City of Hamilton. The exhibits and the operation of the hall are looked after by the league, and the city underwrites the upkeep, maintenance and taxes of the building and property, which it owns. There is a management committee of nine members, including the mayor of Hamilton, two aldermen and three citizens appointed by the city. In 1977, the cost to the city was $82,587. A provincial grant of $18,096 was received to assist in the operating of the Football Hall of Fame.

CONCLUSION

In the main, we think that the special purpose bodies that are currently serving the recreational and cultural needs of the Region are doing a commendable job. Given the recommendation we make about a unified City of Wentworth, we suggest that all municipal appointments be made by that body. Otherwise, we think there is little reason to suggest changing arrangements that seem to be operating effectively and to the satisfaction of the residents of the area.

The one facility that gives us concern is Hamilton Place, with its extremely large deficit of costs over earned revenue. We strongly urge that an attempt be made to bring costs and revenues more into line one with the other.

Recommendation 13.8: Immediate attention be given to reducing the current deficit incurred in the operations of Hamilton Place.

As noted, some of the special purpose bodies are attached to the Region, and some to the city, for both appointments and grants. Under the proposed municipal organization it will be the City of Wentworth that makes appointments to the various boards. In our view it will help improve coordination of the recreational and cultural activities of the whole area if all municipal councillors who are appointed to these boards are members of the Parks, Recreation and Culture Committee of Council.

Recommendation 13.9: All municipal councillors from the City of Wentworth appointed to boards of special purpose cultural and recreational bodies be chosen from members of the Parks, Recreation and Culture Committee of Council.

In general, the need for, and the use of, special cultural and recreational facilities is greater in urban areas than in rural ones. Evidence of this may be found in the number of these special purpose bodies that are currently sponsored by the City of Hamilton. We think that the most equitable approach to funding these bodies under the proposed organization is to charge all costs now underwritten by the City of Hamilton to the urban-rural tax differential, and to general rate all costs now underwritten by the Region.

Recommendation 13.10: All contributions to special purpose cultural and recreational special purpose bodies now made by the Region be generally rated for tax purposes in the City of Wentworth, and all other such contributions be made as part of the urban-rural tax differential.

Chapter 14

The Implementation of Reform

This chapter addresses the issue of how best to implement the Commission's recommendations for a single-tier local government in the Hamilton-Wentworth area. The discussion and recommendations in this chapter are premised on two basic assumptions: first, on the assumption that the Government of Ontario will choose to accept our recommendations; and secondly, that the Government of Ontario will provide an opportunity for the citizens and municipalities of the Region to respond to and comment on our recommendations.

Throughout this report the Commission has emphasized the need for a strong, united government for the present area of Hamilton-Wentworth. Divisiveness has played a role for too long. We are very concerned that any indecision or delay in the implementation of our recommendations will only exacerbate existing problems. Therefore, while emphasizing the need for an opportunity to make comments on this report, the Commission thinks that every effort should be made to ensure that the City of Wentworth is fully operational by the beginning of 1979. Only if this is done will uncertainty and hostility be minimized among the citizens, the political representatives and administrative officials of the area. Moreover, the Commission is concerned that good staff may be lost if the period of uncertainty is extended.

Recommendation 14.1: The City of Wentworth be constituted effective the 1st day of January, 1979.

Few if any immediate changes will be required to enable the major services currently being carried on by the Regional Municipality to continue after the establishment of the City of Wentworth. It is essential, however, that the present level of services, both regional and local, is not lowered because of the establishment of the new municipality at such an early date. Accordingly, it is imperative that the council of the City of Wentworth be elected earlier than the normal municipal election date. Moreover, it should have the authority of a municipal council for the purposes of appointing and organizing its staff. It must not have to wait until January 1, 1979 for this authority. This will enable it to have as much staff as possible in place on January 1, 1979. This authority, however, should not extend to the passing of by-laws for the purposes of any levy nor for the purpose of the general governance of the municipality; existing municipalities should continue until the end of 1978.

>   Recommendation 14.2: The election of the council of the City of Wentworth occur no later than early October 1978.

>   Recommendation 14.3: The council so elected have authority to hire and organize staff.

>   Recommendation 14.4: The major priority of the new council be the development of a system to assure the continuation from January 1, 1979 of all services already provided by the regional and area municipalities at present levels until the establishment of the City of Wentworth is in full operation.

The task of organizing a new municipality in three months is a monumental one. There is a need to ensure that all existing policies respecting the delivery of services are gathered and continue to be implemented on the establishment of the City of Wentworth, so that there will be no disruptions in service. Those policies may also be used as the basis of evaluating any changes in service by the City of Wentworth. Moreover, the establishment of a new single-tier municipality should be viewed as an opportunity to ensure that it has the best possible staff and appropriate policies in this regard must be developed. With so much work to be done, preparations for the establishment of the City of Wentworth should begin even before the election of the new council. Representatives chosen by each of the municipalities in the Region can help in such a task, and a Steering Committee should be appointed as soon as possible for this purpose.

>   Recommendation 14.5: Immediately after the coming into force of the legislation each area municipality and the Regional Municipality appoint one of its members to a Steering Committee, a function of which will be to study and make recommendations to the council of the City of Wentworth on staff, salaries, quality of personnel, early retirement and staff requirements.

>   Recommendation 14.6: The Steering Committee oversee the collection and organization of all policies now used by the Region and area municipalities to provide a basis for subsequent deliberations on, or changes in, policies in the City of Wentworth.

This committee will need a great deal of assistance. It will have to begin an evaluation of all existing staff in order to develop recommendations for the personnel requirements of the City of Wentworth. This it cannot do alone. It should, therefore, have the assistance of the present regional staff and should, the Commission thinks, also have the help of management consultants. The assistance of regional staff can be supplied, and paid for, by the Region. The aid of consultants requires provincial payment and involvement.

Recommendation 14.7: The Steering Committee in conjuction with the Province of Ontario appoint management consultants to aid in personnel selection, organization, and development of management systems, including staff salaries, number of personnel, quality of personnel, early retirement and staff requirements.

Recommendation 14.8: The Province of Ontario provide assistance to the Steering Committee and bear the cost of retaining management consultants.

Recommendation 14.9: The present Regional Coordinator and those of his staff appointed by him assist the Steering Committee.

As has been mentioned, the Steering Committee is to ensure that preparation for the establishment of the new City of Wentworth begins at the earliest possible date before the election of the new council. When the new council is elected, the Policy and Finance Committee can replace the Steering Committee in overseeing the development of recommendations for the administration of the new municipality. Moreover, the Policy and Finance Committee should recommend to council at the earliest possible date the appointment of a Chief Admintrative Officer who can then work with the Policy and Finance Committee and the consultants on all further staff requirements and appointments. This will provide effective leadership in the establishment of the new municipality's administration. Council can then make further appointments to become effective January 1, 1979.

Recommendation 14.10: As its first items of business the council of the City of Wentworth choose the mayor, heads of standing committees, and its representative on the police commission and thus form the Policy and Finance Committee.

Recommendation 14.11: The Policy and Finance Committee immediately upon its formation assume all responsibilities of the Steering Committee and the Steering Committee cease to exist.

Recommendation 14.12: The Policy and Finance Committee, with the help of the management consultants, consider and recommend to council the appointment of a Chief Administrative Officer for the City of Wentworth who will work with the Policy and Finance Committee and the management consultants on all further recommendations on staff requirements and appointments.

The recommendations with respect to the role of the Steering Committee, the Policy and Finance Committee, the consultants and the Chief Administrative Officer are largely intended to ensure that the City of Wentworth appoints the best possible staff. Not all persons now employed by the seven municipalities that make up the Region will be retained by the City of Wentworth. The Commission's views that efficiencies can be achieved in general government by a move from seven municipalities to one means that staff reductions can occur without any disruption in services. It is of great importance, however, that decisions respecting staffing be made in the fairest way possible and that adequate notice and severance pay be provided.

Recommendation 14.13: The existing municipalities freeze, except in emergency situations, the creation of new positions and the filling of vacancies from the date of the release of this report until January 1, 1979.

Recommendation 14.14: Existing staff employed by the Region continue to be employed in the same capacity by the City of Wentworth with the understanding that the staff review referred to in Recommendation 14.5 will include a review of all positions in the city, with particular attention to those areas where service is provided both by the Region and the area municipalities, so that where possible all positions are ultimately filled from the best qualified employees in the total staff of all seven municipalities.

Recommendation 14.15: The Policy and Finance Committee endeavour to recommend all necessary staff appointments by January 1, 1979, and no later than March 31, 1979. All persons interested in pursuing positions not filled by January 1, 1979, be entitled to employment at their present salary in any capacity assigned to them until March 31, 1979. By March 31, 1979, all employees should be notified as to whether they are required by the City of Wentworth. If they are not required they should be given not less than six months' severance pay.

Recommendation 14.16: Negotiations be carried out between the City of Wentworth, the Government of Ontario and the Ontario Municipal Employees Retirement System regarding offering options of early retirement without detriment to interested members of existing municipal staffs who are nearing normal retirement age, and legislation be enacted to accommodate such arrangements.

There are a number of financial concerns that arise with respect to implementation, some of which are dealt with in Chapter 7. The start-up costs of the new municipality, and the small tax increases described in Chapter 7 for the urban parts of the towns of Ancaster, Dundas and Stoney Creek, require attention. It is also important to ensure that no unwarranted disposal of public assets takes place in the period before the establishment of the new local government.

Recommendation 14.17: The Government of Ontario bear all start-up costs of the establishment of the City of Wentworth, such as early retirements costs, road signs, vehicle identification, and stationery costs on a negotiated basis.

Recommendation 14.18: The tax increases for the urban parts of the towns of Ancaster, Dundas and Stoney Creek be phased in over the three years 1979, 1980 and 1981 so that the full burden of those increases not become payable until 1982.

Recommendation 14.19: Subject to any overriding province-wide transitional assistance policies that may be developed to deal with general tax or grant reform, the Government of Ontario pay in one lump sum the full costs of the transitional tax assistance required by Recommendation 14.18, estimated on the basis of the 1977 municipal budgets to total $806,000, and the City of Wentworth place this sum in a Reserve Fund, to be invested and used to reduce the appropriate taxes in each of the three years to 1981.

Recommendation 14.20: No existing municipality dispose of any assets worth more than $5,000 from the date of the release of this report.

Most assets and obligations of the existing municipalities should be assumed by the City of Wentworth without adjustment when it is established. The assets are public property, and no resident will be deprived of the use of them when the new city is created. This is in keeping with the precedent set in 1953 by the Ontario Municipal Board when Metropolitan Toronto was set up, and that has been followed for each regional government established since then.

Recommendation 7.21: All the assets and obligations of the Hamilton-Wentworth municipalities be assumed by the City of Wentworth on the date of its inception.

In legislation establishing restructured governments in Ontario it has been the practice to ensure that any surplus of the pre-existing municipalities are used to the benefit of the taxpayers who have financed them. Similarly, any operating deficits are met by the taxpayers in the areas responsible. We think this is an entirely equitable arrangement, and should be followed in the City of Wentworth when it is established. Apart from the equity involved, it has the effect of removing any incentive for municipalities to run balances down in their last year of existence.

Recommendation 7.22: The audited surplus or operating deficit of each Hamilton-Wentworth area municipality at the time of the establishment of the City of Wentworth accrue to the credit of, or become a charge on, the assessment supporting such surplus or operating deficit.

We think that these implementation recommendations will ensure the successful establishment of the new City of Wentworth. Nevertheless, the council and administrative staff and citizens will have the ultimate responsibility for its success. All will have a stake in the state and operation of the municipality. Of particular concern will be the balance of representation, the functioning of the committee system, the state of finance, and the operation of the departmental organization. By keeping the citizens regularly informed of these matters the City of Wentworth will be better able to determine the need for change. The Commission thinks, therefore, that there should be a formal evaluation of the functioning of local government in the City of Wentworth each year.

Recommendation 7.23: The mayor and Chief Administrative Officer of the City of Wentworth publish a report annually on the state of the municipality of the City of Wentworth.

The recommended annual report will be of interest not only to the citizens of Wentworth, but also to other municipalities, to scholars studying local government, to the governments of Ontario and of other provinces in Canada. Such reports will give all of these groups an opportunity to evaluate the functioning of local government in Wentworth and to determine if the City of Wentworth is able to achieve the Commission's goal of a local government that is able to respond to the needs and wants of its citizens.

APPENDIX I

Hamilton-Wentworth Review Commission

Research Reports

	RESEARCHER
"Economic Study of Hamilton-Wentworth"	George Cordahi
"The Hamilton-Wentworth Review Commission Final Report — Finance Research Study"	Woods, Gordon & Co.
"The Hamilton-Wentworth Review Commission Final Report — Management Research Study"	Woods, Gordon & Co.
"Hamilton-Wentworth Review Commission — Political Life in Hamilton-Wentworth: The Role of Area and Regional Councillors"	Trevor Price
"Health and Social Services in Hamilton-Wentworth"	Hugh R. Hanson
"History of Hamilton-Wentworth, 1788-1974"	Douglas Baldwin
"Parks and Recreation in the Regional Municipality of Hamilton-Wentworth"	Myra Schiff and Reiner Jaakson
"Planning and Development in Hamilton-Wentworth"	John Laskin
"Regional Municipality of Hamilton-Wentworth Review Commission — Transportation Services Component"	I.B.I. Group
"Research Report on a Review of Physical Services in Hamilton-Wentworth Region"	James F. MacLaren Limited
"A Review of the Inter-regional, Inter-municipal Boundaries of the Hamilton-Wentworth Region, based on an Analysis of the Political, Social and Physical Aspects of the Area"	Andrew Burghardt
"A Review of Public Safety Services in the Hamilton-Wentworth Region"	Smith, Auld and Associates Limited

APPENDIX II

Summary of Public Participation

A. Schedule of Public Meetings

1) *November 28, 1977*

   Glanbrook Public Arena,
   Township of Glanbrook
   (over 100 people attended)
   24 people spoke at meeting

2) *November 29, 1977*

   Greensville
   Senior Public School,
   Township of Flamborough
   (approximately 100 people attended)
   10 people spoke at meeting

3) *December 1, 1977*

   Saltfleet High School,
   Town of Stoney Creek
   (approximately 120 people attended)
   26 people spoke at meeting

4) *December 7, 1977*

   Central Park School,
   Town of Dundas
   (approximately 80 people attended)
   14 people spoke at meeting

5) *December 12, 1977*
   Ancaster High School,
   Town of Ancaster
   (approximately 70 people attended)
   20 people spoke at meeting

6) *December 14, 1977*
   Hillpark Secondary School,
   City of Hamilton (Mountain)
   (approximately 30 people attended)
   12 people spoke at meeting

7) *December 15, 1977*
   Sir John A. Macdonald Secondary School,
   City of Hamilton (Central)
   (approximately 30 people attended)
   7 people spoke at meeting

B. Schedule of Meetings with Councils

1) *November 22, 1977*
   Town of Stoney Creek

2) *November 23, 1977*
   Town of Ancaster

3) *November 30, 1977*
   Township of Flamborough

4) *December 8, 1977*
   Township of Glanbrook

5) *December 13, 1977*
   Town of Dundas

6) *January 4, 1978*
   City of Hamilton

C. Schedule of Other Meetings Attended

1) *November 14, 1977*
   Businessmen's groups from Hamilton area
2) *November 15, 1977*
   Jewish Community Centre Ladies Group
3) *November 18, 1977*
   Executive Committee of Waterdown and District Ratepayers' Assn.
4) *November 24, 1977*
   Hamilton and District Council of Women
   Hamilton Jaycees
   Waterdown and District Ratepayers' Association
5) *January 4, 1978*
   7. Optimists Club of Stoney Creek
6) *January 11, 1978*
   8. Hamilton Mountain Rotary Club

D. Schedule of Radio and Television Programs

1) *November 4, 1977*
   CHML: Tom Cherington "Action Line"
2) *November 10, 1977*
   CBC: "Metro Morning" Show Interview
3) *November 14, 1977*
   CHML: John Hardy "Open Line"
4) *November 15, 1977*
   CHCH TV: "Mid-day" program

E. List of Elected Representatives Who Met Individually with the Commission

1. Mayor J. T. Bennett, Dundas
2. Councillor F. Campbell, Glanbrook
3. Councillor J. F. Cauley, Ancaster
4. Councillor J. A. Copland, Stoney Creek

APPENDICES 219

5. Mayor G. H. Dean, Stoney Creek
6. Alderman Kay Drage, Hamilton
7. Councillor J. A. Freeman, Glanbrook
8. Mayor J. K. Harper, Flamborough
9. Alderman B. Hinkley, Hamilton
10. Chairman Anne Jones, Region
11. Mayor J. A. MacDonald, Hamilton
12. Alderman T. McMeekin, Hamilton
13. Controller R. M. Morrow, Hamilton
14. Councillor J. A. Norris, Stoney Creek
15. Councillor J. Orme, Dundas
16. Councillor A. Papazian, Stoney Creek
17. Mayor Ann Sloat, Ancaster
18. Councillor J. M. Southall, Dundas
19. Councillor C. J. Robb, Flamborough
20. Councillor D. W. Weylie, Glanbrook
21. Mr. E. Cunningham, M.L.A.
22. Mr. A. Kitchen (former Reeve of Beverly)

F. List of Group Submissions Received

HAMILTON

1. Lloyd George Community Association
2. Mechanical Contractors Association — Hamilton
3. The St. John Ambulance Association — Hamilton Branch
4. Knights of Pythias (Hamilton Century 55)
5. The Social Planning and Research Council of Hamilton and District
6. Hamilton and District Home Builders Association of HUDAC
7. Hamilton Beach Preservation Committee
8. The Hamilton and District Chamber of Commerce
9. Hamilton and District Electrical Contractors Association
10. Hamilton-Wentworth District Health Council
11. Hamilton West New Democratic Party Riding Association

12. Hamilton Mountain New Democratic Party
13. Ladies Association of St. Paul's Presbyterian Church
14. Hamilton-Wentworth Citizens Committee for the Abolition of Regional Government
15. Canadian Union of Public Employees, Local 5
16. Hamilton Centre New Democratic Party Riding Association
17. Hamilton Public Library Board
18. Hamilton and District Labour Council
19. Women's Progressive Conservative Association of Hamilton
20. Communist Party Civic Committee
21. Family Services of Hamilton-Wentworth Inc.
22. Mohawk College Urban Politics Course, Hamilton
23. CHCH TV
24. E. Parsons and others
25. Walter C. Haynes and others
26. R. F. Puschke and others
27. Mr. L. A. Smee and others

DUNDAS

28. Strabane United Church Women
29. Couples Club — West Flamborough Presbyterian Church
30. Dundas Community Services
31. The Dundas Heritage Association
32. Preserve Old Dundas
33. Dundas Public Library
34. F. Wannenmacher and others
35. Jim Orme and others

ANCASTER

36. The Ancaster Agricultural Society
37. St. Ann's Church
38. Hamilton Region Conservation Authority
39. Carluke Women's Institute
40. Spring Valley Community Association

41. Allarco Developments Limited, Green Downs Developments Company Limited, and Grangmore Developments Limited
42. Women's Institute — Patricia
43. F. H. Junker and others

GLANBROOK

44. Maggie Johnson Women's Institute
45. Wentworth County Federation of Agriculture (Properties Committee)
46. Binbrook Women's Institute
47. Blackheath Women's Institute

FLAMBOROUGH

48. Grand Vista Ratepayers' Association
49. West Flamborough Women's Institute
50. Women's Institute (Lynden)
51. Waterdown and District Ratepayers' Association
52. Wentworth North Women's Institute
53. Wentworth Library Board

STONEY CREEK

54. Winona Women's Institute, Hamilton-Wentworth Region
55. Winona Horticultural Society
56. Niagara Peninsula Fruit and Vegetable Growers' Association (Saltfleet Branch)
57. Stoney Creek Chamber of Commerce
58. Saltfleet Women's Hockey Association
59. Mrs. G. White and others

NO ADDRESS

60. Mrs. C. Sewart and others

G. Municipal Submissions

1. Area Municipalities of the Town of Ancaster, Town of Dundas, Township of Flamborough, Township of Glanbrook, and Town of Stoney Creek. Accompanied by petitions signed by:

Township of Flamborough	1,576
Town of Ancaster	562

Town of Dundas	1,470
Town of Glanbrook	1,431
Town of Stoney Creek	2,446
	7,485

2. City of Hamilton

H. Summary of Written and Oral Submissions

Written and Oral Submissions Analysed

1.	Individual submissions	1,078
2.	Telephone calls to the Commission's office	469
3.	Telephone calls to radio open line	16
	Group Submissions	60
	Municipal Submissions	2
	Individual written submissions from elected representatives	10
		1,635

Prior to the public hearings on the municipal submissions considerable advertising appeared in several of the weekly newspapers from some of the councils urging ratepayers to support the continuation of the municipality as a separate entity within "an improved county or regional system." Open letters to households were used in some municipalities for the same purpose.

The response was as follows:

Town of Ancaster	155 letters
Town of Stoney Creek	48 letters

Summary of Contents of Written and Oral Submissions

	Written submissions	Calls to Commission offices	Calls to radio open line Nov. 4, 1977	Total
1. Too costly	738	285	5	1,028
2. Duplication	337	122	4	463
3. Revert to former system	282	78	1	361
4. One-tier system	133	53	3	189
5. Overgoverned	147	51	4	202
6. No direct vote	96	4	2	102
7. Direct election of chairman and council	90	21	2	113
8. Pro region (usually two-tier)	103	13	-	116
9. More complicated buck-passing	34	4	1	39
10. Ignorance of system	27	15	1	43
11. Full-time paid councillors	2	-	2	4
12. Support review: YES	53	4	-	57
NO	17	4	-	21

It should be noted that some of the submissions included more than one comment, therefore they are recorded more than once in the above tabulation.

APPENDIX III

A Chronology of Activities

SEPTEMBER 1977

19   Announcement of Hamilton-Wentworth Review Commission

20   Review by Commission of Action Plan

29   Review Commission opens office in Hamilton at 20 Hughson Street South

OCTOBER 1977

12   Newspaper advertisements setting out terms of reference, submission dates, etc.

25   Researchers appointed

26   Press release on research program

28   Luncheon meeting with Commission, staff and senior representatives from the *Hamilton Spectator*

     Executive secretary and research director meet with chairman and senior staff of the Regional Municipality

     Distribution of letter to each household in the Region

NOVEMBER 1977

2   Letters to M.P.s, M.L.A.s, present and former elected representatives, ministers of all churches in the Region, groups and service clubs. Also, radio advertising

     Meeting with Commission's research consultants and municipal administrators

     Commission, executive secretary and office manager meet with news media

4   Commission participates on Tom Cherington's "Action Line" radio program

7   Newspaper advertisement regarding public submissions by November 15

10   Chairman interviewed for CBC "Metro Morning" show

14	Chairman participates on CHML radio "Open Line" talk program
	Chairman and executive secretary attend public meeting called by York Street Businessmen's Association
15	Last date for receipt of submissions from individuals
	Chairman interviewed by CHCH TV "Mid-day" program
	Chairman and executive secretary attend meeting of Hamilton Jewish Women's Club
18	Chairman and executive secretary attend meeting with executive committee of Waterdown and District Ratepayers' Association
21	Press conference held at Commission offices
	Commission meeting with regional representatives and Mrs. Yates to discuss procedure for hearings on municipal submissions and to amend municipal submission dates
	Chairman and executive secretary meet with Eric Hardy and E. Simpson to discuss municipal submissions and hearing procedures
22	Commission and executive secretary meet with council of the Town of Stoney Creek
23	Commission and executive secretary meet with Ancaster Council
24	Meetings with: Hamilton Jaycees
	Hamilton and District Council of Women
	Waterdown and District Ratepayers' Association
28	Individual Commission meeting with Mayor J. K. Harper
	Public meeting – Township of Glanbrook
29	Public meeting – Township of Flamborough
30	Commission meeting with Flamborough Council
	Individual Commission meetings with Councillor J. A. Copland and Mayor J. A. MacDonald

DECEMBER 1977

1	Individual Commission meetings with Controller R. M. Morrow, Alderman Kay Drage and Councillor J. A. Norris
	Public meeting — Town of Stoney Creek
2	Last date for receipt of public submissions from groups
7	Public meeting — Town of Dundas
8	Individual Commission meetings with Mayor G. H. Dean and Mr. A. Kitchen

	Commission meeting with Township of Glanbrook Council
9	Individual Commission meetings with E. Cunningham, M.L.A., Councillor J. F. Cauley, and Mayor Ann Sloat
12	Individual Commission meeting with Chairman Anne Jones
	Public meeting — Town of Ancaster
13	Commission meeting with Town of Dundas Council
14	Public meeting — City of Hamilton (Mountain)
15	Individual Commission meetings with Councillor C. J. Robb, Alderman T. McMeekin, Councillor J. Orme, and Councillor F. Campbell
	Public meeting — City of Hamilton
16	Individual Commission meeting with Councillor A. Papazian
19	Group hearings with: The Social Planning and Research Council of Hamilton and District Hamilton and District Labour Council Hamilton and District Home Builders Association of HUDAC The Hamilton and District Chamber of Commerce Grand Vista Ratepayers' Association Family Services of Hamilton-Wentworth, Inc. Hamilton Public Library Board James Orme and others Hamilton West New Democratic Party Riding Association
20	Group hearings with: Stoney Creek Chamber of Commerce Canadian Union of Public Employees, Local 5
22	Commission meeting with the Land Division Committee
	Individual Commission meeting with Mayor J. A. MacDonald
29	Individual Commission meetings with Mayor J. T. Bennett and Alderman B. Hinkley

JANUARY 1978

4	Commission meeting with Hamilton City Council
	Meeting with Stoney Creek Optimists Club
6	Individual Commission meeting with Councillor J. A. Freeman of Glanbrook
11	Commission meeting with Hamilton Mountain Rotary Club
12	Commission public hearing for presentations from Wentworth Library Board and Waterdown Ratepayers' Association

16 Individual Commission meeting with Councillor J. M. Southall
23 Individual Commission meeting with Councillor D. W. Weylie

FEBRUARY 1978
 2 Municipal submissions received
 8)
 9) Municipal submission hearings at Hamilton Place
10)
21 Written rebuttals received from municipalities
22 Commission begins decision-making

MARCH 1978
 1 Basic decisions made by Commission
    Writing of report begins
30 Writing of report completed

APRIL 1978
    Typesetting and printing of report
    Closing of Commission offices

MAY 1978
    Presentation of report